Pool of Life

Kailash Puri

KAILASH PURI
& ELEANOR NESBITT

Pool of Life

THE AUTOBIOGRAPHY OF A
Punjabi Agony Aunt

sussex
ACADEMIC
PRESS
Brighton • Chicago • Toronto

2 4 6 8 10 9 7 5 3 1

First published in 2013 by
SUSSEX ACADEMIC PRESS
PO Box 139
Eastbourne BN24 9BP

and in the United States of America by
SUSSEX ACADEMIC PRESS
Independent Publishers Group
814 North Franklin Street, Chicago, IL 60610

and in Canada by
SUSSEX ACADEMIC PRESS (CANADA)
8000 Bathurst Street, Unit 1, PO Box 30010, Vaughan, Ontario L4J 0C6

British Library Cataloguing in Publication Data
A CIP catalogue record for this book is available from the British Library.

Library of Congress Cataloging-in-Publication Data
Puri, Kailasha Ji., 1926–
Pool of life : the autobiography of a Punjabi agony aunt / by Kailash
Puri and Eleanor Nesbitt.
pages   cm
Includes bibliographical references and index.
ISBN 978-1-84519-602-8 (pbk. : acid-free paper)
    1. Puri, Kailasha Ji., 1926– 2. Authors, Panjabi—20th century—
Biography. I. Nesbitt, Eleanor M. II. Title.
PK2659.P8Z46 2013
891.4'237—dc23
[B]

2013016613

Typeset and designed by Sussex Academic Press, Brighton & Eastbourne.
Printed by TJ International, Padstow, Cornwall.
This book is printed on acid-free paper.

Contents

Series Editor's Preface		vi
Acknowledgements		vii
Glossary		viii
Introduction		1
1	Childhood	6
2	Tradition	21
3	Rawalpindi and Lahore	32
4	Marriage	52
5	London	63
6	India again	73
7	West Africa	88
8	Slough and Southall	102
9	Liverpool	113
10	Writing and Public Speaking	123
11	"A shoulder to cry on"	137
12	Pakistan	153
Afterword		170
Suggested Further Reading		177
References		179
Index		183

Series Editor's Preface

The Sussex Library of Asian Studies Series publishes original scholarly work in various disciplines (including interdisciplinary and transnational approaches) under the rubric of Asian studies – particularly Economics, Education, Religion, History, Politics, Gender, Comparative Studies with the West, Media, and Regional Studies in Asia. The series is keen to publish in emerging topics that demand attention in the Asian context – from the politics of dress to the heteronormative in India and Indonesia for example. Seminal works and approaches will find a home here. The series also welcomes single-country studies or anthologies that explore one important theme across a number of Asian contexts. The series will contribute to scholarly debates on topical issues, highlighting the importance of the region.

This is the first time the series publishes a primary source in the form of a memoir. Kailash Puri, in collaboration with the eminent scholar Eleanor Nesbitt, provides a rich ethnographic account of sixty years of the life and times of a South Asian woman located in a transnational context. The story of Kailash Puri from childhood in what is now Pakistan, to her journeys to London, India, West Africa, Liverpool, and other countries, documents not only the gendered expectations of a woman expected to follow her husband without question, but also the agency of an individual who takes on many roles from cookery and yoga teacher to 'agony aunt'. Feminist scholars in particular will find this narrative useful for analyzing the way South Asian women negotiate their own space in the family, marriage and the diasporic community. In addition, Kailash's self-identity as a Sikh with a unique genealogy (Nesbitt points out that "her family belong to the Khatri caste, the hereditary community that gave birth to Sikh's ten Gurus, but who are a minority among the Sikh population in India, Britain and worldwide"), introduces a novel perspective for those interested in the cultural politics of identity. The transnational location of Kailash's autobiography underscores the importance and distinctive point of view of Asian women in the diaspora. The work is an excellent example of the importance of memoir, autobiography and contemporary experiential account in promoting understanding of the diversity of the Asian region.

MINA ROCES
University of New South Wales, Australia

Acknowledgements

We thank Anthony Grahame and his team at Sussex Academic Press for bringing our project to fruition. Thank you to Dr Akin Oyetade for his help with West African words, and to Dr Doris Jakobsh, Dr Alison Mukherjee and Dr Pippa Virdee for their valuable comments. Any errors are our own.

The front cover photograph of Kailash taken in 2005 is courtesy of Sheila C. Puri; all other cover photographs, and the frontispiece, are from the collection of Kailash Puri.

Glossary

Most of the words listed are Punjabi and/or Hindi. So as to minimise disruption to the flow of the narrative they have not been italicised but they have been translated or explained, at least on their first occurrence. In the glossary, but not in the rest of the book, macrons have been added to assist pronunciation. Thus ā is pronounced like "a" in "large"; "ī" is like "ee" in "need"; "ū" is like "oo" in "pool". However, the diacritic marks, that distinguish (in the roman alphabet) the consonants of Indic languages, have not been added. The letters "v" and "w" are used interchangeably for the single consonant concerned. AG (Ādi Granth) denotes the Gurū Granth Sāhib and the page numbers refer (as per convention) to the 1430-page scriptural volume in Gurmukhī.

Abbājī	(respected) father.
Achār	pickle.
Ajwain	aromatic seed used in cooking; *trachyspermum ammi.*
Akhand pāth	continuous (48-hour) reading of Gurū Granth Sāhib.
Almirah (almārī)	cupboard.
Amaltas	golden shower tree, *cassia fistula.*
Ambras	confectionery; lit. mango juice.
Āmlā	Indian gooseberry, with culinary and medicinal uses, *phyllanthus emblica.*
Anand (Sāhib)	Gurū Amar Dās's "Song of Joy", AG, pp. 917–22; joyful hymn at end of Sikhs' congregational worship.
Angīthī	bucket-like stove stoked with embers.
Angrezī	English.
Annā	coin, one sixteenth of a rupee Ā.
Āratī	hymn of praise, Gurū Nānak's hymn, AG, p. 13.

Ardās	formal Sikh congregational prayer at the end of most acts of worship.
Ark	herbal medicine, swallow wort, *asclepias gigantia*.
Āsana	yoga posture.
Bābājī	respectful title, usually for senior man; also for Gurū Granth Sāhib and spiritual leaders (= sant).
Badām	almond.
Bahin(jī)	(respected) sister.
Baisākhī (Vaisākhī)	mid-April festival celebrating the first Khālsā Sikhs' initiation.
Baithak	sitting room.
Bājā	harmonium.
Barāt	bridegroom's family and friends at wedding.
Barkat	blessing.
Barphī	white sweetmeat made by condensing milk.
Basant Panchamī	Spring kite-flying festival, marked by wearing yellow clothing.
Behr	small fruit, *ziziphus mauritania*.
Bhāīyā	brother, a respectful title.
Bhalā	good.
Bhātrā	caste of Sikh pedlars, the first Sikh community to migrate to the UK.
Bhatthī	shallow furnace.
Bhatthīwālī	woman who roasted grain on the bhatthī.
Brahmin (brāhman)	Hindu priestly caste.
Bindī	mark applied to centre of forehead.
Broni	(Nigeria) brown.
Buba (Yoruba)	loose top, worn by men or women.
Budhsuhāgan	woman whose husband will still be alive when she is old.
Chāchī	wife of father's younger brother; affectionate respectful title for older woman.
Charpoy (chārpāī)	wooden bedstead.
Chaukā	clean area for cooking.
Chaumukhiā	four-mouthed (describing four-lipped clay lamp that holds four wicks).

Glossary

Chhabīl	stall for serving cooling drinks on anniversary of fifth Gurū's martyrdom.
Chīch kichole	children's game.
Chimtā	percussion instrument resembling long fire tongs.
Chīzān	(pl.) things.
Chulhā	shoe-shaped stove made of hardened clay.
Chunnī	long scarf, dupattā.
Chūrā (pl. chūre)	set of mainly red wedding bangles.
Dahī	yoghurt.
Dāī	midwife.
Dandānwālā	travelling dentist.
Darshan	experience of being in a (divine) presence; receiving the blessing of (a respected personage's) benedictory glance.
Dassehrā	autumn festival 20 days before Dīvālī.
Dastārbandī	turban-tying ceremony for boy.
Deorī	entrance.
Dhadd	hand-held, hourglass-shaped drum.
Dhaddī	musician playing dhadd.
Dhol	large wooden drum.
Dholī	palanquin in which bride leaves her wedding.
Dholkī	horizontally held wooden drum.
Dhotī	unstitched cotton garment for men.
Dīvā	wick-light.
Dīvālī	late autumn festival of lights.
Dudh mundarī	ceremonial waving of pot of dilute milk above head of departing bride.
Dumālā	tall turban wound flat across the forehead.
Dupattā	long scarf of fine cloth.
Gachchī mittī	yellowish cement-like substance.
Gaddī	throne, a cushion (for a dignitary).
Gajrelā	sweet made from grated carrot, milk and sugar.
Gallī	alley.
Garam masālā	blend of ground sweet spices.
Gattā	flavoured sugar.
Ghee (ghī)	clarified butter for use in cooking and dīvās.
Ghorā	horse.
Giānī	scholar, title of Sikh preacher.
Gīt	song.

Gīte	pebbles.
Gorā	lit. pale; white male.
Gorī	lit. pale; white female.
Got	lineage.
Grān	village.
Granthī	custodian and reader of Gurū Granth Sāhib in gurdwārā.
Gulāb jāmun	spherical, milk-based sweetmeat soaked in syrup.
Gulīdandā	game of tipcat, using stick and small wooden block.
Gur	unprocessed sugar (brown concentrate from boiling sugar cane juice).
Gurdwārā	Sikh place of worship.
Gurmukhī	script of Sikh scripture and of Punjabi language.
Gurpurab	anniversary of a Guru's birth or demise.
Gurū	spiritual teacher, referring to Sikhs' ten human Gurūs and the Gurū Granth Sāhib.
Gurū Granth Sāhib	1430-page Sikh scripture revered as living Gurū.
Gusal-khānā	bathroom.
Gyān	knowledge.
Handā	food traditionally given, as of right, to a visiting Brahmin.
Hanumān	Hindu god, the monkey-headed devotee of Lord Rāma.
Hār	garland, necklace.
Harāmī	bastard.
Harijan	Mahatma Gandhi's name for people of the lowest caste.
Harmal	*peganum harmala* wild rue, seed burnt (from Turkey to India) as a protection against the evil eye.
Harmattan	winter (West Africa); dry, dusty West African trade wind blowing from Sahara from late November to mid-March.
Hattī	small model "shop" in family's Dīvālī celebration.
Holā maholla	Sikh festival on day after Holī.

Holī	Hindu Spring festival celebrated by throwing colour.
Innū	round support for carrying a pot on one's head.
Izzat	family honour.
Jādū	(black) magic.
Jalebī	golden sweetmeat made by dunking deep-fried spiral of batter in sugar syrup.
Jāmun	damson, *syzygium cumini*.
Janjghar	accommodation for bridegroom's friends and family.
Jat	largest Sikh caste-community, traditionally peasant land-owners.
Jaymālā	marriage garland.
Jot (pl. jotan)	wick-light.
Juthā	food (potentially) impure because of (even indirect) contact with another's saliva.
Jyotisht	astrologer.
Kaidā	alphabet book.
Kājal	lampblack used as collyrium, eyeliner.
Kamīz	tunic top of a woman's "Punjabi suit".
Kangrī	portable heater filled with charcoal.
Karā	steel bangle worn on right wrist. It is one of the five Ks (outward signifiers of Sikh religious commitment).
Karāh prashād	soft golden mixture made by cooking wheat-flour/semolina with butter, sugar and water, and distributed after Sikh worship.
Karhāī	wok-like cooking utensil.
Kartik	lunar month overlapping Oct. and Nov.
Karwā Chauth	day (ten days before Dīvālī) when women fast on behalf of husbands.
Kasbā	town.
Katorī	small metal bowl for portions of vegetable, yoghurt etc.
Kattalāmā	fried dough layered with ghee.
Khālsā	Sikh, esp. in sense of formally initiated Sikh.
Khandā	double-edged sword, hallowed Sikh symbol.
Khāndān	wider family, dynasty.
Khatrī	(from Sanskrit *kshatriya*), Punjabi caste, often associated traditionally with accountancy.

Khīr	rice cooked in sweetened milk.
Khoyā	milk thickened by boiling.
Khūh	well.
Kiklī	girls' game of spinning round in pairs, with wrists crossed.
Kīrtan Sohilā	Gurū Nānak's composition sung in late evening prayer and at funerals, AG, pp. 12–13.
Koel	cuckoo, *eudynamys scolopaceus*.
Kulchā	leavened flatbread made from white flour.
Kurtā	loose shirt.
Laddoo (laddū)	spherical golden sweetmeat often associated with celebration.
Lakshmi	Hindu goddess of prosperity, especially worshipped at Dīvālī.
Langar	Sikhs' provision of free vegetarian meals, usually in gurdwārā.
Lapah (Krio)	wrap (skirt-like garment).
Lassī	drink of diluted sweetened or salty yoghurt.
Lāthī	long, heavy wooden stick carried by police and soldiers.
Lāvān	central rite of a Sikh marriage ceremony, in which couple walk around the Gurū Granth Sāhib four times during singing of Gurū Rām Dās's hymn. AG, pp. 773–4.
Lohrī	January 13 Punjabi festival.
Lohrī de khilone	lit. Lohri toys i.e. animal-shaped sweets eaten at Lohri festival.
Māhā (dī dāl)	whole black lentils.
Madānī	churning pole.
Mahal	palace.
Mahallā	residential area.
Malok	fruit, eaten dried and resembling a prune.
Māmājī	respectful name for mother's brother, (maternal) uncle.
Mambari (Nigeria)	hut in the jungle in which girls were prepared for marriage.
Mammy (Nigeria)	a woman market trader.
Mammy wagon)	a colourful lorry carrying merchandise and passengers.

Masālewālā	spiced.
Māsī	mother's sister.
Mehndī	henna.
Melā	fair often held at annual festival.
Miānī	small upstairs room.
Milnī	ritual introduction of bride's and groom's families, father to father, brother to brother etc.
Mithāī	sweetmeats.
Muzārā	farm labourer, tenant farmer.
Nain	barber's wife.
Navān	new.
Navrātrā	lit. nine night, usually pl. navrātre, the period of nine days before Dassehrā.
Nishān Sāhib	respected Sikh pennant flying from flagpole wrapped in cloth.
Nishāstā	wheat starch.
Oba (Yoruba)	king; traditional ruler.
Oyinbo (Yoruba)	white man; European.
Paisā (pl. paise)	small coin.
Pajāmā	loose cotton trousers.
Pakorā	spicy, savoury chickpea-flour vegetable fritter.
Palang	bed.
Pallā	cloth (to link bride and groom).
Pankhā	ceiling fan.
Pankhāwālā	servant manually operating ceiling fan.
Parāī vast	(of a daughter) belonging to another i.e. to her (future) in-laws.
Parāthā	chapātī enriched with butter and often stuffed with spiced potato, grated radish or other vegetable.
Patāsā (pl. patāse)	white lens-shaped sweet made of refined sugar.
Pāth	reading or reciting scripture.
Pherā	going and returning; bride's post-wedding visit to her parental home.
Pilau	fried rice.
Pinnī (pl. pinnīān)	hard, spherical sweetmeat.

Pīrhā	low wooden stool.
Prānāyāma	in yoga the science of breath control.
Purānā	old.
Pūrī	deep-fried chapati.
Rāgī	Sikh musician (providing accompanied devotional singing).
Rākhī (Hindi)	a thread worn on the right wrist, often signifying a brother's bond as protector of his sister.
Rakhrī (Punjabi)	= rākhī.
Rakshā bandhan	August festival celebrating brother–sister relationship.
Rām, Rāma	divine hero of the Rāmāyan(a) epic.
Rāmgarhīā	respectful title for member of castes traditionally engaged in carpentry, ironwork and construction.
Rasoī	kitchen.
Revrī	hard round sweet studded with sesame seeds
(pl. revrīān)	and eaten at Lohrī.
Richhwālā	travelling entertainer with performing bear.
Rīthā	fruit of soapnut, *sapinda mukorossi*.
Rogan	oil.
Rotī	bread i.e. chapātī.
Sabzī	spiced cooked vegetable.
Sāhib	respectful title for person or venerated place or object.
Salvār	trouser-like garment worn below kamīz.
Samosā	triangular savoury stuffed pasty.
Sangat	Sikh congregation.
Sant	spiritual leader, Bābājī.
Santān sanjan	birth control.
Saperā	snake-charmer.
Sardārnī	Sikh woman.
Sargī	food i.e. mathrī (a savoury fried snack), mithāī, cashews, sultanas and almonds) sent by a wife's parents for her to eat before fasting from dawn on Karwā Chauth.
Sarod	stringed instrument.
Satputrī	bearer of seven sons (blessing for a bride).
Sattū	powder of roasted oats ground with gur and water.
Seer (ser)	old Indian measure of weight = 0.93310 kg.

Sehrā	streamers hiding face of bridegroom; advice read to bridegroom during marriage.
Sej	sex.
Sej ulajhanā	sexual problems.
Shabd (pl. shabdān)	words of scripture.
Shakar	raw sugar.
Shikākaī	*acacia concinna*, saponin-rich bark, leaves and pods used for traditional shampoo.
Shikār	hunting.
Shivālā	(Hindu) shrine dedicated to Lord Shiva.
Shivshakti	creative energy.
Shrāddh	annual period when Hindus commemorate deceased relatives.
Sikhiā	rhyming advice for the bride.
Suhāg	joy of consummation; wedding song; happy state of a woman whose husband is still alive.
Sukhmanī Sāhib	(lit. "Pearl of Peace" or "Peace of Mind"), long poem by Guru Arjan Dev, AG, pp. 262–96.
Suphā	room for sleeping.
Surmā	antimony for eye makeup.
Surmādānī	surmā container.
Sūrya namaskār	salutation to the sun, sequence of yoga āsanas.
Takhtī	hand-held wooden board used like a slate for writing.
Tamāshewālā	travelling entertainer.
Tandoor (tandūr)	clay oven.
Tāyājī	(respected) elder brother of one's father.
Thālī	round metal tray used as plate.
Tīkā	jewellery worn by bride on her forehead; dot of vermilion etc on forehead.
Tillāwālā	made of gold thread.
Tīyān	annual festival during which girls swing.
Tonga (tāngā)	small horse-drawn vehicle.
Tongawala (tāngāwālā)	driver of tonga.
Trederā	room with three doors.
Tribainī (trivainī)	confluence of three rivers, esp. the sacred confluence at Allahabad.
Trikhal	child born after three siblings of the opposite sex.

Urā erā irī sasā	alphabet; first four letters of Gurmukhi alphabet.
Urankhatolā	airborne vehicle for a god.
Vazīr	minister of state.
Wāhigurū	God (lit. praise to the Gurū).

This book is dedicated to our families
to their Punjabi and non-Punjabi
members alike,
and to women worldwide
in all their creativity.

Introduction

Kailash Puri and I met early in the 1980s at discussion meetings in Southall of a group of Sikhs and Christians. I must have mentioned to her that I had recently worked in North India and that I had more recently made a study of the experiences of three Sikh communities in Nottingham. Kailash spoke of her multi-faceted life and mentioned to me that she was planning to publish her autobiography.

I have happy memories of being welcomed by Kailash and her husband, the late Professor Gopal Puri, to their gracious home in Blundell Sands in Liverpool, and I also have a large cardboard box of tape-recordings, plus some manila folders of typescripts and Kailash's handwritten English and Punjabi paragraphs, as evidence of the collaboration between Kailash and myself that followed. In the ensuing years, Kailash's grandchildren, her publications, mostly in Punjabi, and her awards have all increased. (Honours include her Bhai Mohan Singh Vaid literary award in 1982 and her Millennium Woman Award from the Mayor of Ealing in 1999.) The demands of academic life overtook me until I was again able to visit her on her eighty-eighth birthday in 2012 in her Ealing apartment.

During the intervening years my research had taken me deeper into the contested historical development of the Sikh reli-gious tradition, and its scholarly and devotional representation, and into the diverse experience of the UK's Punjabi diaspora. Punjab is one of the two states that were torn apart in 1947 at the Partition of India into India and Pakistan. From then on West Punjab (in Pakistan) has been predominantly Muslim and the population of East Punjab (in India) has consisted mainly of Sikhs and Hindus. Twentieth-century migration from Punjab to Britain before the 1950s consisted mainly of Bhatra Sikhs, a hereditary community from West Punjab, who settled for the most part in seaports such as Glasgow and Southampton and earned money as pedlars. Students, including Gopal Puri who came to London

1

in 1945, made up a much smaller percentage of Britain's Punjabi population at that time. In the 1950s the situation changed dramatically, as post-war emigration got underway from rural East Punjab. The majority of emigrants were young men — Sikhs from peasant land-holding families — who found employment in Britain's industrial cities. Smaller numbers of Punjabi Hindus and Christians came too and families took shape as immigrants sent for their wives and children or returned to Punjab to marry. Subsequently, many more Punjabis (mostly Sikhs from the Ramgarhia community) arrived from the newly independent countries of East Africa. As I explored Sikh migration history my understanding, both of Sikh practice and of life in diaspora, was deepened at many points by recollecting Kailash's anecdotes and insights.

At the same time, the ongoing research by colleagues in Sikh Studies, Punjab Studies and Diaspora Studies, as well as in Women's Studies, provides frameworks for understanding what Kailash so generously shared with me. This introduction, as well as the Afterword and the suggestions for further reading at the end of the book, are intended similarly to enrich and extend the enquiring reader's appreciation of the wider context of Kailash's story.

Darshan Singh Tatla, a specialist in Punjab Studies, commented, in his brief overview of Sikhs' biographies and memoirs, that very few emigrants from Punjab have published their memoirs (2004). Kailash's autobiography is one of that small number. Like Partap Tandon's (1969), Kailash's life-story records patterns of rural life and family religious observance. Like Tara Singh Bains (Bains and Johnston 1995) she is an emigrant Sikh, responding to the questioning of an interviewer from a non-Punjabi background. More recently, Hugh Johnston has shared the "remarkable story" of another Indo-Canadian, Kapoor Singh Siddoo, and three generations of his family (2011). The UK journalist Sathnam Sanghera has written poignantly of growing up in a British Sikh community (2009). Then, too, there are the published accounts of the challenging lives of UK-based Punjabi women, Sharan-Jeet Shan (1985) and "Sita Devi" (Barton 1987) as well as Jasvinder Sanghera (2007), plus two usefully annotated oral histories of Sikhs in Leicester, UK, published by Kiyotaka Sato (2011, 2012). The actress and screenwriter Meera Syal's autobiographical novel, *Anita and Me* (1997) deftly captures the experience of Meena, a Punjabi Hindu girl growing up in the Black Country in the 1970s.

In conversation, Rachel Barton (a pseudonym), the amanuensis for "Sita Devi", shared with me her concern that publishers in the 1980s were keen to give voice to South Asian women qua victims of racism and sexism, but seemed more resistant to acknowledging that a Punjabi woman's self-understanding might not tidily illustrate those concerns of western liberals. A generation later there is space for more voices to be heard. Kailash was the devoted wife of a devoted husband, her life has been stimulating and fulfilling. She does not see herself as a victim, whether of arranged marriage or marital oppression, nor does she perceive her UK experience primarily in terms of racial prejudice.

At the same time reflections on all these aspects of South Asian and diaspora society emerge in her narrative. By contrasting Britishers' attitudes to immigrants in the 1940s and 1960s, and in her disclosure of the pain of women who consulted her as agony aunt and "sexologist", Kailash's lifestory adds to outsiders' understanding of them. (Here it needs to be explained that in British English "agony aunt" is the usual term for a woman who contributes a regular newspaper or magazine column providing sympathetic, motherly advice to readers who contact her for help with personal dilemmas, often about relationships.) South Asian society's endemic devaluing of women runs through her account: her parents' disappointment at her own birth, her awareness of female infanticide, her knowledge — reinforced by ritual, marriages and annual observances — that daughters are destined to be given away to another family's control. (For scholarly discussion of "son preference" see Purewal 2010.)

Much has been written in the past twenty years on the traumatic Partition of India (see, for example, Butalia 2000; Menon and Bhasin 1998; Virdee 2009). Kailash and Gopal were not in India in 1947, but her memoir contributes movingly, if only in passing, to this literature. As readers will appreciate, the oral histories of Muslims as well as Sikhs and Hindus caught up in Partition speak of a frenzy of violence, much of it against women, on both sides of the divide. Kailash reports the suffering of Hindus and Sikhs, and also fondly recalls how hospitably she and her husband were welcomed by Muslims on their return to their roots three and a half decades after Partition.

Kailash's story is not "typical" of UK Sikhs' experience, let alone the wider experience of Sikh women. Individual lives are just that — individual. Stereotyping stalks every community, often with negative consequences, not least the depersonalising of people perceived and labelled in particular ways. A literature that exclusively or predominantly features South Asian women as victims risks hardening stereotypes.

Kailash's life breaks the mould in so many ways: her family belong to the Khatri caste, the hereditary community that gave birth to Sikhs' ten Gurus, but who are a minority among the Sikh population in India, Britain and worldwide. While the more numerous Jat and Ramgarhia families have traditions of, respectively, peasant agriculture and employment as builders, smiths and carpenters, the Khatris' background is more urban and professional. Moreover, Kailash's roots were in West Punjab rather than East Punjab, the ancestral home of most British Sikhs. To take another point of difference: Kailash's sojourn in Africa was as an academic's wife in West Africa whereas, for Ramgarhia families, Africa means East African countries such as Kenya, where many of their forefathers (skilled masons, bricklayers, carpenters and smiths) had been drafted around 1900 as indentured labourers to construct the railway. Like many of her contemporaries, Kailash was (though only briefly) employed in a factory, but she contributed to UK society in many other ways too, notably as an author, agony aunt, and teacher of cookery and yoga. She is committed to improving community relations and has repeatedly spoken out in public gatherings and via the media.

For students of Sikh history Kailash's recollections of her family's association with Damdama Sahib gurdwara in Kallar (in Pakistan) and with members of the Bedi family (descendants of Guru Nanak) will hold particular interest. The religious observances of her childhood convey the close weave of Punjab's social and devotional fabric, a far cry from portrayals of a distinct, homogeneous "Sikhism", severed from its Hindu antecedents and neighbours. At the end of the book pointers are provided to some further reading to pursue this and other aspects of Kailash's experience. An Afterword sketches developments in the UK's Sikh community, including its religious complexity, from 1983 to 2013.

Readers interested in the mechanics of oral history and ethnography may wonder how far what follows is Kailash Puri's verbatim account. As a prolific published author herself, albeit in

Punjabi, she had formulated her narrative but was keen to have editorial help, to loosen the flow of her English. My questions were generated by experience of North India and by my study of Sikh communities in Nottingham, and so they drew out from Kailash more subject matter and more detail. One reader of the manuscript posed useful questions (about her experience of Partition, for example) which resulted in additional text. Rather than append notes, I have incorporated clarifications in the text itself. Kailash and I have collaborated at every stage of the writing process. My life is the richer for this long friendship.

Here is the story of her first sixty years.

1

Childhood

"Another girl!" Despite my two grandmothers' ceaseless prayers for a male child my mother had borne a fifth daughter, me. The dai (midwife) too had hoped to deliver a son. Sons meant ampler payment for her services. She ran to break the unwelcome news to my father, who was pacing up and down the courtyard outside. He did not enquire after the well-being of mother or child. Distraught, he mounted his bicycle and rode off to withdraw his deposit on a piece of land. No need now to increase his property, no sense in doing business. He had no son to carry on the family name — only four daughters (for one had already died), who would all be lost to other men's families. He did not return until after midnight.

Ever since the birth of Vanti, my eldest sister, our mother, on my grandmother's advice, had gone, every full-moon day, to Guru Nanak's shrine at Panja Sahib at Hasan Abdal, 30 miles from Rawalpindi, where his handprint is still clearly visible on the rock-face. Here, in the water that had originally gushed up at the Guru's command to quench his followers' thirst, my mother would bathe, praying for a son. Once more her prayers had been useless, but, undeterred, she taught me to put my tiny hands together and bow reverently before the Guru Granth Sahib, the Sikh scriptures installed in the miani, a small upstairs room, airy and full of light, that served as our family's chapel. Here my mother would intone earnestly:

> Panja Sahib jasan
> Te vir leke asan.
> I will go to Panja Sahib
> And return with a brother.

In the same spirit of determined optimism my parents gave me the name Viranwali, meaning the girl who has brothers, just as my school friend had been called Satbhrai (seven brothers) when in fact she was one of seven daughters. In my case, as in hers, there was no ritual opening of the Guru Granth Sahib to find the initial of my name. I was to be Viranwali, sister of brothers, the idea being in our community that after giving a daughter such a name the next child would certainly be a son.

I was born in my parents' house in Arya Mahalla, Rawalpindi (now in Pakistan), and spent most of my childhood either there or in Lahore. Our Rawalpindi house was a large, terraced family house built by my father who was a building contractor. It had a spacious baithak (drawing room) with two doors opening onto the galli (alley-way), and letting in plenty of light. This baithak was on the right hand side of the deori (entrance), and on the left was a dark gusal-khana (bathroom). There were five other rooms — we did not distinguish rooms further as "bedrooms". A few steps away from the deori was our courtyard which was open to the sky. To the right of that was the rasoi (kitchen). Outside it in the corner was a wood-fuelled chulha (low stove fashioned from hardened clay) on which my mother and elder sisters cooked chapatis and other food at least three times a day. Upstairs were the miani and a storeroom, a refuge from childhood squabbles.

But, when I think of home, it is to Kallar village that I return in spirit. Here in my father's parents' house, with cousins, aunts and uncles, I grew to the village's more primal rhythm, secure in the love of the extended family. My father, Sohan Singh Puri, would happily have stayed forever in his parents' house, but he gave way to pressure from my mother who fancied herself born to a more sophisticated, urban setting. Until the savage dislocation of Partition in 1947, every marriage in our scattered khandan was celebrated in the ancestral village, and we returned here for our holidays. Our khandan numbered about two hundred — a network of kin among whom kinship bonds were still real, renewed at festivals and weddings.

Kallar lies twenty-five miles from Rawalpindi in the foothills of the Shivalik hills, now famous for their fossil remains. In Kallar there were no level roads, but rough boulder-strewn gallis between the houses on the slope to the west of the Kanshi river. The river-bed, more stones than water except during the rainy season, was flanked by berry-covered bushes skirting rows of fruit trees — jamun plums, pomegranates, apricots, amla, as well as orchards of oranges and mangoes. When the greenish bunches of flowers hung from the mango branches the koel (Indian cuckoo) sang exquisitely. There were mulberry trees in abundance as the thin, supple twigs were needed for weaving baskets.

About five hundred people lived in Kallar. It was connected by a fair-weather road to the telegraph office nine miles away and to the railway station of Mankiala twenty-one miles distant. Once or twice daily a bus clattered into the village, raising clouds of dust or spattering the unwary with soupy mud according to the season. It took an hour to reach Gujranwala, a sought after kasba (town), and twice that time to reach Rawalpindi where the nearest hospital was.

My father's family had not always lived in Kallar. My grandfather, Kharak Singh, had served as a vazir (minister) to Raja Sir Gurbaksh Singh Ji, and must have settled in Kallar to be near his princely master. There were close bonds between the Puris, my father's family, and Raja Sir Gurbaksh Singh Ji's clan, the Bedis.

Raja Sir Gurbaksh Singh Ji was respected locally as the biggest landowner, living with his wife and three sons in a mansion known in Kallar as the mahal or palace, decorated with brilliantly coloured murals of Hindu deities. We revered him above all for his spiritual aura as a direct descendant of the noblest Bedi, Guru Nanak. Guru Nanak's visionary message first kindled our Sikh faith at the time that Martin Luther was preaching Reformation in Europe. The pure light of Nanak's Guruship shone next in Angad, his devoted disciple. Guru Nanak's elder son Sri Chand, a deeply religious man, chose the ascetic path of celibacy. His younger son, Lakhmi Das, married. Of his descendants the most famous must have been Baba Sahib Singh, great-great grandfather of our Raja Sir Gurbaksh Singh Ji. The line of human Gurus had ended nearly a hundred years before with the passing of Guru Gobind Singh in 1708, and all Sikhs have since then revered the sacred volume, the Granth Sahib, as Guru. Nevertheless Baba Sahib Singh commanded unique respect. He it was who marked with holy vermilion powder the brow of the victorious warrior, Ranjit Singh, in 1799. Only then was Ranjit Singh acknowledged as the divinely ordained Maharaja of the Punjab.

Sir Baba Khem Singh Bedi, father of Raja Sir Gurbaksh Singh Ji, had been one of the founders of the Sikhs' Singh Sabha reform movement in Punjab. Challenged by the proselytising, educational and medical outreach of British missionaries, and by the activities of the Arya Samaj (a Hindu reform movement), enlightened Sikhs strove to spread education among the Sikh masses. Khalsa High School, Kallar, was one of the first schools to be established. My feeling of pride in my village and our devotion to the Bedis cannot be separated.

My grandfather had indeed been privileged to serve Baba Khem Singh's son, Baba Sahib Singh's great-great grandson and the fourteenth in line from Guru Nanak. Moreover, the Bedis trace their descent from God incarnate, Lord Rama himself — an illustrious family tree by any criteria. Many years before my birth the Bedis and their entourage had settled in Kallar, abandoning Pakka, now a forlorn, rocky site. Raja Sir Gurbaksh Singh Ji enjoyed the blessing not only of his divine antecedents, but also of his foreign masters. He had provided the British with men and money during World War I. He kept race horses, greyhounds and a battalion of servants, including a tutor, Master Hara Singh (of whom more anon), for his sons.

I can picture my grandfather from the framed photograph on our mantelpiece. He wore an imposing white turban and hanging over his shoulders was a white stole such as you still see men wearing to officiate in the gurdwara (Sikh place of worship). To his grandchildren he was Lalaji, and I treasure a loving memory of him, dressed from head to foot in white cotton, sitting in his baithak, while the frills of the pankha stirred the warm air to a more tolerable coolness. The pankha was suspended across the ceiling and moved back and forth as the pankhawala, Fazal Din, outside in the galli, pulled on its cord and kept everyone cool.

My Lalaji died when I was very young. The news broke as villagers heard the call "Lakar suto, lakar suto" (give us a log, give us a log) and then the name of the deceased. Every household contributed a log from its wood-store for the pyre. All the villagers joined the procession and carried any logs that had been put out along the galli. They moved to the percussion of the dhol, a drum beaten at both ends, and the chimta, an instrument like a massive pair of fire tongs with jingling metal discs along both of its arms. Guru Arjan Dev's words sustained the mourners' spirits.

O God, the fulfiller of desires and the knower of hearts, kindly fulfill my desire. I am your humble slave. Make me the devotee of the enlightened saints. Grant me true peace.

Men and women thronged the narrow streets between the houses and down to the riverside. Here the pyre was laid and lit, and the cremation rites were performed to verses of Kirtan Sohila, Sikhs' late evening prayer. Next day my grandfather's ashes were collected to be taken at some later date to the sacred Ganges river at Hardwar or it may have been Kiratpur, a Sikh holy place where the river flows beside the gurdwara as if ready to carry away the ashes of Sikh men and women.

I picture Beyji, my grandmother. Like everyone else over the age of about thirty she wore only white, and passed on colourful clothes to younger relatives. Whether or not male in-laws were there, her head remained covered by a gauzy, white dupatta three yards in length and a yard and a quarter wide. Her loose fitting kamiz reached below her knees and had long, full sleeves. It took thirteen yards of cloth to make her salvar, the pair of loose trousers which tapered at the ankle. (Many separate pieces of cloth were ingeniously fitted together.) Today's salvars are simpler affairs, but in those days it was thought undignified for ladies of her status to wear salvars made of less cloth.

When I think of Beyji I visualise her sitting in the twilit court-yard singing Guru Nanak's evening hymn, the Arati:

> The sky is your silver tray.
> The sun and moon your oil wick lights,
> The galaxy of stars are the pearls studding it.
> The sandalwood is your incense . . .

We grandchildren clustered around her on the charpoy, the wooden bedstead with its jute webbing, and sang along with her:

> You have a million eyes,
> But no mortal eye.
> You have a million lotus feet
> But no mortal feet.

Our young souls were afire with praise for the Almighty, but perhaps rather more with the prospect of tasting some of Beyji's special, soft chapati. She had no dentures to compensate for the teeth she had lost, and all our food required vigorous chewing, so my mother added sodium bicarbonate to the dough to make her chapatis softer. If we pleased Beyji by singing Arati we could eat the crisp edges of the chapati that were too tough for her gums.

> As the bee is ravished with the flower,
> So my mind is ravished.
> O Lord, give the holy water of your grace
> To this little bird -
> The heart thirsting for you.

Darkness had fallen and we had earned our more tangible reward.

Years later I asked my mother whether my grandparents loved one another. "Yes," she said, "Lalaji would call Beyji to sit with him in his baithak. They loved one another very much." My mother looked down shyly as she said this because "love" was not expressed in those days. Although embarrassed, she explained that Lalaji would invite his wife to sit near him on his palang (bed) and to recite the morning hymn. Then they would both go to the gurdwara together.

Lalaji was impressive; he wore a big, loosely tied turban, a white kurta (tunic shirt) and pajama (loose cotton trousers) and a white dupatta around his neck. In his hand he always had his walking stick.

Lalaji and Beyji's spacious house in Kallar was like a museum to us grandchildren, a house full of wonders for us to investigate. During one visit from Lahore we went exploring as usual in the various rooms and wardrobes. I was poring over water colours my father had painted as a schoolboy when I came upon a temptingly beautiful find. It was a kangri, the sort of portable heater carried in Kashmir when temperatures fall far below freezing. Its earthenware bowl to hold live charcoal embers sat in a prettily woven basket decorated with red, blue and green shiny paper. The front of the kangri opened so that the charcoal could be replenished. "Beyji must have hidden something nice in here," I thought, so I picked up the kangri and put my hand inside. The next second I had dropped the kangri and rushed out. My fingers had touched something slimy and soft. A mouse had already fallen for the kangri, and given birth to ten babies.

The downstairs rooms opened off a veranda, covered by a steel roof which could be opened up to allow charpoys (the simple strung bedsteads which served as daytime seating) to be lowered or hoisted up. The staircase was too narrow for furniture to be carried up and down it. On one side of the house was Lalaji's baithak, his sitting room with its manually operated ceiling fan. On another was the cooking area, the chauka, with its hearth, the shoe-shaped chulha for cooking, angithi (a small bucket-shaped stove stoked with embers) and clay-lined tandoor. All our meals were prepared at floor level, and here groceries and brightly gleaming utensils were stored. A veranda led off from the chauka. Sacks of wheat and maize were piled up here ceiling-high in three rows. The muzaras, our farm-workers, beat the cobs and put the loose golden grains in sacks. In two small rooms lentils, rice and wheat flour were stored, as well as mango preserve, pickles and other foodstuffs.

Also on the ground floor was the supha, a long room like a baithak. The family slept here as well as upstairs. Beyji's supha was artistically arranged and I loved to hide away here, looking at her belongings.

Small store-rooms contained trunks, six feet long and three and a half feet wide, for storing quilts, pillows, sheets and heavy winter coats. The trunk-room was full of suitcases, including a special leather one, "Beyji's suitcase". Beyji's small almirah stood there too, and held a range of scent-bottles of different shapes and sizes which she kept locked away.

My grandparents and my parents were overjoyed when, two and a half years after my birth, the dai delivered a baby boy. This was my brother, Gurdip, my mother's first male child. But one superstition bothered them all: when a boy was born after three girls in succession or a girl after three boys the child was "bhara", the possible bearer of misfortune. Such a child was referred to as "trikhal". My elders feared that Gurdip's birth might herald business losses for my father. To counteract this they consulted the family astrologers who said that certain rituals must immediately be performed. A hole was made in one of the circular metal alloy trays (thali) from which we ate. My brother's diminutive body was passed through this hole to ward off any evil. From the roof top we heard the gong being beaten as someone shouted, "Chor agia, chor agia, sade ghar chor agia": bad luck would be driven away by these words: "A thief has come, a thief has come to our house."

My eldest sister, Bahin Vanti, was nearly ten years my senior. Her daughter, Updesh, is nearer my age. In Punjab a woman's parents could not be entertained in the house of her parents-in-law, and when Vanti married this tradition was rigidly observed. Bahin Vanti lived in the house of her father-in-law, a well-known doctor. After a few years of marriage she succumbed to tuberculosis. She never recovered. Heavy with apprehension my parents visited daily. After sitting with her in silence for several hours they would come back home for a meal, then return to be with her for a few more weary hours. Bahin Vanti's parents-in-law felt embarrassed, too bound by tradition to offer any food or drink. Tradition prevented my parents requesting even a sip of water. They prayed for her daily but she did not survive.

Next to Vanti in age was Gurcharan. (A second girl had died within days of birth.) Gurcharan was quiet and submissive and seemed perfectly satisfied to be cooking and looking after her younger bothers (two more were born after Gurdip) and sisters. She was so busy caring for us that she lost interest in her studies. In any case my parents probably never encouraged her.

Amrit was only two years older than me. I admired her smart looks and flamboyant ways. She was clever at her school work and my ideal in every respect. If Amrit did her hair in a new style I would copy her. If she wore a green salvar kamiz so did I. On one occasion my parents brought four pashmina shawls from Srinagar, Kashmir, for us to choose from. Although I was given first choice I wished Amrit to pick one first and then I insisted peevishly that this was the one I had wanted. Amrit wouldn't part with hers and there was no other like it. I sulked disconsolately for hours until Amrit let me have it.

I kept my finely woven and embroidered shawl until Wednesday, because my mother used to say that Wednesday and Saturday were the luckiest days to don new clothes for the first time, just as Sunday was most auspicious for wearing new jewellery. Similarly, Wednesday was propitious for work according to my mother's rhyming folk wisdom "Buddh kam suddh" (Wednesday's work is good). But in the same vein she cautioned us "Don't go to the hills on Tuesday or Wednesday. Even if you have won a game you will lose it." My father was even more superstitious than my mother.

When I was seven or eight years old he contracted TB. To avoid spreading the disease he used separate cutlery and utensils, and even relatives avoided visiting us. His business as a successful building contractor in Lahore collapsed and for a year, on the doctor's advice, he moved to Solan high in the mountains near Simla (now Shimla), the summer capital of Punjab during the British Raj. Recovery would, we hoped, be faster in the mountain air scented with pine resin.

Now that my father's health and business had collapsed he saw omens where none had been before. In particular he regarded the bats which hung in an outer room of the house as inauspicious. He ordered the farm hands to seal up every crack after the last bat had flitted out at sundown. If after that he saw the tell-tale droppings he knew he had not yet eluded his ill fortune. He would reach up, pluck the clinging black body from the ceiling, and throw it outside in disgust. If my father saw a woman as he was leaving the house he would come back, undo his shoelaces and, sitting on the charpoy, remove his shoes and shake them vigorously. Then he would pray and put some sugar in his mouth. If he met someone carrying a load of logs, that was also a bad omen. But if he met a sweeper, good luck would follow. All this was in addition to our commonly held Punjabi superstitions. So, even now, if I sneeze on leaving the house, I come back inside and set out again, praying in my heart.

While my father was convalescing in Solan my mother noticed that a big, black cat was always somewhere in our bungalow. Black cats in India have none of their British reputation as harbingers of good luck, and father was exasperated by the cat's persistent presence. He instructed our cook to remove the cat to the hills beyond the residential area of Solan. The cook obliged, but the cat did not. He was back next day, to Father's fury and consternation. This time he gave some money to our watchman's son, ironically called Chuha (rat), to transport our feline squatter to another village. Pussy never returned and my father's peace of mind was to some extent restored.

Although I attended local schools before our move to Solan, my first school memories are of the mission school there and its Christian teachers. I remember little about it except that we sang hymns in Hindustani. At Christmas we sang:

> Raja Yesu aya, Raja Yesu aya.
> King Jesus has come, King Jesus has come.

We received tiny gifts, and for many years I cherished the colourful chocolate box I was given there.

14

I can vividly picture one teacher, tall, broad and dark skinned with thick-set features, wearing a brightly coloured South Indian sari. She must have been what she seemed — a fresh convert from the lowest caste, the untouchables as we then called them.

From this period also I recall for the first time seeing English ladies, walking in an immaculate garden. I had never before seen western clothes or such pale skins. They were smartly dressed and their light-coloured hair was beautifully arranged. As they walked around the manicured garden they chatted tirelessly, their fingers busily engaged in knitting. From that time I have always admired people who do not waste a minute of their lives.

After several months there my mother's eldest brother, Sardar Bhagat Singh Duggal, a building contractor in Rawalpindi, visited my parents. To ease their burden he took Amrit and me back to Rawalpindi with him. For the next eighteen months we lived in Bai Number Chowki (literally Checkpoint No 22) the house of my maternal grandfather, Sardar Gurdit Singh Duggal. To Amrit and me our grandparents were Dhamialwale Lalaji and Beyji, because the family had moved here from Dhamial village near Rawalpindi. Bai Number Chowki was a small colony inhabited exclusively by the Duggal clan. My mother's three younger brothers' houses were next to Lalaji's.

The house was always lively with cousins, aunts and uncles coming and going, a wonderful contrast to my father's sombre household. One of my two masis (maternal aunts), Masi Basant, had been widowed in her teens. She conspired first with one sister-in-law, then another; the result was always a family quarrel. She would dress up and there were many stories of her friendships with men. One of my mamajis (maternal uncles) had a Rolls Royce and Lalaji had his own tonga, a horse-pulled gig, in which we rode to and from school. Amrit and I had started at a state primary school two miles away in Khalasi Lane near the cantonment. Gheba, the family servant, now in his fifties, escorted us in the tonga. In the afternoon he came to collect us.

Gheba's family lived in a village near Rawalpindi. One of his sons also joined my grandparents' service to look after their cattle, buffaloes and horses. Gheba was like one of the family, and his sons and daughters were married by Lalaji as a token of his recognition of Gheba's devotion to the Duggal family. While Amrit and I were there, Gheba fell ill, and Beyji gave him a bottle

15

of medicine marked up the side with the doses he was to take. When Beyji enquired if he was taking the medicine, Gheba cheerfully replied that he had swallowed the entire bottleful at once. "Can't waste my precious time taking one sip from this bottle every three hours," he said, and he disappeared after paying his respects to my grandmother who smiled at her servant's conscientiousness.

Amrit chattered coquettishly with our male cousins, and spend hours with Gurbir, a girl cousin of her own age, discussing boys. I know, because Gurbir's younger sister and I would hide under the bed where Amrit and Gurbir were sitting. Eavesdropping taught me much in those days. Gurbir knew I was too ignorant and innocent to ask questions or to tell tales to other cousins. So she used to send me with letters to her male cousins and boy friends. Although we had no idea of "boy friends" as such, all the same I remember everything happened secretly, unknown to parents and other older relatives.

As children we were frightened of our parents and elders. This was the norm. Mothers exercised strict control over their offspring and often shouted abuse at them.

Dhamialwale Lalaji's baithak looked out on the main road. He was an impresssive-looking man, and impressively turbaned. Supported by cylindrical bolsters he sat there on his bed with his stick beside him. Every morning Amrit and I visited him in his baithak and he gave us an anna, one sixteenth of a rupee, to spend during the school break. One day we left hurriedly, forgetting to collect our anna. Lalaji sent Gheba with it and chastised us on our return for having set off without our pocket money.

Lalaji always had his breakfast, lunch and dinner brought to his baithak. Beyji or Masi Basant brought Lalaji his food in katoris (bowls) with the chapatis on a round thali. His thali was more than one foot across and made of a brownish alloy, not stainless steel like modern ones. He drank no tea, only milk or lassi (a mixture of yoghurt and water) from a tall metal tumbler.

One day Beyji asked me to carry Lalaji's meal to him. "Couldn't your grandmother find anyone younger than you?" Lalaji shouted in scornful fury, frightening me. "Take it back!" Mortified. I did so and Beyji brought it in for him. Our elders always ate first and mothers ate only after their children. Everyone who was not a child seemed old.

Lalaji often sat outside the house in the shady courtyard. His

16

palang had brightly painted legs, elegantly carved in Kartarpur, the place where Guru Nanak had lived with his followers early in the sixteenth century. Across the wooden frame of Lalaji's palang was a mesh of interwoven white tape. On this his sheet was spread. Lalaji would call me to him and say, "Read me something from your schoolbook." Flattered, I gladly did so.

Mai Bhago's story was a favourite. Early in the eighteenth century the tenth Guru, Gobind Singh, had been defeated in battle by the Mughal army. His followers were demoralised, but not Mai Bhago who vowed she would die for the Guru if necessary. She rallied his men and, wearing men's clothes and turban, rode into the fray. Several of the Mughal governor's men fell to her sword and she won the blessing of the Guru for her heroism. Lalaji listened too as I read out the nursery rhyme:

> Bunde bunde dhara bane . . .
> Drop by drop you collect the water
> Until you have a river.
> Grain by grain you collect the harvest
> Until the storeroom's full.

Lalaji would pat my back and say, "One day this little daughter of ours will also be a famous lady."

It was while I was staying with Dhamialwale Lalaji and Beyji that I first heard about British rule. One January day in 1936 all the pupils in our school were told to sit on mats outside under the trees in the square. A man stood up to speak and sweets were distributed. I did not understand why, although I was informed "Angrez badshah aj gaddi te baithe" (Today the English emperor has come to the throne). England, I later learned, was somewhere beyond the seas, and in some mysterious way India was ruled from there.

After nearly two years in Solan my father was coughing much less and the fever had gone, but he was too weak for active work. He was still under doctor's orders and took his medicines religiously. His personality had changed: he became a violent and angry man.

My parents decided to move to our ancestral home in Kallar with Gurcharan, Gurdip and our two younger brothers, Mukhpal and Gurbachan. Here Amrit and I joined them. Even if no money was coming in at least we could survive on the grain, fruit and vegetables which the muzaras, our Muslim farm workers, brought us from the fields.

Shortly after Amrit and I returned to Kallar from Bai Number Chowki, Rawalpindi, news came of my Dhamialwala Lalaji's death. Whenever we visited Beyji after this we would see her spread a sheet on the floor, cover her face with her chunni (dupatta) and weep. After a long time she would rise from the floor, fold her sheet and put it away. Such was her grief at my grandfather's death. I missed my Lalaji's presence and Beyji's weeping made me very sad.

In Kallar Amrit and I attended Nidhan Kaur's dusty, noisy, government girls school. She was the headmistress, mean, short and shrivelled. Her eyes always looked sad and her brow was puckered in a permanent frown. Saraswati, the only other teacher, had been widowed in childhood. The school consisted of one room and a veranda. Nidhan Kaur perched at one end on her rickety stool while we small girls squatted on jute mats. There was no furniture except a blackboard. We were for ever chattering and enjoyed standing up to chant out tables in a singsong voice. "Two twos are four, two threes are six, two fours are eight." Nidhan Kaur called us little bitches and shrieked at us abusively. I have no recollection of her smiling; she always seemed to be upset and angry. All teachers were like this I supposed.

We had an alphabet book (kaida) but no exercise books for writing. Each of us came equipped with a wooden board called a takhti. Each day we washed it with water and then coated the surface with a clay paste which we made from a whitish block of gachchi mitti (cement-like substance). We waved the takhti around to dry it faster in the warm air. Our pens were inexpensive reed pens, sharpened at one end. When these became worn and fibrous we used to cut a fresh point. Eventually the pen would be too short to hold. We bought our ink as dry black flakes which we mixed with water in an inkpot, putting a scrap of rag in to slow down evaporation. Each day we added a little water. I did not write my exercises on paper until 1939 when I joined the Public School in Rawalpindi. For Geography we outlined maps of India in the mud. British India stretched South and East from the borders of Afghanistan to embrace Burma and Ceylon. We learned of the existence of Bombay, Madras and Calcutta, but little imagined visiting such distant places, with their alien languages, food and silk saris. The journey from Lahore to

Rawalpindi was the longest most of us had experienced, and there no-one wore a sari — the women all wore salwar kamiz and dupatta.

From school in Kallar we would run home and devour leftover chapatis with pickle or onion for relish. Our mothers were expert in pickle-making. Mango achar and chilli achar were top favourites. There was usually a stock of pickled aubergine, lime and carrot too. To make all these achars mother used mustard oil and fenugreek seeds.

Then, if hungry pangs persisted, we put maize from our domestic grain-store into a small basket and headed for the bhatthi, a hollow in the ground filled with burning wood. Fixed over this was a smoke-blackened karhai, an open, round-bottomed pan, containing hot sand. There were bhatthis at two or three spots in the village. For two hours each evening the bhatthiwali would pop corn or roast black gram according to the season. The bhatthi was a wonderful place for hearing gossip and glimpsing boys while the bhatthiwali sang her distinctive songs.

We would give the bhatthiwali a handful of our maize or gram as payment and the rest she tipped into the karhai. The golden maize seeds exploded into fluffy white popcorn which she shook energetically in a sieve to remove particles of sand. Our visit to the bhatthi was the day's high point. Four or five of us girls would go to the bhatthi together, get our popcorn, come home and go on eating and chatting.

Other treats were prepared at home. One was ambras (literally mango juice), made by frying rice flour with gur, the raw sugar (which is sold in great round chunks the colour of coffee, and is made by boiling the juice extracted from the harvested sugarcane until all moisture has evaporated). One tasty sweet was masale-wala gur, spiced raw sugar. To make this our mothers put clarified butter in the pan, added fennel seed (a popular Indian digestive), walnuts, almonds, cashews and some black pepper. When the gur began to melt into a sticky brown liquid the mixture was removed from the pan and moulded into delectable balls.

Mother made all sorts of traditional sweets. Mithai we call them. One of our favourites was round, hard pinnian, the size of golfballs, made with sugar and semolina, almonds, cashews and walnuts. One basic ingredient of these and many Punjabi sweet-meats was khoya, milk condensed by simmering for a long time. This might be mixed with sugar and dried nuts. During the winter when my mother made us pinnian she mixed in some of the nishasta (starch) she had dried and stored for future use. To make nishasta she soaked wheatflour for a week, until it had completely dissolved. The servant pounded it in a mortar until it was like milk in consistency, then strained the mixture through muslin. The nishasta was next spread on white sheets. To prevent lumps forming mother rubbed it with her hands. When the nishasta had dried thoroughly it was ready to be stored to add nourishment to our winter pinnian.

Navan purana means "new and old" in Punjabi. On Navan Purana day near the beginning of June my mother mixed the dough with flour, half ground from the old grain, half from the new harvest. She added clarified butter and syrup made from gur and made mithi roti (sweet bread) from the stiff dough. The mithi roti was cooked very slowly on the gridiron. Otherwise the sugar would have made it stick and burn. One roti was baked in the name of our male ancestors, one for my father, one for each of my three bothers and one for unborn male descendants, "to make them flourish". Naturally none was made in the name of female members of the family, whether past, present or future. We were "parai vast" — another's property. In these unspoken ways we learn our transient place among our kin.

The important thing was that we could all enjoy eating the delicious sweet bread.

2
Tradition

When I was eight or nine I became deeply religious. I suffered from various ailments and during one of my illnesses began to read the Sukhmani Sahib and other Sikh hymns daily. Sukhmani Sahib is the Hymn of Peace composed by the fifth Guru, Arjan Dev. I kept my devotions secret from the rest of the family, reading the hymns privately in my room and gradually memorised all the daily prayers.

Our family fortunes were at a low ebb and sorrow clouded everything. I had heard that God would fulfil the wishes of whoever lit jotan (wick lights) at Damdama Sahib. A jot is a diva, a simple lamp, made by putting a twist of cotton wool in a tiny saucer fashioned from chapati dough and fuelled with clarified butter. I had two wishes: I prayed that God would return my father to his former robust health and restore his hard-earned prosperity.

Damdama Sahib gurdwara stood near the palace of Sir Raja Baba Gurbaksh Singh. This holy shrine was a hall built of white marble. At one end were three copies of the Guru Granth Sahib ceremonially installed, before which everyone prostrated respectfully. Behind these on the wall were pictures. On one side hung a portrait of Baba Sahib Singh, on the other was Baba Khem Singh's picture. Sometimes we saw their living descendant, Sir Raja Baba Gurbaksh Singh Ji with Mataji, his wife, enthroned on the gaddi, a mattress spread with spotless white sheets. With them were their daughter, Kakiji, and Tikka Sahib, their eldest son. I was delighted to have their darshan (the blessing of being in their benedictory presence).

The atmosphere was sublime. From Pothohar, and from as far as Peshawar and Naushaira, devotees came to pay their respects to the Bedis, the heirs of Guru Nanak. In particular we revered the hallowed Nishan Sahib and Palang Sahib (respected flag and bed, respectively) on the marble platform outside the prayer hall. Here at twilight we sang our arati (a hymn of praise) and I lit my two jotan. Our chanting over, we shared as prashad (food blessed for distribution), two rich Punjabi sweetmeats — barphi and laddu — freely given to all who came. We girls sat with the ladies near to the Nishan Sahib. This was the saffron-coloured Sikh pennant which flew from a pole topped by the "khanda", the double edged sword of the Sikh faith. The flagstaff rose from a marble base, and near it, though no longer flying, was preserved an earlier Nishan Sahib, the flag that had flown before Baba Khem Singh's time. We bowed to the ground in reverence in front of this sacred pennant. We also prostrated ourselves before Palang Sahib, a single bed placed in honour of Baba Khem Singh. Inscribed on it were the words:

Ik on kar. Bhai Ram Singh Ji Bharian Kanganwale ne Palang Sahib di seva karai Vaisakh sammat 1911.
God is One. The Respected Bhai Ram Singh Bharian Kanganwale had the Palang Sahib made in the month of Vaisakh (March–April) AD 1854.

Here, of an evening, we performed arati and in exalted exhilaration threw our jasmine and marigold petals towards the Guru Granth Sahib. As I left Damdama Sahib, my spirit bathed in peace, I knew that my two jotan were burning in a steady prayer for my father's health and happiness. Here at Damdama Sahib, in turn, each of my brothers, Gurdip, Mukhpal and Gurbachan, came as a small boy for his dastarbandi. Dastarbandi means turban-tying and is the name for the simple ritual whereby a boy's head is for the first time wound in a turban by his father. Until then his uncut hair is tied back in two tight plaits or coiled in a topknot covered only by a small handkerchief.

Gurdip suffered at the hands of the rowdier boys of his own age. To the village lads he seemed a timid town boy. One day he came back crying and complaining that Mukha had beaten him with his stick, saying, "Why don't you shake hands with my stick?" Mukha was the local ringleader and mischief-maker who played havoc with young lads. Finding Gurdip a towny, and a straightforward young lad, he wanted to extract money from him. Gurdip was terrified of Mukha and his gang.

Near the gurdwara was Sital Singh's shop. He had a dark skin, a goaty beard and had lost his two front teeth. He wore a big rolled up turban. Sital Singh would sit glowering angrily over the balances which he used to weigh out even the minutest amount. From him we bought creamy, snow white milk for four paise a seer (two pounds weight), and firm set yoghurt. He stocked sweet sesame-coated revrian (lozenges of hard sugar) and shrivelled black malok, fruit that was dried up like prunes, but with a seed not a stone in the middle. For half a paisa we could take a handful. Sital Singh lived behind the shop with his plump wife. In their courtyard grew a tree which bore delicious behrs (sweet fresh berries). One of my smaller friends would climb the tree and shake it to make the sweet behrs fall. Sital Singh would shout in fury if he detected us and off we would scamper before he could catch us. Informally we all knew him as Seetla.

Our meals at home were basic. Day after day we ate straightforward dal (lentils), sabzi (vegetable cooked with spices), homemade yoghurt and chapatis. Only on festive occasions did we have khir (creamy rice pudding), gajrela (made from grated carrots simmered in milk till no liquid remained, and then sweetened) and pinnian (the hard sweet balls of semolina). We looked forward keenly to our repetitive repasts. Our teeth were healthy and the ingredients were pure and fresh.

Every morning before we got up my mother would make snowy butter. The water buffaloes' milk had been boiled the previous day and poured into a round earthenware pot to make yoghurt. A little of the previous day's yoghurt added to the warm milk turned it to curd. She churned the curd with the madani, a wooden shaft tipped with a wooden cross in a horizontal plane. A cord was wound around the upper part of the madani, which was specially grooved for the purpose. With this cord it was secured to a sturdy pole set in the ground. Mother squatted beside the pot on a pirha, a multi-coloured stool made like a mini charpoy, and steadied it with her foot while rotating the madani. To do this she pulled rhythmically on the two ends of another cord lower down the shaft of the madani — left, right, left, right left, right. We breakfasted with relish on a freshly cooked paratha with a blob of the recently churned butter melting over it. We drank the cool buttermilk, with a dash of salt or sugar, as a refreshing lassi.

Our house was the only one in the village to boast a lavatory, but we did not generally use it. This job was done early in the morning, before dawn, when we went to the river Kanshi for our daily bath. No-one in our village had running water. At four in the morning a water-carrier brought us water in great tin drums hanging from his shoulder yoke. He fetched the water from the well, Shiva's well, the Shankre da Khuh three furlongs away. Every morning and every evening he carried water uphill to our house. There was another well in the village, but no-one drew water from it. It was unlucky: perhaps someone had fallen down it years before and died there.

My elder sisters were not allowed to carry water, but as a child I loved to put an innu, a ring of firmly wound cloth, on my head and set on this a big pot. I proudly brought this earthenware vessel home full of fresh water, but I always had to steady it with one hand.

Elder women accompanied us to the river, but we always hoped to coincide with some group of boys. In summer as the water dwindled the male and female bathers moved a degree closer. Scared of our vigilant chaperones the men dared not glance towards us. In the first rays of daylight we bathed, stooping to hide our burgeoning breasts, and aware of showing them, as we poured water over our bodies with cupped hands. We young girls would be stark naked, in part wanting to be noticed but behaving as if we were hiding from the watching men. Groups of young lads always timed things so that they were walking behind us to bathe in the Kanshi.

The village women's daily work included washing clothes, sheets and pillow cases in the river, then drying them, folding them and taking them home. The stones of the river bed came in all colours, shapes and sizes. During the monsoon it was impassable. Otherwise the farm-workers would go across and return with their donkeys laden with lentils, vegetables and fruit, the produce from our fields beyond the river. When the farm-workers needed salt or oil they would buy these by selling their own share of the harvest. Fathers and sons walked barefoot together with no thought of a more luxurious lifestyle.

If they needed extra the labourers would come to my mother as she sat preparing vegetables on the jute-strung charpoy in the courtyard. Fazal Din, Karam Din, Ram Dula and the others had seen my father growing up. They were an accepted part of our extended family. Sitting on the floor they would share their domestic problems as they would with an older member of their own household. My parents felt this responsibility and gave them extra cash, clothes and other gifts at the time of marriage, especially when a son or daughter was getting married.

When I was well enough I enjoyed playing with other girls in the village. A sadness hung over our house during the months of my father's illness, but when guests visited us the family looked as cheerful as possible. Food was seasonal and supplies were sometimes low. Then even at festival time my mother could cook nothing more than a wheaten paratha served with sweet, golden, crumbly shakar (pure, unrefined sugar). What confectionery could have been better for us? But we longed for mithai and a better daily menu. When the wheat flour ran out we had to make do with the coarser millet and maize flour. There was no money for buying wheat flour to tide us over to the next harvest.

Our neighbours, Motilal and Soni, were Jains. They would bring pebbles from the riverbed, boil them and drink the water — or so I believed as a child. That was how my elders described the Jains' diet, and our neighbours were Bhavras (Jains). Around my grandparents' house were some ten Jain households, and from Lalaji's baithak you could see the temple. Holy men visited from time to time, mouth and nose covered surgeon-like, by a white cloth so that no insect was inadvertently inhaled or swallowed and so killed. The white wool whisk they carried over one shoulder was to remove unwitting insect victims from their path. Naturally, with such high standards of non-violence, our Bhavra neighbours ate no flesh or eggs. They also avoided ginger, onion and garlic, and tomatoes too because, they told us, tomatoes resembled blood.

Soni and Motilal lived upstairs and stored their grain on the ground-floor. One day one of their muzaras (tenant farmers) came to the house with his donkey loaded with grain. Soni opened the door while we carried on playing outside. Suddenly Soni's shrieks frightened us. My mother rushed out to find the muzara retreating while Soni furiously abused his receding figure. As she calmed down she explained that he had demanded money for bringing the customary share of corn. She had refused, as muzaras were never paid for this portion of produce. He had then turned insolent. That was Soni's story. But the gaggle of housewives bathing at the riverside soon knew better, and word spread that the muzara had seduced Soni.

25

Some Brahmins also lived in the village. One was the only doctor, Ram Charan, a gaunt figure clad in pajama and kurta (loose straight cotton trousers and a cool shirt worn over them). Ram Charan knew a little about typhoid, cholera and quinine, so when my brothers ran high temperatures Ram Charan was called. For most ailments homemade remedies were administered. Mother-in-law's tongue, roasted in hot ashes to remove the skin, cured many conditions. For indigestion powdered amla fruit was mixed with milk. Another medicine was ark, made by boiling ajwain (a pungent seed) with fennel seeds. If a woman failed to conceive the dai recommended some age-old treatment, often with no conspicuous success.

Brahmin families such as Ram Charan's kept away from other castes. I recall one old lady following behind a low-caste woman with a glass of water, so that she could sprinkle it. Water, it seemed, would purify the places where she had trodden. I recall Brahmin ladies who bathed and changed into clean clothes if a sweeper's shadow fell on them. At least sweepers did not have to carry a warning bell, as they did in some other parts of India, but they lived in a separate part of the village and washed further along the river than the rest of us.

Brahmins were entitled to offerings of food, known as handa, in any house they chose to visit. Chachi Rajo, an elderly Brahmin lady who lived alone across the galli from us, exploited this privilege to the full. She was related to Ram Charan the doctor. "You are my daughter-in-law," she would say to my mother. This meant that my mother could not deny her a meal. Chachi Rajo certainly specialised in being given tasty repasts in other people's houses. Wrinkled and barefoot, her head covered, she arrived, bearing morsels of gossip in exchange for abundant helpings of food. Seeing my attractive elder sisters deftly embroidering she would remark to my mother, "Someone will cast an evil eye upon those daughters of yours." Then came the antidote. "I will get a bunch of hair from So and So's house. Then your family will not be affected." She would come with a clump of hair, mutter something and throw the hair into the burning wood fire. As the hair burned she would be jumping with glee, saying, "Now your children are safe and sound. Guru rakhe" (May the Guru protect them). Whenever Chachi Rajo came my mother would serve her parathas, butter and vegetables. After eating these with great relish she would take her leave, blessing the family.

26

With babies preventive measures were always taken to ward off the evil eye. Whether a boy or a girl, the baby's face would be smudged with black and the baby's eyes outlined with sooty kajal. This was beneficial to the eyes and made them look large and lovely. When we were older I remember how, at least once a week, my mother would take seven red chillis and pass them seven times over our heads. Then she used to burn them with black harmal seeds in the fire nearby. Pungent smoke stung our eyes and any envious curse was dispelled.

There were more men than women in our villages. From other villages we often heard how, carrying out a grandfather's muttered instruction, "Palla pa dio", the dai (village midwife) had quietly smothered a newborn girl. Even if such irreversible measures were not taken, girls were more prone to die in childhood than their brothers; fewer delicacies were showered upon them. So, if there was any question mark over a man's reputation, he might be hard pressed to find a wife in our relatively closed society. Alone, with no social standing, he received few invitations to the homes of others. Dyal Singh was one such unfortunate bachelor. From our house at the top of the village we overlooked his terrace lower down the street. He would wake about four in the morning and sing:

> Nange ana, nange jana
> Koi na rahisi raja rana.
> Naked we come, naked we go.
> Not even kings and queens are exempt.

One day Dyal Singh disappeared. On his return word went around, "Dyal Singh has brought back a she-ass." His bride was dark-skinned with a big red bindi (dot) in the centre of her forehead. She wore bright lipstick and rouge. No-one spoke to her or invited her in. Her language was different from ours. We termed her and others like her "banelan". (The word "banelan" was one coined by the villagers to show their disgust at mixed parentage.) Desperate bachelors would go to Uttar Pradesh and purchase banelans. Then at least they might put an end to the whispered gossip, "Dyal Singh mates with cows and horses."

Great was the excitement when a young man was engaged to a girl from Rawalpindi or Gujarkhan. From house to house the word spread, "A city girl is coming to our village." The whole village participated in every marriage in Kallar. The bride's family would borrow a charpoy from here, bedclothes from there. There was no janjghar, the building used to accommodate a bridegroom's kin. Instead villagers offered their spare beds and rooms to the barat, those accompanying the groom to his wedding. Every marriage in the village was everybody else's affair and they all participated and gave a gift of one or two rupees.

On the day after the marriage ceremony the bridal party departed with the dowry. We could all see the procession bearing clothes and furniture given by the bride's family. We all heard the sobbing of the bride and her relatives as she left home for the unknown world of her husband and his family. If the bride did not weep up to the general expectation tongues wagged, "What sort of girl is she, not a tear in sight?" or "Oh, she is happy to leave her parents, she is not like us innocent girls." Innocent! These village girls knew more than the town girls.

Anyone could act as matchmaker and everyone knew everyone else. Marriages were always in the air. From my earliest childhood I overheard my elders speaking of some new bride:

What a wonderful daughter-in-law. She worships her parents-in-law.
Sara din kam lagi rahindi hai. Boldi nahin. (She works away all day without speaking.)

A bride's first priority was to please her mother-in-law. Only then would she be accepted into her husband's family. If a girl was a good daughter-in-law then her husband would be proud of her. There would be domestic peace.

As I grew older I realised that the day would inevitably come when I too would be bundled up in scarlet and gold and given away in marriage. I hoped I too would be a good daughter-in-law.

Nobody seemed to consider the girl from any other angle, not even to say whether she would make a good wife, certainly not whether she would be happy. No-one ever mentioned anything about the couple — their happiness, compatibility or sexual relationship. Sex had always been a taboo, a dirty aspect of life which must never be mentioned.

Marriages apart, festivals were the most exciting landmarks in our lives. Our annual festivals arose naturally from the changing crops and seasons, celebrated family relationships, and commemorated key events in Sikh history, or else their origins were lost in the ageless cycle of Hindu mythology. Many festivals involved more than one of these elements. Most were fixed according to the Hindu lunar calendar. All brought their own excitement.

Every year at wheat harvest time we celebrated our Sikh new year, Vaisakhi, on April 13th. As children we were unconcerned with its special religious importance for Sikhs: it was on this day in 1699 that our tenth Guru had baptised his followers as the first Singhs. What mattered to us was the feasting on light, fried, golden puris that ballooned in the oil, then deflated on our plates, and creamy rice khir and halwa for lunch, shared with countless friends and relatives.

At the hottest time of year our fifth Guru, Arjan Dev, had endured torture at the hand of his Mughal oppressors. He had been forced to sit on a griddle over a fire and expired when his body was thrown into the river. That was in 1606. On every anniversary Sikhs distributed a refreshing drink to all comers. On this day of remorseless heat no-one would go thirsty, whatever their caste or creed, and no matter how big the vessel they brought to be filled. Stalls called chhabil were set up. A mixture of milk, water and white, granulated sugar was poured on to ice in a big pot. Thence it was freely given. For us Sikhs this was a major gurpurab or religious festival. In the gurdwara an unbroken reading of the Guru Granth Sahib would begin two days previously, and on the eve of the gurpurab, all of us — men, women and children — would flock behind the decorated vehicle which bore aloft both the enthroned Guru Granth Sahib and men singing its inspired hymns.

Torrential rains followed the intense heat. For four months the rains fell and the stony river-bed was a rushing expanse of filthy brown water. Boys caught fish trapped in the branches of uprooted trees and bushes. They salvaged wood for fuel. Every morning we returned from our ablutions at the riverside dirtier than we had been before. The rough pebbly street between our houses turned to mud, and leeches stuck to our legs and fell off when bloated, leaving a trickle of blood. I remember my sister Amrit standing screaming for someone to rescue her from a leech which had stuck to the upper part of her vagina.

At this time of the year our drinking water was not only sieved and boiled as usual, but we added potassium permanganate crystals and then filtered it a second time. The water took a pinkish tinge. But after such heat, with all those discomforts, we revelled in the rain. On Tiyan day I would swing with girls of my own age. Stout ropes were tied to orchard trees near the well. There were no wooden seats and the coarse rope left our hands red. We competed to see who could swing highest, knowing that the next such opportunity would be during the Navratra days which precede Divali.

During the monsoon, on Rakhi Day, the day of the full moon of Shravan (August), we reaffirmed the bond between brothers and sisters. Nowadays girls buy elaborate, tinselly decorations to tie on their brothers' right wrists or to send through the post. In my childhood a plain red thread sufficed. We girls got up early and, with "sucha munh" (before eating anything), took plates of sweetmeats to our brothers. We each tied our rakhri (the Punjabi name for the auspicious red thread that is called rakhi in Hindi) around each brother's right wrist, and popped a sweet in his mouth. For us the most exciting part of the ritual was receiving a coin in return for our rakhri. Among Sikhs and Hindus brothers know that they must support their sisters when support is needed. When our parents have gone our brothers will be there. It would be unlucky indeed for any brother who gave no present to his married sister when she left her parental home to rejoin her husband. Unaware as yet of their future responsibilities my younger brothers, Gurdip, Mukhpal and Gurbachan, strutted about proudly showing off their wrists festooned with threads from all their sisters and female cousins. My mother tied the first rakhri onto the Guru Granth Sahib, so seeking an abundance of blessings from Almighty God.

There were also days to remember ties with deceased relatives. On Shraddh days Hindus fasted on behalf of their forebears. In my family only my parents observed this fast, which ended at three or four in the afternoon. Food was sent to an orphanage or given to Brahmins, so Chachi Rajo was in her element, because as a Brahmin she was invited to everyone's house. She ate as much as she could and took home the chapatis she could not manage to devour on the spot. I heard her say, "I keep eating the chapatis I collect during Shraddh until they start to go off. Then I dry them and soak them in water. By adding some gur I make sweet halwa from whatever is left." At that time many people could hardly afford two chapatis a day, let alone fruit and vegetables. Although Hindus fasted more often than Sikhs, the married ladies of both groups rigidly observed the fast of Karwa Chauth which occurred in the Autumn between the festivals of Dassehra and Divali, for their husbands' welfare was at stake. Before the first glimmer of dawn young wives would eat sargi, sweet and savoury items, including sultanas, cashew nuts and almonds, sent by their parents. Throughout the daylight hours my grand-mother, mother and aunts abstained from all food and drink. In the afternoon all the daughters-in-law of the neighbourhood gathered to hear a Brahmin lady read the traditional injunctions:

> Sun bahin piari viran,
> Chanchare te pani pivan . . .
> Na katie, na terie,
> Na ghum charakha pherie.
> Listen, my little sister, only when I see the moon will I have a drop of water . . .
> Don't cut, don't sew, don't turn the spinning wheel.

The ladies wore two chunnis over their heads. The outer chunni was always a red one on Karwa Chauth, and they were decked out in their best clothes and jewellery. They stood in a circle singing and passing round a thali of money and whole almonds. Then each woman returned home with her thali, reverently touched the feet of her parents-in-law and offered them the almonds. The Brahmin lady had received some money for her efforts. None of the ladies of the household ate until she had seen the moon through a brass sieve and flicked some diluted milk through the sieve towards it. Only then could the women sit down to a sumptuous meal.

3

Rawalpindi and Lahore

When my father had recovered sufficiently to restart his business we returned to my birthplace in Rawalpindi. In this he followed my mother's brothers' example — they had moved from Dhamial to expand their contracting business in Rawalpindi. But whereas they had settled in Bai Number Chowki my father built a spacious house in Arya Mahalla. On the main road outside the mahalla (residential area) was the famous Gordon College and on the other side was the extensive Arya Hospital. The houses of the mahalla were terraced with three or four rooms downstairs. None of them was designated dining room or bedroom, but the front room was used as a baithak cum rasoi (combined drawing room and kitchen area) and the rest of the rooms had beds. Trunks were stacked up in every room almost to the ceiling, each trunk covered with a lace-edged, embroidered tablecoth. We ate our food out in the courtyard, sitting on a charpoy with a table drawn up close. Our elders were happier to sit on low stools near the cooking area, eating chapatis fresh from the griddle.

I remember my father sitting in his baithak with its outer wooden door and the inner one of metal gauze. In summer only the metal gauze door was shut, so allowing in a current of air. Daily my mother washed the cement floors. Every morning the postman climbed the three steps to our door and shouted resoundingly, "Sardar Sohan Singh Pureeeeee" before putting my father's mail in the grey letterbox beside the door. No post ever came addressed to anyone else.

I attended Modern Cambridge School, Rawalpindi. One girl in our class stood out against the others. Ranjita, a buxom girl, was always well dressed and behaved like an older girl. When we studied the great Punjabi poet Professor Mohan Singh's anthology *Sanve Pattar* (Green Leaves) the romantic undertones were lost on me. During recess we clustered round her, munching our one anna's worth of starchy kulcha, spicy chickpeas and green chillis or a two-paisa bar of chocolate. Then Ranjita would explain the meaning of Mohan Singh's love poetry. She told us that her knees had rubbed against the English master's under the desk. "It's wonderful. It makes me tingle all over." I wondered why.

In Rawalpindi, as in the village, out entertainments were few and a crowd would gather around any visiting tamashewala (entertainer). We watched in amazed trepidation as the performer advanced barefoot or in ill-fitting sandals across a tightrope, or his son leapt through a hoop of flames and knives. A tamashewala might swallow pieces of glass, nails and crumpled razor blades, then pull them effortlessly out of his mouth. His wife might lie with her head submerged in a bucket of water for ten minutes that seemed endless. How, we wondered, could she go on breathing? Some item in a conjuror's hand would turn up miraculously in a spectator's bag to everyone's astonishment, no matter how many times we had witnessed this feat before.

The wail of the snake charmer's pipe irresistibly signalled his arrival in our galli. The snake charmer (sapera) played two insistent notes on a gourd pipe. He carried two round wicker baskets suspended from the ends of his wooden yoke. We waited fascinated as he carefully lowered these, removed the covering cloth and squatted by the baskets, piping with raucous persuasiveness. Slowly the cobra's hood appeared from its basket and, more or less reluctantly, the huge snake uncoiled and swayed to its rhythm. We could not understand why the cobra did not harm his trickster of a master, and only later heard that most saperas died of snake bite.

The monkey man was always popular. To shouts of "Bandarwala agia!" (The monkey-man has arrived!) we would converge to see his trio of monkeys perform age-old tricks. No-one could resist throwing a few paise when the monkey walked upright around the ring of spectators, hands together, bowing and saluting. In the monkey's act we saw episodes of our own unspectacular lives. Perched in her pink frilly dress in a wooden barrow the bride was drawn by her triumphant monkey bride-groom. But there were no weeping monkey relatives at the departure of this diminutive bridal palanquin.

Less often we gathered to watch the antics of a great black

performing bear. The richhwala (bear man) strode along the roads between the villages and into the towns, his bear lurching behind on all fours, a stout lead attached to his collar. The bear behaved like a perfect biped, obedient to his master's commands, greeting us with raised forepaws, winning the remainder of our pocket money.

One day a family of wandering puppeteers enlivened our galli with scenes from the two Hindu epics, the Mahabharata and Ramayana. On another occasion we heard a bell ringing outside our door and a man's voice singing,

> Bara baras ki ma banegi.
> Bis baras ki beva banegi.
> She will be a mother at twelve.
> And a widow at twenty.

Marriages and festivals, for which we often returned to Kallar, continued to enliven our year. While we were living in Arya Mahalla one of my mother's brothers' daughters got married. For some reason my father refused to participate. It was necessary for all relatives to show their approval by attending the engagement ceremony. When there had been a difference of opinion it was not uncommon for a relation to make his point by conspicuously objecting to the proceedings and absenting himself. I still recall my father's obstinacy and the morose faces of my disgruntled uncles. Everyone begged him, but he would not listen to any Duggal. Finally my Mamaji (maternal uncle) removed his turban and laid it on my father's feet, so accepting unconditional defeat, apologising and inviting him to come to his daughter's wedding. This was my father's opportunity to show that, regardless of their wealth, Rolls Royces and abundance of servants, he was more important than they were.

The festival of Lohri fell around January 13 each year. In addition to the sweets, the good food and the new clothes there was the excitement of a bonfire. As darkness fell we gathered around the fire, munching and feeding the flames with dried rice, popcorn and hard round revrian made of raw sugar coated with sesame seeds. There were Lohri de khilone to enjoy, colourful animal-shaped sweets made of sugar which had been boiled and set very hard. January nights in Kallar were chilly so we looked forward to drinking hot, sweet tea. One year the fel-

low responsible for contributing the sugar mischievously sub-
stituted salt.

Lohri was particularly memorable for families blessed during
the previous twelve months with the birth of a son. The mother
would receive gifts of clothes, food and sweets. She carried the
infant several times around the blazing bonfire, praying for a
blessing on the family. For several days beforehand we children
went from house to house singing Lohri songs and being
rewarded with gifts. To turn away a Lohri singer was deemed
inauspicious.

> Sundar mundarie. Ho!
> Tera kaun vichara? Ho!
> Dulla Bhatti wala. Ho!
> Dulle di dhi viahi. Ho!
> Ser shakar pai. Ho!
>
> Beautiful girl. Ho!
> Who will think about you? Ho!
> Dulla of the Bhatti clan will. Ho!
> Dulla got his daughter married. Ho!
> He gave a seer of sugar. Ho!

And so on . . . with one child singing the first words of each
line and the others coming in with a loud "Ho!" (Dulla is the name
of the Robin Hood of Punjab, Abdullah Bhatti, who was famous
for rescuing girls from being sold into slavery centuries ago in the
time of the Mughal emperor Akbar.)

In February Basant Panchami brought the excitement of kite-
flying with the boys. The mustard fields were brilliant yellow,
men sported yellow turbans, women's chunnis (dupattas) were
all yellow, and we ate saffron-coloured pilau and halwa. From
every flat roof terrace multicoloured kites were flying. They were
made of tissue paper stretched taut over a simple frame
consisting of three splints. We ensured our kites had strong
threads by dipping them in a mixture of glue and a powder made
by grinding down small pieces of glass. That way they would cut
through our competitors' kite-strings without being severed
themselves. When we were with our cousins the boys would
make us grind the glass for this mixture.

Holi falls in March. In those days everyone, high and low, Sikh,

Hindu and Muslim, joined in the merriment in town or village, throwing coloured powders or squirting coloured water through syringes. We wore our oldest clothes, stained from previous Holis, and no-one was exempt. Girls, otherwise demurely distant, daubed the faces of male victims and drenched them in colour. We spent the previous days whispering conspiratorially. Now was our chance to single out touchy individuals for special treatment. If they objected bad luck would befall them. On Holi day we feasted on golden puris and rich sweets: halwa, khir and gulab jamun.

The day after Holi was Hola Maholla, a day sacred for Sikhs. So we visited the gurdwara to make our offerings, listen to the musicians singing hymns and enjoy the soft, sweet prashad which we received in cupped hands. No more colour throwing on Hola Maholla, but for several days our pillows and sheets were stained with rainbow colours, however assiduously we washed our hair.

Melas were fairs. Dressed in our finery we darted among the crowd. We milled around the temporary stalls, met our friends and marvelled at this exciting world. At the Dassehra mela in the Autumn there was an extra attraction. On the outskirts of Kallar village the story of Ram (Rama) and Sita was re-enacted with towering, colourful figures of Ram, the noble king, Sita his virtuous wife, Lakshman, his loyal brother and Ravan, the menacing king of Lanka who treacherously abducted Sita. In Rawalpindi there were extensive Ramlila grounds where crowds flocked to see the gigantic images of Ram, Sita, Lakshman and the ten-headed Ravan. Children loved to scamper along as Hanuman's monkeys who assisted Ram in his quest for his abducted wife.

In readiness for Divali the house was thoroughly cleaned. There could be no Divali without divas, the lipped clay bowls an inch or two across, used as oil lamps to illuminate the house on the darkest night of the lunar month of Kartik (October-November). On Divali day the divas rose in price, so we bought them the day before and soaked them all day in a bucket of water. That way the porous clay absorbed less oil. We checked the supply of mustard oil and sat twisting the fluffy raw cotton into wicks. Then we arranged the divas on trays and thalis. Every room must be illuminated, even the lavatory. Divas would twinkle all around the flat roof top.

On Divali day even the poorest families cooked meat and there were lots of sweetmeats. We wore fine new clothes and waited impatiently for dusk when we could set off our fireworks. Not everyone had enough self-discipline and the day was punctuated by bangers exploding in the street.

At night the menfolk drank and gambled. For each of my brothers my mother made a hatti (shop). This was like a small wooden dolls' house, painted green and divided into compartments. In each compartment she put a plate of sweets. Walnuts were a must, and we children later used these to play.

Some Sikhs who read this will say that this is a Hindu custom, and so it is. In Kallar, Beyji would go to the Shivala, the local Hindu shrine. She performed both Sikh and Hindu rituals. Probably her parents had been Hindu and Lalaji too was the first Sikh on that side of the family.

We would put coins in a thali, and among them one dating from the time of Guru Nanak which was inscribed in Arabic script. Beyji mixed saffron with milk in a silver bowl and added it to the fresh milk and water in the thali, then dipped in the fourth finger of her right hand to mark the "Nanakshahi" coin. She chanted "May God bless us and grant us success in this happy new year." We bowed our heads in prayer and ate festival sweets.

At home we kept the four wicks of the chaumukhia ("four-faced") diva burning all night by refilling it with oil, and we left the door of every room open, including the one to Babaji's room. We hoped that Lakshmi (prosperity) would enter. Our more immediate concern as children was the fireworks: I loved the spinning Catherine wheels.

One of my uncles had been a building contractor in Naushaira in the North West Frontier Province near Peshawar. He had a shop too in the Cantonment stocked with "angrezi chizan", things for the Army officers. He gave my aunts bottles of unforgettable perfume, and for us children there was chocolate, a box of tiny racquets and balls and plastic dolls. We cooked them food, pretending with toy utensils, taught them their Gurmukhi alphabet, ura, era, iri, sasa, nursed them back to health when they were ill, and performed their marriages. To be married honourably my girl doll needed a dowry. So with my daily pocket money of one anna a day I got toys, little dresses, pieces of cloth and sweets.

One of my older cousins played tennis in Gordon College, so there were plenty of tennis balls to bounce as we sang:

Thal pavan, thal pavan
Vich motianda har pavan . . .

Bouncing ball, bouncing ball,
Put on a necklace of pearls.
My necklace bobs up and down.
In the garden a small bird sings.
Sing little bird, I am your sister-in-law,
Wearing red bangles (of a new bride).

We skipped with lengths of rope, and played hide and seek, as well as chich kichole: two of us would hide in different places and make as many marks as possible on a brick or stone. Each of us had to find the other's marks. The winner was the player who managed to make the most marks before his or her brick was found.

We girls enjoyed playing kikli in pairs. Each girl crossed her hands over at the wrist and seized hold of her partner's hands, similarly crossed. Then we spun round and round faster and faster. Gulidanda (tipcat) was really a boys' game, but I used to play it with my boy cousins with a brightly coloured stick, pointed at both ends. The players had to strike the pointed end of a similar shorter stick so that it jumped in the air and landed somewhere else.

All year round boys played at marbles while girls preferred gite (pebbles). Four or five of us would sit on the doorstep with our five pebbles. We played it like dibs: with one pebble in your hand you had to pick up the remainder individually, then two pairs, then all four together, finally catching them on the back of your hand. The hard shiny kernels of the soapnut (ritha) could double up as marbles or gite. If you shook a soap nut you heard it rattle inside.

Soapnuts look like nutmegs. They were soaked in water to produce a thick lather and we removed any bits of broken nutshell with a sieve. We had no soapflakes or washing powders in those days. Blocks of hard soap were adequate for laundering most of our clothes, but for the fine embroidered shawls woven from Himalayan pashmina goat fleece we used soapnut lather and we washed our hair with it too. Ladies who wished to strengthen their hair and keep it black longer would boil shikakai pods and use this water. These pods were four to six inches in length and grew on big trees in the jungle, but people who did not go out to gather them could buy them. The dry brown pods were boiled, seeds and all. Nowadays Indians buy ready-made shikakai shampoos and soaps.

A newborn baby's hair was first washed with soap and then with freshly made dahi (yoghurt). If this was rubbed in well the baby's hair would grow strong and shiny, and it was also thought to be beneficial to the brain. It was certainly cooling and soothing. My parents always used dahi to wash their hair, and my father was very particular about having a bowl full of yoghurt for this purpose.

Providing the weather was neither too hot nor too cold, women sat cross-legged chatting together on the veranda and massaged babies firmly and lovingly with mustard oil. Adults rubbed almond oil (badam rogan) into their scalp and onto their faces. Milk too was good for the complexion: I would bathe my face in it, washing it off only when I had finished my bath. We made an excellent astringent by drying orange peel in the sun, then grinding it in a small mortar and adding cream from the pans of boiled milk. My mother made a facial mask from chickpea flour and cream. She applied this mixture to her face each day, scraping it off when it had dried. After churning butter in the early morning she rubbed her greasy hands with coarse wheat-flour or chickpea flour and applied it to her face, so cleansing her hands and beautifiying herself.

Surma was kept in a little brass container (surmadani) with an elaborate applicator. Surma is a dark grey substance used as eye makeup. My mother or aunts made it by soaking a special piece of metal on the days immediately following a full moon. With the addition of a drop of rosewater the surma was ground intermittently over the next forty-one days in a separate pestle and mortar reserved for this purpose. Surma was applied to the surface of the eye inside the lid as it was believed to enhance both vision and beauty.

Kajal too resembled mascara and was applied with a deft stroke of the fourth finger. I always associate kajal-making with Masi Basant. She would prop a dish above the four-wick chau-mukhia oil light that burned throughout Divali night in front of the Guru Granth Sahib upstairs. To the accumulated soot she addded a drop or two of butter. She distributed this among the family for our beautification and for protection from the evil eye.

Until I was fifteen I saw almost no other cosmetics. A fair complexion was coveted and no-one wanted a dark skinned daughter or daughter-in-law. As one Punjabi saying has it:

> Gora rang kise nu rab na deve sara pind vair pai gia.
> The whole village is jealous of anyone to whom God gives a fair complexion.

From cosmetics to confectionery: in Rawalpindi I saw animals and birds of all colours fashioned from flavoured sugar called gatta which was as pliable as plastocene. The vendor picked up the mixture rolled around a big stick and deftly moulded it into into a peacock, swan, cat or monkey, a miracle too beautiful to be eaten — or almost ! Old woman's hair (buddhi mai da jhatta) was our name for candyfloss which came in all colours.

Kulfi is India's icecream. The kulfiwala carried his icecream in a wooden box on his head — none of us then dreamt of domestic refrigeration. Each round chunk of kulfi was wrapped in an insulation of tweed tape. He scraped the pale green kulfi off with a knife, and served it on a banyan leaf, or dabbed a free sample on the back of our hands.

At home in Rawalindi my mother made icecream throughout the summer, using blocks of ice from the ice stall. Caustic soda stopped it melting too fast. Mother put the ice in a wooden pail which contained a pot with a handle attached to it. Into the pot she poured milk thickened by boiling, then she added crushed pistachio nuts or golden mango pulp. After she had turned the handle for forty minutes the kulfi, fragrant and creamy, was ready. However relentless the sun outside, the kulfi had no time to melt.

When I was about thirteen my father brought us back to Lahore, to the fine house called Puri Nivas which we had evacuated when TB ruined his business. We lived upstairs over the shops, in the heart of the bazaar. Despite paternal disapproval we girls used to sit on the sofa-shaped cement seats projecting inwards from the parapet of the roof terrace, commanding a grandstand view. We watched the arrival of the dandanwala or travelling dentist. Fair-compexioned, red-cheeked, dressed in a loose-fitting black kurta-pajama, the dandanwala approached the central shopping area, heralded by his own resounding patter. "If you have toothache, come here, come here. See this magic potion. One drop and you'll never have toothache again." He held up little golden-yellow bottles. From the crowd clustering around him a patient came forward. With a quick twist of the pincers the dandanwala extracted the tooth, and brandished it. Another dozen sufferers would come up to him for relief. Once he had pulled out a tooth he inserted cottonwool in the socket. Nobody screamed or even complained of discomfort, and not a drop of blood was shed.

My health began to fail and my parents feared I was consumptive. My head ached, my stomach weakened, dysentery ruled my life, and my parents tried a succession of remedies. An astrologer drew up my horoscope, and I was seen by the best city physicians. One traditional practitioner recommended a blue tika, an inkspot in the centre of my forehead. My father applied this daily with his pen. Sometimes when I look in the mirror I think I can still discern an indelible blue mark. An astrologer gave me a big paisa coin with strict instructions to keep it on my person. "If you lose that paisa your father will lose everything," my mother impressed upon me. With total faith I guarded the paisa for many years.

In Lahore I continued my private daily devotions with deep sincerity. One Baisakhi day my mother returned from the gurdwara at midday to make puris and halwa. I was outside chanting my path (sacred words) when I saw a glorious, flashing light. I felt perfect atunement with God and sensed myself floating. That moment I made a solemn promise to myself: I would recite the Sikh hymns daily and endeavour always to help others. My experience left me dazed. I confided it to no-one. Under my shawl I hid an ivory rosary. As I moved each bead I uttered God's name, Wahiguru, under my breath. I vowed that when I was fifty I would devote my life exclusively to worship.

My brothers had fewer restrictions than we girls did. If we went downstairs we had to draw our chunnis over our heads. We never questioned this discipline, but despite Father's orders not to peep out into the street we took every opportunity of furtive eavesdropping on the man's world that surrounded us. Late at night we quietly opened our window and listened in on the café life below. Taxi drivers, tongawalas and bus drivers dropped in

41

for tea, joked, swore at each other and exchanged anecdotes unedited for adolescent female ears.

In Lahore we bumped through the bustling bazaar in a tonga. Some days we passed the pale-faced, khaki-uniformed Tommies on their bicycles. Their faces were identical. Their light eyes stared in at us, but we knew we mustn't speak or even glance up. "The Tommies are all harami (bastards)," said our elders. Once a Tommy wrote on a piece of paper, crumpled it into a ball, and threw it into our tonga. Harami or not, at Christmas time my father and my maternal uncles sent fruit and wine for these fair-skinned soldiers. Such was my second encounter with the British. We guessed that the crumpled paper was a love letter, but couldn't make out the English handwriting.

My parents seemed uneasy if Gurcharan, Amrit and I walked together to the gurdwara. Perhaps they feared malicious comment on their three nubile daughters. Our parents usually proceeded to the gurdwara separately, one or two of us walking with each of them.

One day my father was reading the newspaper when his eye dwelt with particular pride on the photograph of a distinguished young scientist. Gopal Singh Puri had obtained the highest mark in the whole of Punjab for his master's degree. He was a student of Gordon College where my cousins were studying. Above all he was a Puri, a member of our got (clan), so we could bask in his glory. In passing curiosity I glanced at the newspaper photo-graph — showing a good-looking young man with a big, well-tied turban and manly features — and then thought no more about him.

One morning through the thin bedroom wall, I overheard my parents discussing a marriage proposal from a man who wanted to marry me. I had seen him in the village and felt an instant aver-sion. I was disturbed and downcast and could not picture myself marrying this man. If this was to be my fate I would die before the day came. Clothes no longer interested me and my appetite disappeared, but I never voiced my fears to my parents. My mother was worried and asked my elder sisters what could be the matter with me. What they replied I do not know, but my parents dropped the idea of the marriage.

When I was fifteen Gurcharan and Amrit were married to two cousins, the sons of two sisters. This was unusual in those days, as was the joint marriage ceremony in Chadha's gurdwara in

Kallar, where we always returned for family marriages. One week we were carefree children; the next I was alone with my parents and brothers, the next in line for matrimony. My sisters had left, amid traditional songs and the customary tears, for their in-laws' homes. Their fine new clothes and bangles, the scarlet and ivory chure, marked them out clearly as recently married women.

My mother stayed a few days after the celebrations to sort out some accounts, but my father hurried back to Lahore, taking me with him. After two weeks, a letter arrived from my mother. As usual my father sat down and asked me to read it to him. When I read the names of Master Hara Singh and his son Gopal Singh Puri, and that I had been betrothed to him, I dropped the letter and fled in embarrassment. A girl never uttered the name of her husband or father-in-law and she would be far too shy to declare in her father's presence that she was engaged to be married.

Later I learned the background to this bewildering turn of events. As a talented scientist Gopal was much sought after as a son-in-law. His parents had earned a hard-won living as primary school teachers in Peshawar. (Previously Master Hara Singh, Gopal's father, had taught at Khalsa High School, Kallar.) His parents moved with their daughter and younger sons to Kallar, the family home, where in due course his father died. Meanwhile Gopal stayed with some relatives in Rawalpindi. Here a succession of girls from richer, more prestigious families were offered to him in marriage. To escape this increasingly irksome pressure Gopal joined his mother in Kallar for a day, having told his cousins to deal with further proposals. My sisters, Amrit and Gurcharan, had just married and Gopal accompanied his mother on a visit to my father's house to offer congratulations and good wishes.

Although I had left for Lahore with my father Gopal remembered seeing me as a carefree schoolgirl at his sister Gian's marriage and decided that here was the answer to his matrimonial dilemma. He had no wish for dowry from wealthy in-laws and my parents were only modestly well-to-do. He had no wish for a university girl with a mind of her own and here was an innocent, malleable girl.

His mother tried unsuccessfully to dissuade him, protesting, "You can't marry Viranwali. She could be my granddaughter, not my daughter-in-law, she is so young." There was another serious objection: according to Hindu and Sikh tradition husband and wife must come from the same caste, but from a different got. Each caste consists of many clans (got) and marriages are arranged between members of different clans of equal standing, never between members of the same got. So Puris could marry into eleven other gots including: Sahnis, Tandons, Bindras, Oberois and Anands. No Puri boy or girl could marry anyone whose mother or grandparents had been Puris, let alone someone whose father was a Puri. My parents addressed Gopal's mother as Chachiji, that is "respected wife of our father's younger brother", so clearly we were not very distant cousins. Probably Gopal's grandfather and my great-grandfather were brothers. His father had served as house tutor to Raja Sir Gurbaksh Singh's children. Like my forebears his family had migrated to Kallar from Pakka in the Bedis' entourage.

Gopal was not to be put off by the fact that we were blood relatives: Puri men are notoriously chauvinistic. Westerners suggest that Indian women dare not show initiative, yet mother settled my marriage without even consulting my father, and Gopal's mother showed a similarly independent spirit. Father left me in Lahore and attended my engagement in Rawalpindi with the usual exchange of gifts in the presence of the Guru Granth Sahib. In particular karas are exchanged at the time of betrothal. The kara is a plain steel bangle, one of the five outward signs of a Sikh's religious allegiance. Gopal asked for no dowry and his requirements were simple.

On the surface my existence in Lahore with my parents and brothers had not changed. In my heart I hoped that I would be worthy of my wonderful fiancé. Would the older women be able to say of me, "What a marvellous daughter-in-law. She works hard for her mother-in-law"?

My mother's relatives in Rawalpindi were delighted to hear of my engagement. The Duggals regarded it as a good omen for further strengthening their ties with the Puri family. But, I was to learn in due course, Gopal's relatives were less enthusiastic. His mother received anonymous letters telling her that "the girl is squint-eyed. She is sickly and suffers from many ailments." Gopal's sister, Gian, and her husband were disturbed by these allegations and came from Shekhupura to Lahore to meet me. Luckily for us they realised that the anonymous letter-writer's sole motivation had been malice.

In particular, Sundar Singh bitterly opposed the planned marriage. Since Gopal's father's death Sundar Singh had regarded himself as head of the family with a decisive say in all decisions affecting Gopal's future. He was Gopal's cousin by marriage, having wed Bahin Jaswant, Gopal's father's sister's daughter. Ever since Jaswant's father had died, her widowed mother had lived with Gopal's parents, often overruling Gopal's mother. Jaswant had been brought up as Gopal's elder sister. Sundar Singh, had a beautiful, recently widowed sister whom he intended Gopal to marry. However, since Bahin Jaswant disliked this idea, she had been independently negotiating with several other eligible families.

As a widow herself Gopal's mother could not afford to annoy her relations. Without any family consultation she had agreed to Gopal's betrothal to me. Gopal was the eldest son in the family and his senior relatives felt entitled to play their part in planning his life. Amid the criticism of his mother's decision his aunt Katari spoke up: "Gopal is going for an interview next week for a post in the army. If he is successful we will consider that this girl has brought good fortune to our family."

By God's grace Gopal was appointed to a wartime job as Malaria Officer in Malir Cantonment Hospital, Karachi. Without my knowing this at the time his aunt's words had clinched my acceptance into his family. They welcomed me as Lakshmi, bestower of wealth and blessings.

Gopal flouted convention in more ways than one. As a wartime malaria officer in Karachi he lived in a big bungalow and was waited on by two servants. He wrote to my father asking him if I, as his fiancée, could spend two weeks with him there. Such a thing was unheard of and my father was furious. "What an outrageous suggestion! Who on earth does he think he is? We shall not marry our daughter to a man who behaves like this." But Gopal insisted and my mother eased the deadlock by suggesting that, instead of my going to Karachi, Gopal could spend a few days with me in Lahore. My elder sister, Gurcharan, was to stay with us, when Gopal arrived in Lahore.

This was agreed and Gurcharan arrived from Rawalpindi before Gopal was due to reach Lahore. As we waited for him Gurcharan told me, in a fashion more motherly than sisterly, how well the betrothal ceremony had proceeded in our parents' Rawalpindi house, despite opposition from Sundar Singh. He

45

had tried to prejudice Gopal's mother against me, refusing to attend the ceremony. But he eventually agreed, reluctantly, to join in the preparations. Gopal's friends, Yog, Prem, Tilak and Dalip, took upon themselves the responsibility of performing the engagement. A group of Gopal's relatives and friends arrived, dancing to the music of a band. My parents feasted them lavishly, as custom demanded, and presented gifts to them.

I listened to all Gurcharan said as if this were someone else's story, not mine. She explained about Gopal's visit, and I felt just as detached. A fiancé visiting his betrothed was totally unheard of, an event I could never have anticipated. I had no idea what I was supposed to do or say or how I was meant to behave towards a person who was so learned and well-travelled. My mind flew back to the time I had seen him at his sister, Gian's, marriage in Kallar, joking and laughing. I was lost, out of my depth.

"He is bringing an engagement ring for you," Gurcharan was saying. I could take in no more. In any case there was no more time for her patient attempts to prepare me. Gopal had arrived. Dressed in my best salvar kamiz I went downstairs, clutching the tillawala har, the gold tinsel garland, supplied for the occasion by my thoughtful sister. I put it around Gopal's neck somehow and in exchange he gave me the most beautiful ring I had ever seen. Gurcharan, my tactful chaperone, left the room, leaving the two of us together. I was bewildered, not knowing what to say or how. Gopal did the speaking and I was impressed beyond words.

For two days I was in an enchanted world, marvelling that so important a person had chosen to marry me. My father retired to bed early and we two climbed up alone to the moonlit terrace. Gopal asked me about my school and which subject I liked best. I snuggled in the folds of his tweed dressing gown which he had bought in Kashmir.

Gurcharan's mother-in-law was also staying with us. When she discovered that I had spent the night on the terrace with my fiancé her rage knew no limits. My father claimed ignorance of the whole affair, while my mother maintained a tactful silence. Gurcharan's mother-in-law vowed never again to be the guest of a family which permitted such shameless goings-on. Perhaps she had noted my upper lip, swollen, to my acute embarrassment on looking in the mirror, by Gopal's tireless nocturnal kissing. Then I cut my forefinger on a sharp tin in the kitchen, my mother shouted and Gopal came running. Flouting every convention of hygiene and social propriety, he put my finger, dripping scarlet, in his mouth to suck the wound better. This episode further fuelled Gurcharan's mother-in-law's sense of outrage and she murmured to my mother that such intimacy could lead only to my becoming pregnant.

After those two days I was left with my memories and my engagement ring, the first ever given or received in our khandan. It was the first time an engaged couple had met in this way. But Gopal's reputation for scholarship and family responsibility won him many concessions.

I knew that Gopal would not forget me, however pressing and important his work, because he had taken my green chunni, kissed it, and put it around his neck, kissing me passionately and promising, "I'll always keep this with me for the lovely fragrance of my darling Vino." Soon afterwards I received this letter, something unheard of for fiancés in my day. He addressed me in it as Vino, the affectionate name that he always used and he alone.

Military Hospital
Malir Cantonment
Karachi
15 August 1942

My dearest Vino,
It was heavenly to pass two nights with you. I still feel although a thousand miles away I am living with you. I have kept your chunni under my pillow so that I have your flavour all the time with me. I hope we will be able to meet soon again and I am writing separately to your parents to send you here to spend a few days in Karachi. This is a beatiful city. Clifton beach is glorious. The sea breeze towards the evening makes the place ever so delightful. Moonlit nights are really loveable. Please consider visiting next month. You will be free for your Easter holidays.

You must be wondering why I was so sad the first day I met you. The recent death of my uncle and my own family responsibilities make me think if I will ever be able to provide for you the comfort and luxuries to which you are accustomed in your parents' home. You must realise that you are going to marry a poor man with heavy responsibility. My mother is our first duty. She needs all our love and protection. We will have to discharge our duties to her together. Won't you agree this is the test of our love? Love does not only lie in gazing towards each other, but it is looking into the future together with four eyes. I think this is the test of our love.

I certainly wish my brothers and sister to get higher education. You also have got to contemplate yours. The only thing I can give you is education. And what is love? It is nothing but unselfishness giving. In this case there is an item of selfishness also — because education will give you capacity to help me in discharging my responsibilities. So I want to exercise the right of my love right now. Won't you darling write an essay on love? Or any other topic which may be uppermost in your mind and send me. This will keep your mind occupied with at least some of me. And I will have your writings to inspire me to live here alone for as long as I have to be here. I love you darling more than my life. Write soon,

Ever yours,

GOPAL

To hasten my education Gopal wrote in English, a practice he continued over the years. He also wrote to my father inviting me to stay in his bungalow in Malir. When my father refused to consent to anything so scandalous, Gopal said he would marry straightaway. My parents were plunged into hasty preparation for a marriage in only four weeks' time.

Gopal's doctoral thesis had been sent for examination to London. In due course it had won him the Ruchi Ram Sahni prize and he was appointed to a post at the university of Agra. However, release from his war work as Malaria Officer was possible only on medical grounds, so Gopal's robust health was for the first time a handicap. At medical colleagues' suggestion, he took large doses of aspirin and ran fast for thirty minutes. After each stint his heart was tested and the abnormal cardiac activity was duly recorded. After a week of aspirin, running and tests a panel of doctors approved his discharge from Malir.

Within days of taking up the Agra post a better offer reached him from Lucknow University — a fellowship funded by the Burmah Oil Company. On arrival in Lucknow he immediately applied for leave to come to Kallar for our marriage.

For the final week before the wedding women of all ages gathered in our courtyard every evening to sing the marriage songs known as "suhag". Suhag means the joy of consummating marriage, and these songs were to wish me joy in my marriage. They expressed the feelings which none of us would have dreamt of voicing in conversation. One still popular suhag song is a dialogue between father and daughter. In real life no girl would have aired her hopes so brazenly.

My daughter, why are you standing behind the sandalwood tree?
I am standing here father, because I want a good marriage
What kind of husband should we find for you, daughter?
What kind of husband would you like, my child?
Someone who is bright like the moon among the stars,
Like Lord Krishna among men.

Sitting crosslegged the women sang shrilly to the quickening beat of a dholki, a cylindrical drum, which one held in her lap. She was striking both ends with her fingers while another beat loudly with a spoon on the wooden part of the dholki. I sat quietly in a corner. I would never have dared to speak to my father like the girl in the song, but I had no need: my bridegroom was indeed like the moon among stars.

Some songs were more risqué, at least in the accompanying mime. An elderly lady was in the centre of a ring of singing women. She was capering about with her chunni bundled up in a roll which she moved to and fro suggestively between her legs. In another song a woman banged a rolling pin up and down on the floor, then round and round as if grinding something. She was enacting the sadhu (holy man) who is not too holy to have a keen interest in women. For some songs ladies, otherwise staid, danced in drag, donning a man's suit, tie and turban. All this was the traditional way of exciting the bride's interest in sex and preparing her for married life. Late in the evening the ladies would go home, clutching the patase (white sugar sweets) distributed by my mother.

As the days passed the excitement in the household mounted. On the eve of my wedding day my hands were decorated elaborately with mehndi. Powdered henna leaves had been soaked in water to make terracotta-coloured vegetable dye, and the decorations were intricately worked. My skin was treated with a cool compress of turmeric powder mixed with water to lighten my complexion. I sat upstairs, my right arm heavy with the eleven scarlet and ivory bangles given by my mother's brothers. I listened intently for indications that my bridegroom had arrived from Lucknow. It was August 28th, the day he was to arrive.

Downstairs cooking was underway. Gopal's relatives and friends, all two hundred of them, had arrived from Rawalpindi and must be feasted that evening by my parents. As Gopal still hadn't come my parents didn't know what to do. My father was blaming my mother for allowing their daughter to be engaged to a rascal who insisted on a hurried marriage, then left her in the lurch. The eyes of our entire world were upon us, and my father dreaded the unimaginable shame. My mother, though agitated, still believed that Gopal would not humiliate us like this. Sitting upstairs my own confidence never wavered, though I had no practical ideas of why Gopal had not appeared or how he might arrive. Why should he let us down? He had expressed the desire to marry me, with no incentive from my family or encouragement from my parents. He loved me and would most certainly come. I prayed fervently. The barber's wife, the nain, a key figure in village marriages, came to my room. She wound a red and yellow raw cotton thread around my right wrist and said, "You must pray hard for your parents' izzat — their reputation." Punjabis value nothing more than their izzat. If Gopal did not come in time my parents' izzat would be ruined. My feelings were irrelevant. Sundar Singh had all along disapproved of Gopal's betrothal to a girl ineligible on so many counts. As the hours passed he sat with his companions, on the steps outside our house, gloating at the likely embarrassment to my parents. He was heard to say, "If Gopal marries that girl I will shave off my beard in dog's urine." For any Sikh this was the most outrageous proposition imaginable, as the unshaven beard is a sacred symbol of Sikhism.

My uncles went to Mankiala, the nearest station, to await the next train. The morning trains came and went. No trace of Gopal. They returned to Kallar without their prospective brother-in-law. There was an evening train which stopped only at Rawalpindi, but there was no evening bus to bring Gopal to Kallar. The marriage party had arrived and my parents, the hosts, were ready with the food, but there was no news of the bridegroom. As evening approached despondency spread. Guests prepared to leave. Some felt hurt, others suspicious, many looked angry and humiliated, but my mother retained her usual composure. That night hardly anyone slept and my mother remained sitting on her charpoy while my father paced up and down. At every slight sound breaking the nocturnal silence our hopes rose and fell.

4

Marriage

Eventually, the 29th August, my wedding day, dawned. In their anxiety no-one had gone to the station at Mankiala or Rawalpindi. Everyone was in Kallar offering advice to my family. A few guests had already left when someone brought the news that Gopal had arrived. It was already midday and no-one had eaten since the previous day. There was glad commotion on all sides.

Later Gopal explained the cause of his delay. The visit of the Chief Geologist from Assam had kept him busy until the last minute. His colleagues drove him to the station, and he leapt on to the train as it was already moving off towards Delhi. He had brought with him almost nothing apart from a single change of clothes. In August, despite monsoon rains, the heat is still intense. Gopal passed an uncomfortable night in the train. He could only afford to travel third class. In Delhi he found that the train for Lahore had already pulled out. The second train to Lahore would leave later that afternoon and he would have to change trains again at Lahore for Rawalpindi. At five in the morning of the 29th Gopal jumped down at Mankiala. There was no one there to receive him. The only transport to Kallar was a bus due to leave Rawalpindi at nine o'clock. The bus was packed with passengers, among them a few guests bound for Gopal's marriage. They looked astonished at the bridegroom, weary and travel-stained, struggling aboard the bus. He squeezed past standing passengers to the crowded rear of the bus. There was no seat. When the bus started he heard two of his friends in the front of the bus telling their fellow passengers that they were sorry to have missed their friend's marriage party the previous night, but hoped that they would still reach Kallar in time for the wedding ceremony in the gurdwara. Gopal could not resist shouting from the back, above the roar of the engine, "You aren't late. I am the one who is late." For the rest of the journey to Kallar everyone was joking and laughing.

At midday, dirty, hot and tired, Gopal reached his family home. Here he hurriedly bathed and his sister tied his new pink turban. In accordance with custom the barber had rented out the mare for him to ride the short distance to his bride's house. Relief spread through our house on learning of Gopal's belated arrival. With my sisters' help I changed hurriedly into my bridal clothes which were, like my mother's outfit, a gift from my maternal grandmother. Excitedly I pulled on the golden yellow salvar and knotted the draw-string at the waist, fumbled my way into the matching kamiz and was relieved when my sister pulled the veil, a yellow chunni, heavy with silver fringe and decoration, well down over my face. Little had Dhamialwali Beyji visualised the ordeal of suspense we would suffer before putting on our finery.

At last, Gopal had reached our house. He was mounted on a brown mare. From his pink turban streamers of freshly threaded jasmine and rose petals, the sehra, hung over his face. That was the tradition. His clothes were rather less conventional for a bridegroom — a blue and red check shirt and corduroy trousers faded with wear.

Milling around him were his friends and relatives, a noisy barat. Local musicians played raucous wedding tunes on wooden flutes and drums. The expression of Sundar Singh's face had changed — to one of chagrine. When he noticed that no-one was paying any attention to his objection to our marriage he joined in the festivities without any further complaint.

When the bridegroom arrives, provided his family aren't known to be unusually touchy, the bride's relatives taunt him with songs of traditional abuse:

> Our daughter is like a gold thread;
> Your boy is crude like a potter.
> They aren't a suitable couple —
> How shameless you are to bring him.
> For six months you had a goldsmith
> Making the jewellery,
> But we find only gold film on it —
> You should have got new jewellery.

My father has found a match for me;
He is small and fat.
He doesn't know how to tie his turban,
He is so short he doesn't even reach my plait.

However, such was my parents' relief at knowing that Gopal had not brought disgrace upon them that I have no recollection of any such songs being sung. In any case there was too little time.

Hurriedly my father, then my uncles, male cousins and brothers embraced their nearest counterparts from Gopal's side, nearly lifting them off the ground. This was the milni or introduction. On the threshold I put the jaymala, the marriage garland, around my bridegroom's neck and he reciprocated by garlanding me.

The marriage party flocked to Chadha's gurdwara. Here I sat tremulously on Gopal's left facing the Guru Granth Sahib, enthroned below its canopy. My hands were the only bit of me visible to my bridegroom. As I was wearing socks on my feet I was totally covered from head to toe.

From the countless weddings I have attended I know what must have happened at my own, but the familiar words and clamour hardly interrupted my train of thought. Utter nervous and physical exhaustion could not block out my relief that my parents had narrowly escaped ineradicable embarrassment, that I had been spared the stigma of being known for life as an abandoned bride. The future was unknown: I could have no inkling then of the financial difficulties, the delicate intermeshing of relationships, the strangeness ahead. Tired or not, I was happy. With such a knowledgeable, delightful person as Gopal there could only be bright prospects. I felt safe under his protection, warm in his love, confident that he could overcome any problem.

The gurdwara was packed with hundreds of friends, relatives, fellow-villagers. It was ringing with the Gurus' hymns sung lustily to the accompaniment of the harmonium player, one hand skimming the keys, the other working it to and fro like bellows. My reverie was broken. We stood while the man officiating prayed for God's blessing on our union. As we subsided again on our floor cushions the musicians sitting to one side of the canopy sang:

Before any undertaking
Seek God's grace . . .
With the True Guru
We taste the nectar of immortality . . .

Then the officiant explained the significance of matrimony.
Mechanically we bowed our assent towards the Guru Granth
Sahib. One of Gopal's male relatives placed a garland of orange
flowers on the still covered Guru Granth Sahib, then garlanded
each of us as we still sat in front of the whole congregation. He
took one end of the saffron-dyed palla (cotton length) and put it
in Gopal's hand, brought the palla up over his shoulder and
closed my trembling hand over the other end. We were linked
together for life. The officiant drew back the silky coverings and
opened the Guru Granth Sahib to read the first verse of Guru Ram
Das's marriage hymn, the Lavan. Then the musicians sang the
same stanza and Gopal slowly led me round behind the Guru
Granth Sahib's canopy. Gurdip, my mamajis, my father and other
male relatives stood behind the Guru Granth Sahib. They
supported me and blessed me as I followed Gopal. We moved
clockwise until we again reached our cushions and sank down
while the second verse was read:

In the second round the Lord has caused you to meet the true Guru
The fear in your hearts has departed
And the filth of egoism has been washed away.

Again the singers took up the same words, again we rose, and
holding tightly onto my end of the palla, my head veiled and
bowed I followed Gopal with small steps around the enthroned
volume of scripture. There are four stanzas of Lavan and four
times we walked like this while a thousand faces watched. As we
sat down for the fourth time we were pelted with orange and
crimson blossoms and petals, the fragrant ephemeral confetti of
marriage.

I heard little if anything of Giani Hakm Singh's sikhia, the
conventional, rhyming lines of advice that he had composed and
now proclaimed. This was counsel for the bride's ears in particular, composed according to the general formula. He later
presented me with a copy, like a certificate, neatly printed in
Gurmukhi script on a page with a trim, purple border. I need not

be educated or clever, but I must please my mother-in-law, my brothers and sisters-in-law. Above all I must recall the three words with intital "bh" in Punjabi — bhala, bhuli, bhana. All would be well, the words meant, if I showed forgiveness. Hakm Singh reminded us, as all Sikh couples are reminded, that as husband and wife we were, in the words of Guru Amar Das, "ek jot doi murti" (two bodies with but a single light).

The sehra is advice read out to the groom: Gopal must not neglect his mother. Everyone sang the joyful hymn that concludes all congregational worship, the Anand, and stood for the solemn Ardas prayer. After a verse had been read at random from the Guru Granth Sahib, the Guru's words of guidance for the day, sweet helpings of karah prashad, our sacred food, were distributed to everybody who had come to witness our marriage. Chattering and rubbing the ghee of the karah prashad into their palms, people got up and moved in noisy groups along the gallis to our house to feast.

The dholi, a wooden palanquin covered with red cloth and white trimmings, was standing near our door. The barber hired it out for marriages. As I sat alone inside it I wept and my mother, aunts, sisters and cousins wept as they sang:

> Father you have put your daughter in the dholi;
> People shower blessings on you.
> Bless you father for all you have showered on me,
> Bless you mother who bore me.

Whenever I attended weddings in future the pathos of the dholi songs brought back that moment.

> Ours is a flock of sparrows, dear father.
> We'll fly away
> On a long, long flight.
> We know not to which land we shall go.
> In your mansion, dear father,
> Who will do the spinning?
> There is my unfinished embroidery —
> Who will finish it, father?
> My grand-daughters will do that, daughter.
> Go to your home.

56

Four men lifted the palanquin and bore me along the steep, uneven street that separated our family's house from Gopal's. Here I was set down and the ritual of "dudh mundari" was performed. Gopal's mother waved a pot of diluted milk (dudh in Punjabi) over my head as I sat inside the dholi. She pretended to sip from it but, as custom required, Gopal intercepted the jug, for, people said, whoever drank the milk would have power over the bride.

My mother-in-law then poured mustard oil on both sides of the threshold and blessed me as "satputri" (the bearer of seven sons), "budhsuhagan" (one who would still be wed in her old age) and twice-fortunate. I touched her feet and my in-laws sang:

> You have filled our house inside,
> Outside in front and behind.
> The beautiful daughter you have given us
> Will be its ornament.

It was a hot, humid day. Gopal's family home was bursting with people, among them Sundar Singh, self-important and intent on mischief. Everyone was thronging round me, peering at my veiled face and passing comments. Gopal asked for food to be brought for us, saying to everyone's horror, "We will eat from the same thali." At this unheard of proposal Chachi Fidi, a lady from the neighbourhood, shouted in disgust, "All your sense has gone to your heels, don't you know this, if you eat food touched by somebody else." (Indians are very careful usually to avoid eating food that is jutha, meaning that it has been polluted by anything that has come in contact with another person's lips.)

Generally guests drift away to allow the newly weds to retire for the night. But Prem, Yog, Tilak and the others stayed in the close room while Sundar Singh joked interminably. He deliberately went on sitting and talking till it was past midnight. Eventually he departed to his own room and I was escorted to the place where I would sleep with my bridegroom. It was a small, hot room, lit only by a kerosene oil lantern, and the charpoy was barely large enough for one person.

Next day was the day for phera, when a bride returns to her parental home to receive clothes and other gifts before setting out to her husband's place. In the past, when brides were only children, they customarily stayed for several years before rejoining their husbands. Gopal decided that, until our departure to Lucknow, we would be more comfortable sleeping in a large upstairs room in my parents' spacious house.

After a week I set out with Gopal and his relatives to my new home in Lucknow, where I would live with him, his mother and two younger brothers, Harbans and Surinder. A telegram had arrived in Kallar the day after our marriage ordering Gopal to return immediately to Lucknow. I was surprised at this telegram ordering him to return immediately after his wedding, but his professor, Dr Birbal Sahni, did not like his students to "waste" their time.

Soon after our arrival Professor Birbal Sahni, the son of Ruchi Ram Sahni, invited his favourite research student and his young bride to his home for dinner. I was in another world where conversation moved, interspersed with assured English, from one subject to another of which I knew nothing.

In my father's house even my brothers were discouraged from reading and my own studies had been cut short. Now I was determined not to embarrass my brilliant husband by betraying my terrible ignorance. I could not bear to let him down. For his part Gopal never commented on my immaturity or lack of education, but instead he brought books for me to read. The first was a book on geology, written in Hindi. I read it all, fascinated especially at discovering how coal was formed underground over many centuries. It had never occurred to me to wonder about such things before.

I was in a world of dynamic young academics. Gopal's colleagues, Dr Verma, Dr Sitholey, Dr Misra and the others were married men with children. They all spoke Hindi and ate only vegetarian food. Although a number of Punjabis had settled in Lucknow I hardly ever saw women clad in salvar kamiz. In Pothohar, a sari would have been equally extraordinary. Daily I met and mixed with people of a type I had never previously imagined existed.

As a city Lucknow differed from my previous homes, Rawalpindi and Lahore. The mosques and Muslim tombs, and the fine muslin drawn thread embroidery, are constant reminders of the courtly Islamic style of the Nawabs of Oudh, princes in whose courts classical dance, Persian poetry and elaborate courtesy flourished. Much had changed. Luchnow's former glories had faded. But elephants still lurched laden over the Gomati bridge and the bazaars reverberated with the haggling of centuries.

"Have pity on me, have pity on me": my curiosity was aroused by this wailed entreaty and I stopped to hear more details. A man was standing in the street, holding some animal hairs in his hand. "Please give me money, Bahinji. Respected sister, I have committed a great sin. By accident I harmed a cow. God will punish me. Have pity on me, Sister. Please give me money to go to Hardwar to wash away my sins in the Ganges. Have pity on me, have pity on me." The animal hairs were, he claimed, those of the unfortunate cow. I remained unconvinced. During the next few months, in turn a young boy and an elderly man came past our house with identical pleas for charity.

I read avidly. Gopal was teaching his students palaeobotany and took them to visit mines three months after our marriage. Before he left he brought me some books of Urdu and Hindi short stories and said, "Wouldn't it be nice, Vino, if you wrote me a story before I come back?" Amazement left me dumb. How did writers put stories together? Why did my husband imagine that I, of all people, his inexperienced, uneducated young bride, had sufficient knowledge to select appropriate vocabulary and weave a plot that others would enjoy reading?

He outlined for me a tragic plot, a tale of passionate love between a holiday maker (a Brahmin from Sindh) and a local Muslim beauty, set in the breath-taking scenery of Kashmir. Here, as he had collected fossils, the clear skies, snowpeaks, grassy slopes and dancing reflections of boats and timber houses in the Dal lake had captured his romantic spirit. His descriptions kindled in me a lifelong yearning to see Srinagar and the Dal lake for myself. His suggested storyline drew too, as he frankly admitted, on his own romances with girlfriends. Years later I published this story as "Situ di Nilam" (Situ's Nilam).

From time to time my father fetched me back for a brief stay in Lahore. On one occasion I had packed my jewellery, including my prized engagement ring and the gold bangles lent me by my mother. On returning to my room to pack my clothes I realised that my jewellery had disappeared, among it my tika (forehead jewel) which my mother had bought for me. Probably the maid-servant was responsible — she never came back to work and we did not have her address. Nothing could ever compensate me for the loss of my first treasured gift from Gopal.

My husband talked chiefly of education and books. With the money he received for his research we employed a maid to sweep the house, scour the utensils and launder our clothes, but there was little money to spare, as Gopal was supporting his mother and paying for his brothers' education. I recall waiting several months before spending one rupee on a new comb. Gopal spent almost nothing on himself; if he had a spare pair of trousers or sandals he gave them to his brothers. He had won scholarships since the age of twelve when he was in class eight. He seemed able to survive on a cup of tea and a handful of chickpeas and to save unnecessary expense he had often studied under the street light. To earn extra pocket money he had, as a schoolboy, tutored British soldiers in Peshawar for their compulsory Urdu examinations.

Now, as a research fellow, a palaeobotanist concerned with microbotanical remains of Assam Tertiary Sediments, to be precise, his life was still gruelling, for in Professor Birbal Sahni he had a hard taskmaster, one who expected work to continue regardless of weekends, holidays — or, indeed, marriage. Like his illustrious father, Birbal Sahni was a distinguished scholar. He had studied at Cambridge where one of his class fellows in fossil botany was a young woman, later a household name in Britain and overseas. At that time her name would have held no significance for me, even if I had heard it. The fossil botanist in question was Dr Marie Stopes. Little did I realise that I was destined to follow her as a community worker.

I accepted Gopal's single-minded dedication to the laboratory and his long hours away from home. But one luxury I craved — never in my life had I seen a movie, and I longed to go to the cinema. When I suggested going, Gopal invariably said, "No, I have work to do." In any case we had no money to spare for such frivolities. One evening, however, with three or four rupees in his pocket, Gopal agreed to take me. To save money we walked. It took us two hours to reach the cinema. The film was *Chalchalre Naujavan* (Youth on the Move). Our excitement soon flagged and turned to disappointment as we watched the hero falling from horses and performing mindless feats of spectacular valour. True, Naseem, the heroine, had a pretty face, but we had hoped for a plot. Disappointed we left the crowded cinema and counted out our paise. We had one rupee left and I refused to walk back. Food we could dispense with but I must have a tonga to take me home.

The pony jolted us through pitch-black streets. Absorbed in our own conversation we registered nothing of our whereabouts until the tonga stopped abruptly. "Why are you stopping here?" Gopal asked the tongawala. We were outside Isobel Thorburn girls' college, notorious for the inmates' rendezvous with local boys. "Memsahib ko hostel jana hai?" (Isn't Memsahib going to the hostel?) said the driver. Emphatically Gopal replied, "Ye meri bivi hai" (This is my wife, not a girlfriend).

Gopal was sensitive about my childish appearance. My parents had never allowed me to wear my hair in two long plaits, the style I liked best. One evening I came down to the drawing room where my husband was waiting to accompany me to the home of Dr Sitholey, another palaeobotanist, for dinner. My hair was hanging in two braids. "Go back, unplait your hair and arrange it properly in a bun — and clean your face." Tears rose to my eyes but I did not retort. Perhaps I had powdered my face too liberally. I should have guessed that he did not approve of teenage fashion or behaviour.

In Lahore I had bought a pair of high-heeled sandals. Now my husband of a few months declared, "I don't think you should wear those sandals. We are not wealthy middle class people." We might break with some conventions, but in some ways he was as rigid as any custom-bound husband. If I came out without covering my head he would stare at me in disapproval and become moody and silent.

In those days, if I made a suggestion with which Gopal did not agree, it did not occur to him to discuss it further. "No" was a sufficient answer. Nor in those early years of marriage did I think of contradicting or protesting. He had been his own master during his years of university study and the decision-maker in matters concerning his mother and brothers. As his young wife I learned to accept a sometimes peremptory manner and I remembered Dhamialwali Beyji's advice, "No matter what sort of a boss or a husband you have, never speak ill of him in front of others." But it was not easy.

My sisters also accepted their husbands' ways. For Gurcharan this was not as easy as for Amrit. Gurcharan's husband married her after a period of army service, a period which changed him from the young man to whom her parents had engaged her. Whatever problems she had she kept to herself. By publicising their grievances among friends and relatives I have seen how

61

some wives aggravate the difficulties in their relationship, difficulties which might otherwise have dissolved with time.

For each of us the greatest reward would be the awareness that some observant relative might be saying, "How lucky her parents-in-law are to have such a daughter-in-law. How devotedly she serves her husband's family day in day out."

No-one in those days spoke of either husbands or wives finding fulfilment in their relationships. No-one mentioned whether a husband and wife loved one another. We knew that our husbands would think well of us if our parents-in-law were happy. Of course husbands had their own way, informing their wives, not consulting them. As a wife one accepted this and complied. No-one had thought of women's rights to independent decision making or intellectual development. Certainly I never asked myself whether I was happy. I sought simply to please. But I remember my feelings as my tentative suggestions were swept brusquely aside by my husband.

One day a fortune teller came to our house. He looked at my palm and pronounced, "While your name begins with V you will never get on with your husband. You must take a new name beginning with K." "Krishan? Kamal?" We thought of all the possibilities. I wanted nothing too striking, just something well worn and ordinary. So I chose Kailash. But for my parents I was happy to remain Viranwali and I felt glad that relatives carried on calling me "Wali", not my professional name, Kailash.

5

London

In 1945, when we had been married for two years, Gopal gained a government of India Research Fellowship in Plant Ecology to study for a second doctorate at University College, London and the Kew Herbarium. He booked his passage on the Cape of Good Hope, a huge ship carrying several thousand soldiers home from the war. It was too large for Suez and so would travel around South Africa. With no source of income we had to sell our house in Lucknow and I returned to my parents' house in Lahore.

There was also Harbans's future to consider. With a third class degree in Geology he could expect to find only undistinguished clerical work. As a respected Fellow, Gopal approached his senior, Mr Coates, and said, "I am leaving for Britain and have no means of supporting my family. Now that my brother, Harbans, carries this responsibility I know that he will work hard at any job you can give him. If he fails you I will bear the blame." Harbans was appointed to a university post and subsequently transferred to Calcutta to work for the Geological Survey of India. He lived up to Gopal's high expectations.

Gopal had promised me, "As soon as I have enough money you shall join me in London." When my parents offered to pay my passage he refused to accept their money. "You can give your daughter clothes and jewellery, but it is for me to find the money for her passage."

In Britain, having paid his own fare, he had no money, so he appealed to Mr Coates once more. He pointed out that by now some bonus must rightfully be his for his two years of service. "I desperately need five hundred rupees so that my wife can join me here," he wrote to Mr Coates who was now in Calcutta. Gopal was also in correspondence with my parents. My father was angry: "What business has he to ask my little girl to spend thirteen days alone with no companion? If the sea is rough she will fall ill and have no one to look after her. What sense is there in Viranwali going? He will only be away for two years." As I was their youngest daughter my parents were happy to have me at home again. But my mother felt that I should, if possible, rejoin my husband.

Meanwhile I listened and said nothing. I was a married woman, but I never resented the fact that no one consulted me. My husband loved me, but he addressed his letters to my father. My father loved me and was sure he knew my best interests. I was quietly jubilant that my husband loved me enough to want me so desperately. Silently I longed to be with him.

One day I visited Gopal's cousin, Sundar Singh, in Rawalpindi. There Gopal's aunt further fuelled my resolve to rejoin my husband. "You know what sort of a man Gopal is. If you want to keep your husband you must follow him. Otherwise, you mark my word, he'll marry a gori." Gori means fairskinned and it is the word most commonly used by Punjabis when speaking of a British woman.

I was later to discover touching evidence that Gopal had not forgotten me. With him he had taken my green chunni, the one he had taken with him to Malir as a keepsake. Now it accompanied him on his expeditions to collect soil samples. Great was my excitement when a cheque for my fare came from Mr Coates. Thanks to the cooperation of a friendly high court judge I soon had a passport. My father could let me go without losing face, as a chaperone had materialised. Mrs Pradhan, wife of an officer in the Pusa Agricultural Institute, who like Gopal had won a Government of India Scholarship, would be travelling to Britain with her three-year-old daughter and I could share their cabin.

Now that my passage to Britain was settled my mother took me to Amritsar. There in the Golden Temple (Harmandir Sahib) we said our prayer for blessing on my sojourn far away. The railway station was two or three furlongs away, through the farms, from our house in New Dharampura in Lahore. We left home in the early morning. The milkmen were about and men in the fields were out ploughing with their hump-backed, off-white oxen. My thoughts were rudely interrupted as my mother's pent-up irritation exploded. "Cover yourself properly. Cover you head up. Cover your chest decently. See how people are staring at you." I said nothing, but angry questions welled up inside me.

"Who is staring at me? What fault is it of mine? I am a married woman, about to leave home, even if no-one in my family has ever married so young before. Why is my mother rebuking me unjustly like this?" I listened quietly as befitted a daughter, whether wed or unwed.

As travel alone — especially for a young girl — was unheard of, my middle brother, Mukhpal, escorted me to Bombay where I boarded the Princess of Scotland, my world for the next thirteen days. Many of the passengers were Indians going to Britain for further study. Some were businessmen and there were several girls going to study medicine. One young man from a well-known Punjabi family had come well-equipped; he had decided to find a gori — an English bride — and had brought the gold bangles with him in readiness. (He succeeded in marrying a British wife, but was soon divorced.)

The passengers asked each other about their plans for life in Britain. To their enquiry, "What are you going to do in England?" I answered, "I am a writer." Why I did so I was not quite sure. Mrs Pradhan told me stories of Gopal and his girlfriends, stories her husband had related to her. I was thankful that soon I would be with him again.

At last Liverpool docks came into sight through a grey veil of English drizzle, a gloomy scene. After so many long months I again saw Gopal, and together we travelled to London on the dock train. For the first time I saw large black hackney cabs. One took us to my new home, number 8 Cleveland Gardens. In this three-storeyed Victorian house close to William Whiteley's department store, Gopal was renting a second-floor bedsit for two pounds ten shillings a week from his annual scholarship of £300. Each floor was divided into bedsits with Mr and Mrs Shipley, our landlady, their daughter, Avril, and Mrs Shipley's brother, Leslie, in the basement. In their living room was a long table. Mr Shipley buttered the loaf before slicing it, something I had not seen before. His clothes were untidy, his nose dripped in cold weather and a cigarette hung out of his mouth. He had, I was to discover, a heart of gold.

On the top floor lived a Bengali, Dr Dun, with his French wife, their daughter Ushali, and his mother-in-law. Dr Dun's anger one day shattered the peace. His mother-in-law had taught Ushali to greet her mother, but not Dr Dun. In fury he hurled abuse at the old French woman.

Mr Kasim was the Shipleys' wealthiest lodger, and the eldest. A Muslim, now in his sixties, he had left his flourishing business in Karachi, his wife, children and grandchildren and had come to London solely to enjoy himself. No doubt the tall, Greek beauty, Christina, in an adjoining room on the first floor contributed to this enjoyment, as did his other female visitors. Later Gopal's colleague, Chandra, moved in to replace Mr Kasim.

Freda, a woman of nearly forty years, also lived on her own in a single room on the first floor. I had never seen a woman behave as she did. Cab drivers and others would bring her home blind drunk and take advantage of her. Sprawling on the staircase she abused the world indiscriminately. Leaving Gopal engrossed in his books, I sneaked out of our room to watch the astonishing drama. Mr Shipley clearly did not share my interest in her novel behaviour. He reacted angrily when he saw her in this condition. On our floor, the second floor, lived Janet with her baby boy and an unmarried girl called Rosa. Each weekend an English boy came to stay with Rosa. Even more surprisingly, in the waste bin each Monday we would see a saucepan or a frying pan. Gopal explained, "Such women are interested only in enjoyment. They don't love anyone, nor are they home makers." Money was too scarce for me to understand such waste. To save money we moved into a smaller room across the landing which cost only one pound ten shillings a week and was completely filled by our bed. The fitted wardrobe contained all our possessions. For cooking there was a small gas ring and a meter. I kept our two pans sparkling and removed every speck from the floor. We had a bucket and a wash basin for washing. The only problem was Gopal's turban. Each turban was a six-yard length of fine patterned muslin which had to be starched. I washed and starched it at night, then hung it up in the hallway to dry while the other residents slumbered unawares.

People ask me if I was lonely or homesick. I can truthfully say that I was neither. I missed my parents, sisters and brother, but not too much. My new life totally absorbed me. Alone during the daytime I recited my Sikh prayers and embroidered runners and cloths to beautify our humble home. To buy most fabric you needed coupons, so I bought army surplus white nylon.

Certain experiences were initially disconcerting. The first sight of carcases hanging in William Whitely's repelled me and I hated the smell of the meat as it cooked. When Gopal first explained war-time rationing and coupons I was bewildered. There were, he said, coupons of different colours for tea, for soap, sweets, socks, towels and so on. When Gopal went to Cambridge for a few days I panicked. "What shall I do? I don't understand a word about the coupons." He reassured me that the shopkeepers would not cheat me. They would simply take the requisite coupon in exchange for whatever commodity I bought. To my relief his words proved true. Everyone was polite, courteous, helpful and friendly and I did not experience any prejudice.

Fish was not rationed, but we were allowed only one egg each per week and one pound of meat apiece. I had less experience of cooking than Gopal had, and our diet was simple, with bread, milk and unappetising dried egg as our staple. By adding different vegetables to the meat each day we eked it out for the whole week. Only from Chatawal's emporium in Euston could we buy spices, and at a high price, but our meat tasted better cooked with turmeric, chilli and garam masala. We bought small pots of yoghurt from the milkman. My favourite delicacy was Weetabix with hot milk and sugar as this reminded me of home since it tasted just like sattu, a mixture of roasted oats ground with gur and water. On summer days in Punjab we used to serve it cooled with ice. We had no money in London for a more elaborate diet. If all other food ran out we survived contentedly enough on bread and jam and tea.

When I ventured out women would stop me in the street to admire my colourful salvar kamiz or my sari which I wore more rarely. "How lovely you look. Are you from a royal family?" I told them that I had come over to join my husband who was a student. This warm interest made me feel humble.

My husband had been struggling as a young man and he would become angry for no apparent reason. His quick temper scared me. If I was unable to eat he would become furious and throw away the food. I kept quiet, weeping inwardly, as Gopal could not bear my crying. But soon he would return to his normal self.

I never asked myself whether I was happy. Happiness lay in the fact of being married. Soon I was expecting a child and my hopes were high. In queues for lifts and escalators kindly folk gave me priority as a pregnant woman, and I was officially allowed extra rations of milk, vitamins and orange juice. The local greengrocer kept back Jaffa oranges and bananas for his regular customers. He would take my bag behind the shop to fill it so that less fortunate customers did not feel upset. For half a crown I enrolled in county classes in cookery and leatherwork and appreciated the helpfulness of the others who attended.

One day I returned to Cleveland Gardens bearing an exciting piece of news. In Kensington I had spotted two Sikhs driving in a private car, not a taxi, a sign that they were residents, and well-to-do ones, in London. We made enquiries and discovered that these were the Dhingras, two brothers whose family managed a large paint business with branches in Karachi, Lahore, Delhi, Bombay and Amritsar. With their wives two Dhingra brothers had come to Britain to start a branch here. We were welcomed to their fine house but, conscious of the social gap between us, Gopal said, "We won't visit you again. We aren't in a position to return your hospitality adequately." The Dhingras were undeterred in their kindness. They came to our cramped room and, while I played with Jiti, their baby boy, the Dhingra ladies, hefty sardarnis, prepared a meal. We forged a close and lasting friendship.

As the day approached for the birth of our child we moved back into the larger room. Perhaps in part due to the exertion, on the next day, October 21st 1947, I gave birth to a baby boy in St Mary's Hospital. We called him Shaminder — Shammy or Baba to the family. Now we had a British son and Gopal recalled an epsode in Kallar village when he was five or six years old. A white sahib had arrived with his entourage including a small lad of about Gopal's age. Gopal's village friends advised caution. The gora (white boy) would kick if you went too close. But Gopal was kitted out in the same style as the English boy and felt no qualms about initiating a conversation. Soon they were quarrelling. In his rage Gopal shouted, "You may be an English boy, but I am the father of English boys." A quarter of a century later his thoughtless boast had a prophetic ring.

When I came home Mrs Shipley kindly looked after Shammy if I needed help. "You are so young and look so tired. Can't I wash out his nappies for you?" While she mothered me her husband helped in other ways.

Many a night Shammy cried continuously and Gopal would nurse him. When I went shopping Shammy would refuse to lie still in his pram. So I would put him on my shoulder and push the shopping along in the pram. If I had to use a lift passers by volunteered to push the pram. They seemed to treat me with more affection and respect because I was Indian.

In those days, Indians were relatively rare even in London. I never experienced racial prejudice at first hand, although Gopal had told me, "When Indians look for houses white people won't give them rooms. Most landlords refuse to take coloured lodgers." I thanked God for the Shipleys.

When Shammy was a few weeks old I took him to Shepherds Bush gurdwara. In the 1940s it was the only Sikh temple in Britain and we would have been amazed had anyone predicted that there would be three hundred gurdwaras on British soil only fifty years later. We referred to the temple as the Bhupindra Dharamsala. Dharamsala means a place for worship and relax-ation, and in Guru Nanak's time this was the name for the buildings in which his followers gathered to sing his hymns. Bhupindra was the Sikh Maharaja of Patiala who attended the coronation in London in 1911 and then responded generously to the local Sikhs' appeal for funds to establish a temple.

One of our cherished Sikh practices is called akhand path, continuous reading of the scriptures. An unbroken reading of the 1430 pages of the Guru Granth Sahib takes forty-eight hours. Any Sikh proficient in reading the Gurmukhi script may take part and the reading is divided into shifts of an hour or two each. So few Sikhs lived in London that I was called upon to participate in the akhand path, something I had never done in India. My religious commitment deepened while I lived in London and I enjoyed going to the gurdwara with the Dhingras. During religious services the scriptures were read aloud by the granthi whose son-in-law, Gurbachan Singh Gill, was to become well known among Sikhs.

The other Sikhs of that period in London stand out clearly in my memory. There was Dr Diwan Singh, Britain's only Sikh to be in general practice. His son Indarjit Singh (now Lord Singh of Wimbledon), a prominent Sikh, respected by all the community, went on to be editor of the *Sikh Messenger* and frequently offers his Thought for the Day on BBC Radio 4. There were Ravel Singh, whose sports business subsequently extended to America, and Ram Singh Keith and, from the Bhatra (pedlar) community, now so numerous in Britain's seaports, there was Bhil Singh. I recall too Sajjan Singh Grewal and his father, Baba Asa Singh, a shrewd, peppery old Jat. The Jats are Punjab's peasant farmer caste. In

Britain, as in India, Sikh temples provide a free, cooked vegetarian meal. This is the langar, and it was Baba Asa Singh who cooked the Shepherds Bush langar. Despite strict rationing and the scarcity of Indian ingredients the langar never ran out of maha di dal (whole black lentils), wheatflour and butter. There were always ample supplies in the basement kitchen, and before we left he would press a paper bagful of bananas into our hands, a great treat in those days. Indian men brought their English wives and girlfriends along and we sat laughing as they carved up their chapatis with a knife and fork instead of using fragments to pick up the vegetable curry with their hands.

In November Sikhs commemorate Guru Nanak's birthday. For the first time the BBC was planning to broadcast the traditional Sikh hymns to India. Ram Singh Keith played the harmonium, Surinder and Jagjeet Dhingra sang and I beat on the side of the dholak with a spoon. According to the others my rhythm went from bad to worse. Ram Singh would laugh, saying, "Kailash, go with the rhythm" — to no avail.

Not long after this Kartar Singh Dhingra and his wife returned to Karachi leaving his brother and sister-in-law and the growing Jiti. One evening Mr Shipley called us to the communal telephone. It was Mrs Dhingra saying, "Will you come over? Your Virji (respected brother) is not well." We set out for her house. A doctor came and pronounced that her husband must go straight to hospital. He was exceedingly pale and his feet were swelling. We learned that his kidneys had failed. Day by day he deteriorated visibly. While his wife sat at his bedside I looked after Jiti. Gopalji's days and nights were spent looking after Mr Dhingra and giving encouragement to his wife Jagjit Kaur.

Jiti, it transpired, had been adopted at birth from a third Dhingra brother. Later Jiti was to tell me, "I have three mothers — my natural mother, the mother who adopted me and Kailash Aunty." Sadly the doctors could not save the life of Jiti's adoptive father and he died in hospital.

In 1948 Gopal's research grant came to an end and we prepared to leave London for India. I was disappointed that we could not visit Europe on the return journey. Mrs Pradhan, Mr Chandra and Mr Saxena had all visited Paris and Germany. Gopal had attended a conference in Sweden in February, but I had stayed behind in London. We could not risk exposing a four-month-old baby to such a cold climate.

Gopal reacted to my disappointment with his usual loving optimism. "Don't worry. This is only the beginning. We shall be returning here again and again. Mrs Pradhan may have been to Paris once, but you will be going there many times and you will travel all over the world. There is more than Europe on my list. Just you wait and see. I shall take you to so many exciting countries."

We had no money, but with characteristic foresight and generosity Kartar Singh Dhingra, now in Bombay following Partition, sent us money. He asked us to buy a Hillman car too for him to sell in India, and gave us all the profit.

From newspapers and the radio we learned of the Partition of India, the creation of a new country, Pakistan, where we had lived before. Our home state of Punjab, the land of five rivers, the granary of India, had been sawn in two, gashed by a boundary at odds with its geographical integrity, its fan of mighty rivers.

We feared for our relatives' safety as news of communal bloodshed reached us, so far away and yet so desperately involved. Gopal, Saxena, Chandra and Pradhan spent long hours reading the newspapers, listening to the radio and arguing politics. I listened, more and more bewildered and upset. Never until now had I known anything of the antagonism dividing Muslims from Hindus and Sikhs. Muslims were our neighbours and friends. They were like family members, whether they worked on my father's farms or in his business. How could Muslims and Sikhs be killing each other? Only later did I learn that in our part of Rawalpindi district, in Kallar village itself, hundreds of young girls and women jumped down wells to escape being raped by Muslims. To spare me Gopal had tried to prevent me seeing in the gurdwara an illustrated account of the atrocities. This booklet described cruelty and unimaginable pain: women were being raped and their breasts were cut off, and children were being boiled in oil.

I was haunted by the cruelty of Muslims and cried for the safety of my parents and brother who were in Lahore at the time of Partition. I thought of Seetla, the old gentleman who owned the shop where we used to buy little things for a paisa or two, and I imagined him killed in his own shop. I thought of Rama Terna, and Master Kishan Singh and Bahin Nidhan Kaur, the head mistress of the Girls' Primary School. I remembered Ma Ajabi, who had been born a Muslim, but did not believe in any religion and was there for everybody. Was she still alive?

In the months before our departure, we waited fearfully for letters. There was no telephone and so we depended on letters. We were relieved when at length we knew that none of our family had been killed or injured. All had reached India. From now on their homes must be on the eastern side of this until recently unimaginable frontier which forged its way remorselessly across fields and irrigation canals, roads and railways, regardless of human suffering.

In 1948 we set sail from Liverpool to Bombay, wondering anxiously in what condition we would find our parents.

6

India Again

Many and long were our conversations on board the ship carrying us back to our independent, decimated homeland. We docked in Bombay where nothing seemed changed. Before proceeding to join my parents we spent a week there as guests of the ever-generous Dhingras. Kartar Singh sold the Hillman car and gave us the profit of over two thousand rupees — riches indeed in those days. His wife had trained a nanny specifically to look after Shammy during our stay so that we could both go out with them sight-seeing and visiting their friends. My parents were now living in Dehra Dun, so after over a week with the Dhingras, we took the train north. Travellers to this gracious hill resort are usually in high spirits, looking forward to a respite from the heat of the dusty plains. We too were happy to be seeing my parents after three years of study successfully completed, and carrying their new grandson. But I dreaded finding my worst fears confirmed. My father had faced too many reversals of fortune. Surely he could have been spared this latest blow. We had no money and no source of income. I prayed fervently that God would quickly bless Gopal's efforts with a salary. I could not bear to be a further burden on my parents. Nor could Gopal feel at ease if we stayed with them with no prospect of financial independence. First and foremost he urgently needed to find a post, in a university, in a research institute, anywhere at all.

One great relief was knowing that Gopal's mother and sister, Gian, and her family plus her two younger brothers were safe and sound in Calcutta.

The train was climbing the winding mountain track. Among the milling passengers and coolies on the platform we recognised my parents waiting for us. I had not thought they could look so changed. They were thin and their tearful eyes full of worry. But the relief of reunion was all that counted that day. I had been wondering where they were living. When we jumped down from the tonga that had brought us from the station it was depressing to discover. None of their former servants had ever been housed in such miserable quarters as they now occupied. With my three young brothers they were cramped in two small rooms. My father was over fifty, too old to find work easily. My brothers were still studying. How they found enough money to live I do not know. In 1947, as the communal violence increased, my parents had realised that they must leave Lahore. They had taken some cash and a few personal belongings. Certain that the arson, rape, looting and murder would soon cease, and that they would then be able to return, my mother had locked everything in the house, saying, "We will come back when the disturbances die down again."

Little had she realised that they would never again see the houses that my father had built in Lahore and Rawalpindi, nor his family home in Kallar. In this she was like millions of others who fled for sanctuary beyond Amritsar. Bhaiya Sundar Singh, Gopal's cousin, now manager of the Hindustan Mercantile Bank, had also been rehoused in Dehra Dun, in a spacious bungalow forsaken by its Muslim owners. It stood back from the Rajpur Road in extensive grounds. Bhaiya Sundar Singh made up unstintingly for his ungenerous sentiments at the time of our wedding. He and his wife, Bahin Jaswant, welcomed us into their house, assuring us of a home with them until Gopal found work. Great was our relief, for we shrank from adding to my parents' difficulties in their oppressively claustrophobic two rooms.

Social agencies had struggled to help the millions of displaced people. My father was eventually compensated for his fields in Kallar with a piece of barren land near Ambala in Indian Punjab. As it was unfit for cultivation he sold it.

Many families suffered far greater reversals than the Puris, although my Mamaji Avtar's son had been murdered, we learned to our sorrow, and my mother told me that another aunt, uncle and two of our cousins could not be traced. One day I was in a tonga in Pulton Bazaar near the clock tower when I heard the voice of an eight- or nine-year-old Punjabi boy. "Bibiji, lelona, buy something please, Sister." He carried a tray in front, suspended from a strap around his neck. He was selling pins, combs and tapes. "Isn't anyone else earning in your family?" I asked him. He told me that his father had been killed, leaving his mother with several children of whom he was the eldest. I needed nothing, but moved by his plight, offered him a rupee. Furiously he hurled it back. "I'm not a beggar," he cried, "if you don't buy I won't take anything." His sincerity touched me and I recalled the Guru's teaching: "kirt karni, nam japna, vand chhakna" (earn your living, share with the needy and pray to God).

Millions of people had been uprooted. All had lost their homes, many their dear ones. Some died in the violence, others of heart failure from the trauma of losing their all. There were hundreds of West Punjabis in Dehra Dun alone. But no-one begged. All showed enthusiastic determination to work hard and put down new roots. It was said at that time that the traders of Karol Bagh in Delhi complained to Pandit Nehru, "These Punjabi refugees are earning much more than our shops. They have come as refugees but seem to have taken over the place." Panditji replied, "OK. Give them your shop and you hawk your wares as they are doing."

Gopal's search for a suitable academic post took him to Patiala one day, to Delhi another, visiting ministries and universities. His perseverance was rewarded with an appointment as forest ecologist and technical secretary to the Indian Council of Ecological Research in the Forest Research Institute, New Forest, Dehra Dun. We did not have to move far after all.

For the first months we were accommodated in empty barracks, a thatched building with servants' quarters. Then we moved into a fine bungalow appropriate to Gopal's rank as a first class gazetted officer. It had a double garage, though we never possessed a car, and six servants' quarters. (There is always a difference between the various categories of people. The first class gazetted officers' bungalows were on Schalick Road and the second-class officers' bungalows were on Trevor Road.) Our bungalow was situated in the Forest Research Institute itself, with its extensive buildings, expansive lawns and brilliant avenues of purple-blue jacaranda, luminously yellow amaltas, cascading like laburnum, and acacias, pink, blue and red. Our gardener grew vegetables for us in plenty and planted two dozen fruit trees. At night Mussoorie's lights twinkled above us. The rising and setting sun flushed with pink the Himalayan snow-peaks. During the flowering season the garden was abuzz with bees. Colourful butterflies and birds shared the garden with us, and tawny monkeys played on the lawns and leapt through the branches.

On a trip to Kulu we stopped in Amritsar to buy a full size copy of the Guru Granth Sahib. From now on one upper room, wherever I lived, would be Babaji's, a place set apart for daily prayer and reading of the scriptures.

I looked forward keenly to making my first proper home, but I had not realised how much I had to learn; I had no experience of full-scale housekeeping, let alone in the style expected of a scientist's wife. I must not only attend, but be hostess at, dinners and garden parties. I had never seen such glamour and sophistication of dress and entertainment. The challenge excited rather than disheartened me. I had bought a Tricity cooker for use in India and experimented with baking all sorts of cakes, cookies and puddings, and continued to enjoy embroidery and sewing. I was studying for an Arts degree through a correspondence course, but it came to nothing as I had no time to study.

From Professor A. Roy I learned to play the sitar. Chandu, Professor Roy's sickly looking son, amazed me with his prodigious versatility and mastery of sitar, tabla, sarod and banjo. Social life revolved around the Forest Research Institute, generally known by its British name of New Forest, and everyone belonged to a club. I joined the New Forest Ladies Club and was elected Miss New Forest and was soon asked to be secretary as younger blood was needed and fresh ideas. As New Forest was a residential institution everyone knew everybody. In the Doon Club members devoted their days to mahjong, bridge, rummy, dancing and flirtations. Traditional festivals were still highpoints of my year, but the style had altered in some instances. For example we ladies continued to keep the annual Karwa Chauth fast on behalf of our menfolk, but the evening meal was washed down with alcoholic accompaniment.

Very few people had cars. We thought nothing of a two- or three-mile walk home in the early hours after a party. There was no local public transport either: khaki-uniformed peons carried our messages from one part of the Institute campus to another, escorted our children to birthday parties and ran our errands. Telephones were almost as scarce as cars, but all rang one Saturday evening as one officer after another succumbed to the curiosity that spread like an epidemic from bungalow to bungalow. "Have you heard about Rita, yar? What have you heard about Rita? How are her parents bearing up? Will you be there too?"

Rita was Dr Mehra's elder daughter, the eldest of his three children, and Mehra was Director of the Officers' College. Rita was devoted to her work and had been happy for her younger sister, Supna, to marry before she did. As her parents always explained at parties, Rita was a serious girl. She taught in a school in Dehra Dun, and in the evenings practised classical music. A music tutor came to the house. What Rita's parents did not know was that while they socialised at the interminable succession of farewell parties, parties of welcome and parties held because no-one else was having a party, Rita's companion was Dr Mehra's head clerk's son. Rita loved him and she conceived a child by him.

So, on that Saturday evening Mehra's peon went from house to house inviting everyone to Rita's marriage the next morning. Bewildered, we signed against our names on the peon's list. There had been no engagement, none of the customary excitement and preparation, no rumour even of romance or scandal.

On Sunday morning we proceeded to the director's house. The ritual was conducted as tradition required, but the mood was subdued, sad. We observed the morose, embarrassed faces of Dr and Mrs Mehra and felt the deadly silence. We could hardly begin to imagine the shame endured by Rita's parents. For a few months Rita did not see her family, but in due course her child was born and contact was restored.

One of my mother's male cousins one day visited us in Dehra Dun. He insisted on not having even a cup of tea in our house. But Gopal would not take "no" for an answer, and on his insistence my relative drank some tea, but paid us handsomely saying, "Parents do not have even a sip of water in a daughter's house." I remembered my parents' dreary vigils in Bahin Vanti's parents-in-law's house in Rawalpindi. In rural areas this custom may still be unchallenged. (But in England, for at least thirty years parents have been staying with their married daughters for three to six months at a time, and no-one minds.)

Among those who worked on Gopal's scientific team were Ved who joined the FRI as a BSc graduate and, later, Bhatnagar, who obtained his PhD there. Little did we then suspect how tragically their promising careers would end. We found out some years after leaving the Institute that Vaid had committed suicide the day that he heard that Bhatnagar had been promoted to a position above his. On learning of his colleague's tragic death Bhatnagar sank into a deep depression and would not tell anyone the reason. One day, after waiting a long time for her husband to have his breakfast, Mrs Bhatnagar went to her bedroom. Her husband had hanged himself from the ceiling fan. In her grief she followed his example, leaving their children orphans. The rivalries of the Institute blighted many lives and brought untold sorrow.

Another colleague was Babu Sharma. By scrimping and saving he had given his only son, Raj, the best of educations. Great was his pride when his son qualified as a doctor. But others in the Institute were jealous and ensured that Dr Raj, the apple of his parents' eyes, was posted to a remote village in the hills. Here at least the shikar (hunting) was good and Dr Raj and his friends could improve their aim at cost only to local wildfowl. On one expedition he shot at a plump duck. It plummeted into the gorge below. Realising the peril of steep rocks and rushing current, Raj's comrades urged him to forget this bird and try for another. Dr Raj was determined in sport no less than in study. "No, just wait there, I'll be back soon," and he scrambled down the stony ravine. He sprang onto a boulder to grasp the duck and slipped into the turbulent water. His friends watched, mute, as his body was swept downstream, stunned and cut by rocks — rocks until so recently part of an enchanting mountain scene.

Unable to rescue their companion they dispatched his servant to Dehra Dun to break the news to his parents. His father was out of station. As neighbours heard the sobbing and wailing of Raj's mother and sister they rushed in and joined in the lamentation. Soon everyone in the Forest Research Institute knew of the tragedy. They knew, too, that Sharma suffered from asthma and a weak heart. Somehow he must be intercepted before reaching his house, now thronging with mourners. The Institute doctor accordingly went down to the station to meet him. He insisted, to Babu Sharma's puzzlement, on accompanying him to another house where, as gently as the facts would permit, he broke the shattering news.

Some days later the doctor's body, retrieved by his friends, and carefully covered to prevent their seeing its grievous injuries, returned to his parents' house. Raj had been married only eighteen months. His young wife's grief was heart-rending. She begged to be given a last glimpse of her beloved husband, but her friends and relatives decided that the shock would be too great for her, as the body had swollen beyond recognition in the river water. We all shared in the funeral rites beside another mountain river.

From Dehra Dun I accompanied my husband on the tours that were essential to his forestry research. We would reach a Forestry Commission bungalow set on some conifer-clad mountain slope. Awaiting us in punctual welcome would be a pannier of choice fruit, vegetables, eggs and poultry. Our peon would disappear inside to re-emerge with tea neatly set out on a tray. He would remove Gopal's shoes and massage his feet. On one occasion I succumbed to dysentery. Stationed outside my bedroom door our peon must have realised my embarrassing plight. We had no medicines, but he extracted the juice from an onion and a root of fresh ginger. He gave me this mixture to sip and my stomach returned to normal.

In 1950 we visited Nagar, a minor hill station in Kulu's Parvati valley. Here we spent two months amid the peaks that inspired the Russian-born artist, Roerich, whose sharp Himalayan vistas are admired in the art galleries of the distant, dusty plains. In Nagar we met Roerich and his very beautiful wife, Devika Rani, Rabindranath Tagore's actress-granddaughter. We also visited Jean and Jeannette, two English sisters, spinsters then in their late fifties whose resolve to stay on had been unshaken by Independence.

Nothing could induce them to leave their trim flower garden, their orchards of pear and plum and apple. They welcomed us warmly, and we sat down to an English tea of scones, cakes and sandwiches set out on china plates on the starched, crochet-edged table cloth. To bake they had a simple oven, consisting of cooking trays above a layer of embers. They asked us for "news" of England now that the war was over. Had the British treated us well while we were in London? Before we left they gave us apples from their sweet-smelling store, all picked ten months earlier. Every apple was wrapped in its own sheet of newspaper.

Next day we were visited by an Indian family who had seen us sitting on the lawn of the Rest House bungalow and invited us to tea. As we sat around chatting and relaxing, the lady of the house, a pleasant-looking, middle-aged, childless woman, took Shammy from my arms, a very normal action, saying she would bring something from inside the house. My heart leapt sickeningly to my mouth. I snatched Shammy back and made some excuse about having to leave in a hurry. To my surprise, far from upbraiding me for my irrational behaviour or laughing at my terror, Gopal admitted to a similarly overpowering conviction that Shammy had been in some sort of danger. I remembered my mother's seven red chillies. This kindly looking woman must have cast the evil eye on our son. We thanked them and hurriedly returned to our Rest House.

In the Civil Hospital, Dehra Dun, on 6 May 1950 at 2 a.m. our first daughter was born. We called her Kiran, a sunbeam, and she certainly proved to be our ray of hope. Some of our friends found the news of her birth hard to believe. On 5 May we had entertained fifty guests for dinner. After eating we sat chatting and singing in the drawing room. After midnight an elderly lady patted me on the back saying, "You look tired, we must go now." Soon after our guests' departure I felt the onset of labour pains. Gopal went to Mehra's house to ask for transport to the hospital and I left home at 1 a.m.

Subsequently, Kiran was voted Baby of the Year in the competition run by the New Forest Ladies Club. Begum Hamid Ali, President of the All India Women's Council, who had achieved much for women's organisations, invited me to be secretary of the Dehra Dun City All India Women's Council, but on account of my parental responsibilities I declined.

In countless way we had been blessed, but jealousy consumed many of Gopal's colleagues and their wives. They would not stop their envious scheming until their rival had been destroyed professionally, if not literally. Gopal was distressed by the vicious intriguing and was intent on furthering his research and his career, but his letters of application to other institutes were intercepted and all leave of absence for interviews was refused. To all appearances we were leading happy, successful lives, the parents of two healthy infants, in a garden paradise against a backdrop of Himalayan splendour. We chaffed at the frustration of imprisonment in this gilded cage.

Gopal was the youngest but the most senior silviculturist. His colleagues' daughters and daughters-in-law were my age. Gradually we realised the intense envy that his early success had generated. Our bungalow was another source of jealousy. With no thought of arousing antagonism I had made our home as attractive as possible. We had ordered a magnificent table, sofa set and fabric to match the upholstery. Across the bay windows I arranged the curtains in the British butterfly style. When visitors entered and looked around I had noted their start of surprise. "The house is as beautiful as the lady of the house" rang in my ears as a compliment. In my innocence I did not at first perceive the undertones of resentment.

Not only guests from the campus but distinguished scientists from further afield enjoyed our hospitality and I responded to the challenge of catering and entertaining them to the best of my ability. I happily rose to the challenge, knowing that Gopal was pleased with our style.

Five years after our return to India we were privileged to meet Maharaja Yadavindra Singh of Patiala, eldest son of the maharaja whose generous patronage had in 1911 provided Sikhs with their first place of worship on British soil. His Highness Maharaja-Dhiraja Bhupindra Singh Bahadur of Patiala had been generous in ways other than financial. Reputedly Yadavindra had ninety-nine younger siblings. The maharaja's sister was engaged to marry the son of one of our friends. As wedding guests we stayed for several days in the gracious Motibagh Palace. At that time Patiala retained its princely ethos. PEPSU (Patiala and East Punjab States Union) had not yet merged with Punjab. The palace suites were luxurious in scale and in detail. On our writing table were a silver blotter, silver paper knife and silver pens.

Some of our acquaintances at that time had not reached their subsequent pinnacles of fame. In 1955 at the Doon School, where Shammy and Kiran were among the youngest pupils, we met another parent, Pandit Nehru's daughter, Mrs Indira Gandhi. Her sons, Rajiv and Sanjay, were boarders in the senior school. That day pupils were receiving their certificates and trophies. Indira Gandhi, sharp-nosed and olive-complexioned, was sitting quietly, and I wondered how many people had recognised her.

But the exhilaration of our social encounters could not mask the underlying malaise, knowing that Gopal's promise was being stifled and thwarted, that envy enmeshed us. In my sleep one night I saw two quivering flames irradiating the darkness. They were, I knew, the flames of my two jotan, the homemade ghee lamps that I had so often offered in my distress at Damdama Sahib. Someone in my dream was approaching me, handing me a burning light, a little ghee-soaked cotton wool wick in a pastry-fashioned saucer. I realised the profundity of the crisis we faced, and knew with total certainty that our path would be lit. We need not fear. This dream recurred over the years whenever Gopal faced acute problems.

He was going through an agonising period, as the President of the Research Institute had favourites and Gopal was not one of them. The President planted informers to report on who visited our bungalow. When, in 1956, Gopal was offered the post of Regional Director (Botanist) in the Botanical Survey of India in Poona (now Pune), we gladly left the Forest Research Institute. Gopal now had a higher position, and the president was furious with his informers for misleading him.

In Poona Shammy's dastarbandi took place. This means that his first turban was tied. Our son was a young man of nine years and, like Kiran, he attended a local English-medium convent school.

We were housed in a spacious, pleasant bungalow with Maharashtrian servants to do the chores. In the kitchen I continued to increase my repertory of tasty dishes. When *Femina*, a popular Indian women's magazine, ran a cookery competition my stuffed cabbage won first prize. Encouraged by this unexpected success I entered the *Femina* pickle and fruit candy competition, and again came first. Inspired with new-found confidence I wrote features on cookery and sent them to Punjabi magazines published from Jullundur (Jalandhar) and Preetnagar near Amritsar. The editor of one literary journal wrote to me, "You may have three pages each week to write whatever you like." I submitted articles on cookery, women, husband-wife relationships, interior decor, indoor plants and gardening. When women readers sent letters about backache, marital problems, or the menopause, editors passed them to me. From the encouragement of men such as Sardar Gurbaksh Singh, editor of *Preetlari*, and from readers' letters, I knew there was a responsive public to be catered for and I determined to start the first ever Punjabi-language magazine specifically aimed at women. I remain forever grateful to S. Gurbaksh Singh and Prof Mohan Singh, the poet and editor of *Panj Darya*, for their support.

When I discussed the idea with Gopal he was enthusiastic. From Poona we had access to a Punjabi press in Bombay. Gopal would publish and I was chief editor. When I embarked on the first issue I found I had material enough for six.

Subhagvati is the beautiful name for a bride blessed with good fortune, a wife whose husband is alive. This was the title I chose for the Punjab-language women's monthly that I launched in Poona in 1956. I was expecting our third child, but Shammy and Kiran were less dependent now and housework and gardening are not daunting when shared with enough servants. *Subhagvati* consisted of articles on domestic matters, recipes, marital relations, children, gardening, current affairs, poems and short stories. Government officers had begun talking publicly of santan sanjan — birth control. *Subhagvati* aired the arguments for this policy. I began to receive abusive letters. "You are ruining our family life", "You are prejudicing our daughters-in-law," wrote the more restrained.

One elderly man went round his village every publication day to confiscate every copy of *Subhagvati* he could find to burn. "We do not want our daughters and daughters-in-law to learn anything more than the family wishes them to know," he told me.

One of the short stories I published was "Situ di Nilam", the story I had written as a girl-bride for Gopal ten years earlier. In my story I came to Srinagar in the summer months. The Dal lake was astir with houseboats and I got talking with my boatman, Nurdin. Why, I asked him, was there a small blue flag flying from the centre of the lake between two lotus flowers. "Memsahib, that is a very unhappy story, which I myself witnessed:

"One summer a visitor arrived here from Sindh, from the desert land there. He was a handsome man, a Brahmin, Situ by name. To him this mountain valley was a paradise, not only because of the scenery, but because of a beautiful girl he had seen, a Muslim girl called Nilam. Situ spent the whole summer here. Every night he passed the moonlight hours by the lake and Nilam would slip out secretly to join him. As I said, she was of our faith and he was a Brahmin, yet somehow her parents consented to their marrying.

"That very week Kashmir was flooded and the lake burst its banks. Situ and Nilam took part in the effort to save victims of the flood. They were rescuing the unfortunate, ferrying them to safety. But their boat overturned and Nilam fell into the turbid water. Situ plunged in to save her but, crying her name, he too was swept away.

"As news of their drowning spread our whole community lamented that two such young people, so soon to marry, had died like this. In their memory local people set this flag in the water, a blue flag, since Neelu, Situ's name for her, means blue, and two lotus plants."

My mail brought not only hostile criticism but an ever increasing number of pleas for help and advice. When I answered readers' questions I drew on knowledge gleaned from books, from discussion with Gopal and from intuition.

Sometimes the praise I received left me with an odd sense of unworthiness. One evening, while Gopal was abroad attending a conference, a visitor arrived unannounced. Below our residence, on the ground floor was Gopal's office with marble floor, palm trees and fountains. The chaukidar (watchman) came upstairs to announce the unexpected arrival. Hearing the name I vaguely remembered that our caller managed a cloth shop. But why, I wondered, should he be disturbing me at home at five o'clock in the afternoon?

"Send him up," I instructed the chaukidar. I opened my door to greet the elderly shopkeeper and his wife.

"Sat Sri Akal": we exchanged the distinctive Sikh greeting.

"We have come to meet Kailash *Subhagvati* Bahinji," they both said.

I told them that I was the person in question. Their faces registered disbelief. They were expecting to consult a wise, experienced person, not some young woman. They had come for help. Their daughter and son-in-law had been quarrelling with her mother-in-law and brother. While we talked their daughter and son-in-law arrived. Till late at night we sat talking, and the feuding parties left pacified and conciliatory.

I might lack the years that my readers and correspondents expected but wisdom depends on breadth of experience, not on length of life alone. My experience was constantly enlarging as my guidance was sought, as I read more and as I met different people. Kiran and Shammy were growing up and, on 27th September 1956, I gave birth to a second daughter, Risham. Kiran and Shammy were overjoyed to have a little sister and they got us to distribute laddoos in Dadji's office and throw a party for our friends.

Of the many individuals I encountered Sant Singh Smith was definitely one of the most translucently holy. ("Sant" is a title reserved for spiritual masters.) With his two sons he came to our house in Poona, participated in reading the Guru Granth Sahib, and preached. He gave a simple exposition of the Guru's verses and, unlike most of our Sikh preachers, he did not digress with a string of anecdotes (sakhian) about the Gurus. After the religious part of the proceedings, while we chatted around him, he continued to sit erect, cross-legged on the floor, apparently entranced, a devout presence in our midst, appropriately clad in white turban and white clothing. Visiting saints are prone to dictate their culinary preferences. "Babaji will eat only almond khir" and so on. But when we questioned his two sons they replied that Sant Smith Singh ate almost nothing. Following their instructions we gave him two spoonfuls of plain yoghurt, a little vegetable and a half-size chapati. Quietly in his corner he ate our scanty offering, which would suffice him for twenty-four hours. Sant Smith Singh never spoke about himself. From his name, his features and from rumour, we knew his origins were British. His life-story remains a mystery. But we could guess from his composure, his limited speech and his superb kirtan that he meditated most of the time.

After three years in Poona Gopal moved north to Allahabad as Director of the Central Botanical Laboratory. Allahabad has a Muslim name and a unique status for Hindus, for whom it is holy Prayag and marks the tribaini or confluence of three sacred rivers, the Ganges, the Jamuna and the Saraswati. Only the first two rivers can still be seen, the Jamuna clear and blue, Mother Ganga tired and muddy. Every twelve years at Prayag yogis, beggars, the saintly, the sanctimonious and the curious gather on a moonless night early in the year for the most ancient and best-attended religious assembly on earth, the Kumbh Mela.

Allahabad is known too as the home city of India's first Prime Minister after Independence, Pandit Jawaharlal Nehru. Whenever Pandit Nehru came to Allahabad his home city, his residence, Anand Bhavan, was decorated with vases of red roses. The finest roses grew in the Government of India's Central Botanical Laboratory. One morning we joined the fifty or so people waiting, as people did every day, to meet the Prime Minister. Pandit Nehru came through the door and across the room straight towards us. He enquired who we were and how we liked his city. Gopal told him, "Sir, I have the pleasure of sending you roses each day." Panditji gave a charming smile, saying, "Now I know. They are very fragrant and beautiful. Thank you for thinking of me."

Shastriji, another distinguished native of Allahabad, promised to introduce us to Sathya Sai Baba, who later became India's most internationally acclaimed holy man. In many Hindu shrines his picture hangs garlanded among longer established forms of godhead. His celebrated miracles excited devotion and controversy, as watches and religious pendants materialised in his empty hands. There are countless stories of miraculous cures attributed to this orange-cassocked, Afro-haired incarnation of the divine. But in 1961 he was less well known.

We had not heard of him and knew only that Gopal's departmental problems were becoming unbearable, and that our future was uncertain. Would we have to return to Dehra Dun, at the cost of demotion, to escape the vicious in-fighting? In this mood we were glad of help from any quarter. We reached the hall where thousands were awaiting Sai Baba's imminent arrival. Only Indians can crowd together so tightly, as if they have no bones in their bodies. We managed to squeeze ourselves in and waited. A young man, hardly more than twenty, in a long saffron robe entered the hall. His face was half framed by thick, fuzzy black hair, like the negative of a halo. Sai Baba came straight towards us. He was South Indian and spoke neither Hindi nor English. His interpreter translated, "Don't worry about anything. Soon you will be in a better place with no worries." And they moved off towards someone else.

About the same time we consulted a Brahmin clerical officer on the Laboratory staff. His name was Shukla and he was acknowledged to be something of an astrologer. He examined our foreheads and pored over Gopal's right palm and my left, as is the way with fortune tellers. Then he said, "You need not worry. You will have a secure and respected position. You are going to a big building with a prayer room above the entrance." My worries persisted despite his reassurance.

At a conference in New York Gopal met a scientist from Nigeria who asked if he would set up a Botanical Laboratory in the University of Nigeria, Ibadan. Gopal gladly accepted. Later, when we were established in a new house in Ibadan, and our travelling edition of the Guru Granth Sahib was installed in the small room over the doorway, we remembered Shukla's prediction.

There were many calls to make before leaving for Nigeria. In 1961, at Gurmukh Singh Musafir's suggestion, I again met Yadavindra Singh, Maharaja of Patiala, not, on this occasion, in his palace but at his less sumptuous Delhi mansion, Patiala

House. As I entered the room where he sat he rose, tall, courtly and magnificently turbaned. His ADC saw to my comforts. When I left, the maharaja escorted me to the outside gate, bowing repeatedly in farewell with the courtly politeness of bygone centuries. I said, "May God bless you. You are a real Maharaja."

Our departure had to be kept secret. We had to lock up our beautiful bungalow on Park Road, with its lychee and mango trees, and only Bidiya, our trustworthy cook steward, knew where we were heading. We could not leave the country without seeing my mother-in-law, Beyji, and so she came at our request from Calcutta for a few hours. I did not tell any relatives about our departure, none of Gopal's staff were informed and we contacted no-one in Delhi before taking off.

7

West Africa

In 1961 the University of Ibadan was still affiliated to the University of London. Travel from India to Nigeria to take up the appointment entailed sea travel from London, and necessary shopping (we had received a list of articles that were unavailable in Ibadan) before boarding the ship to Africa. In London we stayed in a tiptop hotel. From Liverpool we boarded the MV Apape to Lagos. There were many Nigerians on board and I was initially appalled and puzzled by the deeply scored tribal marks on the men's faces. But it was important to communicate with them and we made a few friends aboard the Apape.

With us in a special case we carried a travelling edition of the Guru Granth Sahib, smaller than the full size volume we had used hitherto. Respect for the scriptures, the physical embodiment of the Guru's word, requires a Sikh to carry them with the utmost reverence. By tradition the volume is carried, ceremonially wrapped, upon the bearer's head. When we travelled we took care that the scriptures should not touch our shoes or anything made of leather. When later we travelled by air Gopal always took the Guru Granth Sahib with him in a box.

At Lagos the Professor of Botany, Professor Eni Niokku, welcomed us and accompanied us to Ibadan. The vivid blue of the sea and the brilliant colours of the lush vegetation reminded me of South India, the red clay soil, the crotons and frangipani, the fringed palm leaves shimmering in the sunshine and the coconuts overhead. Motionless and white, the slender-necked herons stood on one leg. The university campus was particularly beautiful.

Gopal was the first Indian to be appointed to the university, and his turban aroused friendly interest as Hausas from Northern Nigeria have similar headgear.

"Are you an Arab?"

"No."

"Hausa?"

"No."

"Then what else?"

"Indian."

Because of our fairer skins the Nigerian people called us "oyinbo".

All three children started to attend local schools. Risham and Kiran went to the university primary school. Shammy travelled by taxi to the boys' grammar school three miles away until we engaged Nicholas Balewa to drive him. Nigerians welcomed us hospitably. They showed their happiness if there was cause for rejoicing and uncomplainingly accepted deprivation. Tempers flared quickly if provoked. They erected no barriers of reserve.

With British staff in the University there was more tension as Indians and Britishers cultivated the Vice-Chancellor's friend-ship in competition for high position. At this game the British were the winners. Nigerians might be snobbish with members of their own tribe or towards those less well-off, but to us expatri-ates they showed friendliness. Department Heads at times resented the continued presence of British officers who had stayed on, but towards Indians they showed only kindness. Of Gopal I often heard them say, "He is helping our country" — a compliment to Gopal and his subjects of Botany and Ecology.

On the road each passing mammy wagon (lorry) faced the world with its own cheerful message emblazoned across it: Show Love; First is God; Fear Woman; Not too Late; Here I am still Happy; Kill me and Fly; Life is Precious; Jesus is Mine; Indian Girl; Service is always Happy; Praise God. Outside a café was the advice "Never mind your wife — come here with your girlfriend and dance." There was a huge poster of a woman with her child tied at her back, the traditional way of carrying one's child.

In Dugbe market, Ibadan, mammies sat behind little tables displaying some twenty carrots and similarly small quantities of stubby okra, only one and a half inches long, aubergine and red peppers locally called "pepe". "Put out hand! Pay money!" they called. We moved along the narrow passage between their tables.

Soon after our arrival I went shopping with Kiran, then about nine years old, and Risham, who was now nearly three. A middle-aged Nigerian customer was sitting on a chair in the shop. Seeing me enter the shop he greeted me and shook hands. "Is this your daughter, Madam?" he enquired, looking at Kiran. "Yes," I said. "I want to marry her" came the reply. Furious at his unprovoked effrontery I demanded what on earth he meant. The shopkeeper was an Indian. He explained, "It is meant as a great honour when a Nigerian says this." This was only the first of many such situations.

Often Nigerian and Indian cultural attitudes were at variance. One of Gopal's students was Goke, the son of Oni of Ife, the Obah or king of Ife. Goke's mother, queen though she was, kept a trolley of condensed milk, flour and similar commodities for doing "trade" in her drawing room. Goke invited us to his ancestral home, the "palace" where his aunt and uncle lived. We arrived to find a mud house. His parents had gone ahead to entertain us. On the steps was an emaciated, sickly man with a child of six months lying on the floor. Was he a relation too, we wondered? Goke's relatives were inside, waiting to be introduced in turn. We met his great aunt, a senior wife. She was a sixty-year-old Christian in white socks, white buba (loose-fitting top) and lapah (a loose skirt). Her head was covered. Last of all we were introduced to a subdued, unhealthy looking Muslim girl not yet twenty. She, we learned, was married to the old man on the steps, Goke's great uncle. This new bride would serve the senior wife as a domestic slave for the rest of her life without uttering a word. That was the plight of women in Nigeria.

I became more and more interested in the peoples of Nigeria, especially the women. Yoruba women were prized by their parents even if they had wanted a boy. When girls married they received a bride-price (often locally termed a "dowry"). The better educated they were the more they could command. The dowry for a mammy (a successful business woman), a nurse, a hairdresser or doctor was particularly high. As soon as Yoruba men started earning they saved up, hoping to win a working woman. If the girl became pregnant before marriage there was no question of illegitimacy. The father would bring the child to his own house: whether married or not the woman was his prized wife.

A man seeking marriage would ask the woman of his choice. He took with him a calabash and kola nuts, the most essential part of any dowry. A calabash is a large hard-shelled gourd of varying size: it can be a small bowl or a large flat vessel for carrying all sorts of foods. Even at the time of proposing a man must bring a calabash of palm wine and other gifts for his future wife and her mother. Especially if she was beautiful or earning a wage, her parents would refuse even to look at him until he brought more dowry. The bride-price paid by an average bridegroom was forty kola nuts, thirty or forty bitter kola nuts (orgobo), one calabash of sugar, one of salt and one of honey, a box of beer, five or seven bottles of schnapps (very popular in Nigeria), one or two boxes of Guinness (also very popular) and a gift of clothing for his parents-in-law. For his bride he must bring two expensive dresses, a bible, a ring and cash.

At the marriage, and at funerals too, all the ladies on the bride's side wore clothes of one fabric, all their counterparts on the bridegroom's side were decked out in another design. The bride wore bright colours. At parties wives often wore a three-piece costume of the same cloth as their husband's turban. They loved expensive brocades and cloth imported from Japan, Holland and Germany. Each wife had a plot of ground on which she cultivated cocoa, yam, okra and chillies and grazed a goat.

Fat women were the most desired for sex and child-bearing. As men remarked freely, "If she is big enough, I don't need a second mattress." In Northern Nigeria in Hausaland and Yorubaland, the "mambari" was a popular institution: in mud houses on the outskirts of the village girls were fattened on rich food. After three months they came out and processed, clad only in a tiny skirt, around the village square where young men had gathered with calabashes of wine. The fatter the girl the better her matrimonial prospects. Many were already pregnant, as boys from the village would sneak out to the huts for the night. If a girl decided that she did not want to marry the father of her unborn child, the man who took her at the time of the procession became the legal father by paying sheep, cows or cash to the natural father. There was no stigma involved for any of the parties.

Using my observations and literature in the university library I compiled *Kala Manaka* (Black Bead), a Punjabi University publication describing West African customs. Kiran, at that time twelve or thirteen and an excellent untutored artist, drew the illustrations — outlines of golden tribal thrones and tribal marks — and I included photographs of memorable encounters.

I wrote of the carefree people of Nigeria. Whereas Indians dread the shame when a relative breaks time-honoured convention, and live in fear of community gossip and ostracism, the people I met in West Africa were gloriously emancipated, however precarious their living. They danced and sang. Even at funerals, praying to the departed soul, they danced and drank all night in their gorgeous new clothes. "You'll have a good funeral for me, won't you?" I heard old folk say. There were pictures of women dancing, with a calabash on their heads and a child tied on their backs. Women were uninhibited in their dress. African and European styles were both acceptable. Husbands did not stint themselves in their choice of wives or abundance of children. They had mistresses who bore them children and these children were considered to be legitimate. None of the wives would share their earnings with their husbands, as they were notorious for spending their money on concubines. I discussed this on West Nigeria TV with a group of men who insisted, "This is our culture. Our fathers and grandfathers did it. We have to carry on in the same way."

From Nigeria we travelled to other countries. One trip, when Risham was five, was to Ghana where Gopal had been invited to attend a conference. On our return journey students sat in front with the driver and several more students were in the jeep with the other driver. At eight o'clock in the evening we reached Togo's border with Dahomey (now Benin). It had been closed two minutes earlier and would not reopen until eight the next morning. Our driver, a Nigerian, begged the man on duty to let us through. We had known nothing about closing times. No entreaties would induce the officer to reopen the barrier and he retired to his barracks. The heat was stifling. If we lowered the windows we were at the mercy of thousands of invading mosquitoes. Our driver and the students talked and joked loudly throughout the night. Every so often they would leave the car to relieve themselves in front of me. I felt sick with heat and frustration, powerless to soothe Risham's fretfulness.

Gopal's work kept him in Nigeria when I set off for Calcutta and Delhi, enjoying en route hospitality in Sudan and Aden. In India we went first to Allahabad where I had the unpleasant task of sorting out furniture and other belongings. I knew who would help me to deal with this huge amount of work — Bidiya, our former cook-steward. The previous year Gopal had secured him a job in Swarup Rani Hospital, and when I telephoned the hospital he was sent over straightaway.

Baba, Kiran and Risham were all over Bidiya, in their delight at seeing him once again. Risham, now nearly four, climbed up to him and he took her in his arms. The four of them talked and talked. Bidiya was our children's favourite servant: when I had sent their lunch to school with the peon or with Piarey Lal they refused to eat anything and sent the food back home, but when Bidiya took their lunch it would all be eaten, because he told them stories. Now that we had come back, it was Bidiya who decided what was to be sold and what we should give away. He showed the children his living quarters and the children reported that they were full of things that I had given him. He packed up the large trunks and the suitcases, and we left after three days, after meeting old friends. Our parting with Bidiya was very sad. He kept hugging the children and crying.

When we arrived in Calcutta it was humid, hot and pouring with rain. My sister-in-law, Gian, was at the railway station with a truck, as we had decided on the phone. We immediately went home to meet my mother-in-law, who had been waiting patiently to meet us, and we all cried and embraced.

We stayed with Bhaiya Sundar Singh, his wife, Bahin Jaswant and their five daughters and five sons. Each looked stunning, with fair skin and clear-cut features. Sundar Singh's widowed mother and widowed mother-in-law shared their flat in Wellington Road, Park Lane. Besides the drawing room and kitchen there was a long room with eight manjis (charpoys woven from jute string) where all the little children and the two old ladies slept.

As one son was already married he had a room for himself. Next was Jiti, who went to live with her in-laws. When Dr Jindi got married, where was he going to sleep with his bride? Bhaiyaji put up a partition in his elder son's room, so making a sleeping space. It continued like this until all five sons were married. During the day they were in and out of several rooms. The dining hall was furnished with a huge table, surrounded by eighteen chairs. At meal times, while the servants brought food to the table, there were arguments and one or two of the children would get up angrily and leave the room. This was the daily pattern.

After nearly two years in Ibadan Gopal took up an appointment in Ghana, as Professor and Head of the Botany Department in the Kwame Nkrumah University of Science and Technology, Kumasi.

Only a few months before leaving Nigeria we saw a massacre. The Chief Minister, Abubakar Tafawa Balewa, and many important Government officials were murdered in a single night. Everybody was frightened, not knowing what was going to happen in the future. The country lost its stability and the currency fell in value. Law and order collapsed and robberies and pick-pocketing soared.

When we arrived in Kumasi everything was peaceful. Like Nigeria, Ghana had recently got rid of its foreign Government, and all departments were being nationalised. The university was similar, but qualified people were few and so the university depended largely on expatriates. Dr Balfour, the Vice Chancellor, had been successful in persuading my husband to help him to establish the Botany department of his university. Gopal enjoyed his freedom as Professor, Head of Department and Dean of the Faculty of Science.

Once again we lived in a pleasant bungalow on campus. From my study at number 43 Akodee Road I gazed at verdant downland where Ghanaians crouched to gather mushrooms. Next to our bungalow stood the Vice-Chancellor's, and on the other side was Dr Chumbrima's bungalow. I remembered Ooty in South India. Vividly patterned birds and butterflies flitted about the garden, which remained veiled in romantic haze until midday. Frangipani blossom hung in delicate pink and yellow clusters. Gulmohar, the flame of the forest, blazed brilliant red. African children ate the almonds from the katapa tree. Our nights were pierced by the wailing of the bushbaby, wailing like a teething infant abandoned by its mother.

Our months in Nigeria had done little to change our Indian notion of social boundaries one dare not cross. For us social class and occupation were still clearly demarcated. So we were surprised to find that, like Goke's highborn mother, even the Vice-Chancellor's wife took pride in her trade, selling small items. A professor's brother might be his chauffeur, his nephews and nieces would stay with him working as cooks and vendors. All his fellow villagers basked in his importance. A woman whose father-in-law was an oba (chief) and whose brother-in-law was a Minister of State was proud to hawk condensed milk, cigarettes and cakes which she herself had baked, saying "This is my trade."

Fascinated though I was by the people and land of West Africa, my attitudes remained unchanged towards couples' behaviour. I still believed that men should appear to be dominant in the family. When Shammy was sixteen he accompanied me to do some holiday shopping. I slipped money into his pocket, so that he could pay. I had allowed Gopal to dominate me just as my father had dominated my mother. One evening we were at a Rotary Club dinner and dance when Gopal said to me, "It is time to go now." Kiran knew I was having a good time. "Why do you make all the decisions, Daddy?" she said. I could not have challenged him like this but thanked Kiran inwardly for voicing my feelings. Later Gopal and I discussed our relationship and I became conscious of greater freedom, although he continued to dominate in some matters.

As I had been teaching Indian cookery in Nigeria I started classes in Kumasi. These became very popular and my classes were full of university professors' wives. They enjoyed learning and it was satisfying to teach them how to make korma, chicken tika masala, pilaus, vegetable dishes and Indian sweets.

I was still working on *Kala Manaka* and began writing articles on food for the *Ghanaian Times* — how to make pilau rice and chicken with vegetables, for example. In a Christmas issue I described how to tie a sari. As English was the lingua franca the *Ghanaian Times* was widely read.

West Nigeria TV (WNTV) was the first television station in West Africa. In honour of Pandit Nehru's visit to Lagos, Kiran and Risham were televised giving a Bharat Natyam dance performance. Later, Lagos had its own television station. For six months I conducted a weekly women's programme on WNTV, then embarked on a series of cookery demonstrations, appearing on alternate weeks on Lagos Television and WNTV. Elsie Olushala, who was in charge of the Women's Programme, asked me to do the Indian cookery programmes, which were very successful.

Parties and socialising still kept us busy. One evening we were chatting over our drinks before eating. Outside it was raining heavily. Our guests included the Dutch ambassador, the American ambassador and Peggy Appiah, Sir Stafford Cripps's daughter, who was married to a Ghanaian barrister, Joe Appiah. Suddenly, Peggy sprang to her feet and all eyes turned to the carpet. Immediately everyone else leapt up. The room was full of hundreds of black millipedes, some more than two inches long. They had crawled the length of the portico and under the closed

French windows. Joseph, our cook-steward, began to spray insecticide. When he reached the portico he realised why the millipedes had moved indoors. A column of soldier ants, several feet long and at least three inches across, was advancing from the lawn. We knew that soldier ants would swarm all over any obstacle. No-one could risk standing in their path. Joseph told us to go and let them march wherever they wanted. Would they go into the bedrooms? We could relax only one and a half hours later when the last soldier ant had left the house.

This episode brought to my mind a similar instance in Kallar. Long-legged ants were swarming in their thousands and the elderly ladies advised against interfering with them if they invaded the house. Instead we should try to find their nest and sprinkle grain or salt there. Some astrologers suggested feeding the ants or giving them black-eyed beans as alms on Saturdays to ward off ill omens or difficulties.

The winter season of harmattan, was cool, fine and sunny. As Christmas approached everyone working for us expected a tip, a "dash" in local parlance. I recollect one workman calling on us for his dash. I intended to tip him, but only in exchange for educating him a little.

"We aren't Christians," I told him.
"Are you Muslims?" he asked in bewilderment.
"No, we aren't Muslims either."
"Oh, what else are you then?"

I told him that we were Sikh, a name that was totally unfamiliar to him, and gave him his dash. To Ghanaians all expatriates and white people in general are "broni" (brown). They know that there are only two religions, Christianity and Islam, and so the workman was astonished to hear that there was also another religion, the Sikh religion.

Traders in the market used the word "dash" for any free gifts. Gopal was clearly a favourite with some stall holders. "Massa, I give you dash," and the fruit-seller proffered him a banana. For Madam there was never any dash on offer.

With the Vice-Chancellor's wife, Mrs Emma Balfour, and the ten other professors' wives I was invited to Flagstaff House in Accra, the capital, to meet Dr Kwame Nkrumah and his Egyptian wife, Madame Fathia. There were detectives everywhere and the bouquets we had brought were whisked away for examination before we could present them to the President and his wife. Security was strict and each of us was individually questioned before we were allowed to see the President.

We were ushered into a spacious room where I noted photographs of Mahatma Gandhi and Pandit Nehru. Given his rumoured arrogance, the President was surprisingly affable, joking and smiling. Jocularly he instructed Madame Fathia to give us good food and drink. He showed us the vegetable patch which he personally cultivated. We guests must have numbered about two hundred, yet he found time to ask me how many children I had, whether I liked Ghana. "And what do you do?" he enquired. My reply that I wrote for the *Ghanaian Times* apparently delighted him.

The President, Dr Kwame Nkrumah, Dictator of the country, seemed to be a virtual prisoner in his own house, with not dozens but hundreds of bodyguards. Neither his children nor his wife, Madame Fathia Nkrumah, were free to come out of their residence. When Nkrumah went to Mali to attend an African conference the local paper showered him with congratulations. The *Daily Graphic* said: "Thousands bid farewell to Osagyefo, Chiefs wish Kwame safe journey. MPs say goodbye to the Father of the Nation." All the papers were full of praise for him. Every company and business showered their congratulations on him and it was the same on his return.

On February 27th the Rotary Club held their President's Guest Night. The City Hotel was full of guests for the dinner and dance. I sat next to Colonel Kotoka, and on my left was the King of Ashanti, Nana Prempeh Ashantihana. As President of the Rotary Club Gopal sat between Nana (who was in his nineties) and Queen Mary (who was less than fifty).

Early in the morning we received a phone call from a friend asking, "Do you know what happened last night?"

"Oh, it was the Rotary Club ball in the City Hotel," I replied.

"No, no, you don't know yet? There was a coup d'état. The army has taken over and Nkrumah is not allowed into the country any more."

The totally unexpected news shocked us. Col Kotoka was appointed Major General and the Lieutenant General was J. A. Accrah. Young men like Col Afrifa became Major General. Now Ghana was ruled by the army. The celebrations went on for the whole day. The *Ghanaian Times* and *Daily Graphic*'s headlines were "Day of Redemption, Chiefs grateful to Armed Forces" and "Nkrumah is a thief, say the demonstrators. They dance and sing NLC [National Liberation Council] praises."

Amazing. Yesterday Nkrumah was there as Father of the Nation, full of virtues. Today he was a thief. The cry went up: "We will boil him in oil. We will cut him up in pieces. He has exploited the country and people." His photographs were thrown out in the streets, spat upon, cursed and torn to shreds, while people called him the most awful names in the world.

Women traders and men put on white clothes, danced and sang songs in praise of the NLC and reviled Osagyefo (the "redeemer" in Twi language) shouting, "Nkrumah is a mad dog", "Nkrumah is the greatest tyrant", "Get Nkrumah and destroy him", they praised Kotoka, and books by Marx, Lenin and Nkrumah were burnt in the town centre.

Fathia and her children had been thrown onto a plane in their night clothes and sent back to Egypt empty-handed, without even a toy. In those days I was writing poetry as well as short stories and novels. My second poetry book *Lahor da Safar* included a long lament for Fathia leaving Flagstaff House with her three children, and travelling in her nightie and house coat.

Every summer we left West Africa for Europe, travelling aboard one of the then famous Elder Dempster lines. We enjoyed these voyages immensely on the luxury liners, Auriol, Accra and Apapa. While Gopal attended scientific conferences in America and Eastern and Western Europe we would spend two weeks in India.

There the family planning injunctions that had earned me abuse were now daubed as slogans wherever we looked. Huge posters proclaimed: "Family planning is essential", "Ham do, hamare do" (There are two of us, and we have two children), "Use condoms". This surprised me as my magazines had been burnt for carrying such slogans. But I was ten years ahead of the Government!

I would stay with my parents until the day we all dreaded when the farewells tore at our hearts. On our last day together my father would ceremonially open the Guru Granth Sahib, as is our Sikh custom, and read out the Guru's special message — those verses on the left hand page wherever the 1430-page volume opens at random. I would carry these words in my heart as a blessing on my journey. Father would intone the Ardas, the Sikhs' petitionary prayer, and as ever include the verse that unites those who know the sanctity of Damdama Sahib and the Bedis of Guru Nanak's line:

Dhan dhan Guru Baba Sahib Singhji
Dhan dhan Guru Khem Sahib Singhji
Damdama Sahib namaskar
Palang Sahib namaskar
Nishan Sahib rukh rukh var namaskar

Great, great is Guru Baba Sahib Singh.
Great, great is Guru Khem Sahib Singh.
Obeisance to Damdama Sahib.
Obeisance to Palang Sahib.
Again obeisance to Nishan Sahib.

Then we would share the sweet karah parshad, trying to push back the intrusive knowledge that for at least another year we would be unable to share it together.

In 1967, as ever, our joy at reunion was boundless, but as my departure drew closer my father grew visibly more upset. He was too distressed to read from the Guru Granth Sahib, and requested me to take his place. Why, I wondered, was parting so much crueller this year?

Sometimes Gopal had to travel overseas leaving me in Ghana with the children. On one such occasion Gopal left for America in the morning and in the afternoon my daughters had been invited to a birthday party in Kumasi city. On the road from the University a Ghanaian woman, her head piled high with fuel logs, strayed in front of the car. Logs fell everywhere and she landed on my bonnet. From the nearby police post I was taken, frightened, to the police station, although the woman mercifully seemed to be uninjured. I told my driver who had been sitting beside me to drive the woman to the hospital and pay any neces-sary expenses. This was not the end of the story. For days the woman's kinsfolk came to me demanding gin, Schweppes and food. Had she been hurt I would have had to hand over a much bigger recompense. I had to make payments to the police as well.

On visits to Europe we went to many ancient churches. I breathed the atmosphere heavy with history, piety and incense.

The Pool of Life

Where possible I lit a candle, a new flame to flicker briefly until it too sputtered out in the pool of wax that had been other supplicants' prayers. I had travelled far since my girlhood in Kallar, but, as I lit my candle, in spirit I set my two burning jotan on the marble platform of Damdama Sahib.

Rome and Athens became favourite holiday places. In those days (1963–1965) there were very few European and American tourists there. We travelled first class and all the airlines gave gifts to the children. But in Rome and Athens, more than any other cities, passers by stared at us in our Punjabi clothes. Sometimes cars and tourist coaches stopped and people got out to shake our hands enthusiastically. Once in Rome an Italian lady rushed up to Gopal, put her arm firmly round him, kissed him, and shouted to her husband to photograph them together. Shammy seized the opportunity, so we too have a photographic record of Gopal's blushes.

In 1967 all five of us paid one of our three brief visits to Amsterdam en route between London and Ghana. We stayed in bed and breakfast accommodation, wandering at will during the daytime and dining in restaurants of an evening. On one of our expeditions Gopal became acutely embarrassed. In every doorway ladies were waiting alluringly dressed, made up and perfumed. I giggled at their display and was curious to know more, but Gopal hurried us away quickly. I had not realised that it was a red light area and that the women were enticing men. We all started laughing when we discovered the secret.

I was glad of this opportunity to see for myself how these women tried to entice their clients. That evening, in Punjabi, I committed my thoughts to verse:

Young made-up, perfumed girls
Smilingly saying, "I'll tell you the way,
If you're confused."

Gopal's contract in Kumasi ended in March 1966. Shaminder was studying hydrogeology as a postgraduate student in the University of Warsaw, and we were anxious to be able to see him from time to time during his three years in Poland. If we returned to India we would probably be unable to see him during that period. Current Government of India restrictions would prevent us from sending him money if he needed it. Gopal's younger

100

brothers were both in Florida, so we thought of finding work there. Harbans was working for the Geological Survey and assured Gopal that he would have no difficulty in finding a suitable position if he decided to settle in America. But we felt more at home in Britain. It is also nearer to India. As Gopal had six months paid leave entitlement we were confident that before his salary payments ended, his qualifications and experience would win him an appropriate position in Britain.

We shipped our furniture and smaller belongings to Liverpool to be stored in a warehouse there pending long term decisions. Meanwhile friends in Slough wrote that they had found rented accommodation for us, two rooms with a shared kitchen and bathroom.

Shortly before leaving Ghana, at a cocktail party given by the then British High Commissioner in Nigeria, we met Edna, an English woman. She was wearing Nigerian dress including the headgear known as onilegogero. I said hallo when I saw her sitting on her own, sipping water. She proceeded to tell me her story as the seventh wife of a Ghanaian building contractor. She seemed happy living with her small daughter in her private quarters. She explained that all the wives lived separately. "We are all very happy. The lady who cooks for "Kofi", he spends the night with her. We all take turns. We are a very happy lot. At least two or three of us" she told me "are always pregnant."

Shortly after that we embarked on the Auriol and docked in Liverpool in April.

8

Slough and Southall

We reached London as we had so many times before, but not this time for the luxury hotel, West End shopping and Embassy engagements. We headed for Slough and our rented rooms. Before long a letter arrived from Shaminder. He regretted that he could not come to Britain until the Summer vacation. As our stay would now be longer than originally envisaged, and neither Kiran nor Risham could afford a longer interval in their studies, Kiran commenced her A level course at Slough Technical College and Risham started at the local school.

It was hard to believe that this was the same Britain which I had first seen as a naive young bride twenty years before. At that time the local people had stopped me in kindly wonderment to marvel at my unfamiliar clothes and ask if I was a maharani. Now, as then, Britishers initiated conversation with: "Looking better now, isn't it?" "Think it'll clear up soon?" or, more embarrassingly, "Do you speak English?"

I had forgotten about weather talk, and it was disconcerting to be told, "Oh! You speak English. Must have learnt in the evening class!"

Now there were Punjabis on all sides, but Punjabis who were strange to us in background and outlook. During our years in West Africa several of our acquaintances had told us about the growing Asian population in the United Kingdom, but I was unprepared for this new scenario. Our home had been in West Punjab, now West Pakistan, and our dialect was Pothohari with its distinctive vocabulary and turn of phrase. Our Slough neighbours hailed from East Punjab, in most cases from peasant farming families around Jalandhar between the Beas and Satluj rivers. To them we were "Bhapas". (Bhapa is the word we use for "brother".) Whereas these East Punjabis refer to their villages as "pind" we Pothoharis say "gran". In some respects our dialect resembles Gujarati, though I do not know the historical reason for this.

Their experience and expectations of life were so different from ours that, despite the gurdwara, the Indian food shops and so forth, we felt strangers, but we admired their determination and resilience. Men struggled on nightshifts in factories and let out rooms or did business on the side to raise sufficient money to bring over their wives and children. Women also found employment in the factories. When they talked to us in the gurdwara they asked us why we were not working in factories too. Our landlord, a Punjabi factory hand, was pleasant enough, but his wife's way of speaking seemed unbearably disrespectful to me. In North Indian languages respect can be expressed in so many little ways, among them by the ending of the verb, and, as in so many European languages, there are different ways of saying "you" to convey familiarity or deference. She insisted that among Jats (her own agricultural caste) "tu" (you) and a singular verb were good enough for anyone. But it hurt me to hear her speak like this to Gopal. In my mind one's husband and father have a special respected place at home, and this was what I expected of Jinder, our landlady. Jat women must have been born as feminists, I mused.

I attempted to impress upon her that it was not nice to show so little respect when speaking to one's menfolk. She listened attentively, then burst our laughing. "Respect. What sort of respect? We don't want them to feel superior to us. They don't need to be addressed in any special manner." To my surprise she had dismissed my point of view totally, leaving me thinking, "These women know more about keeping their men in their proper place than the rest of us!" .

In shops the Indian shopkeepers never handed us goods nicely wrapped or said "thank you" like their English counterparts. Instead they stared at me and thrust the goods aside at the till. It was very annoying. They were selfish and rude to the core, I thought, and I tried to avoid Indian shops.

The mini skirt was at the height of its popularity. Regardless of their vital statistics women and girls were showing their thighs, and Kiran was not going to be left out. However long her skirts seemed to be when we bought them she invariably succeeded in converting them to the miniest of minis. I felt mortified. What would our relatives say if they saw her exposing herself in this shameless way? What sort of fashion was this which required girls to dress so disrespectfully in front of their elders? I remarked on her appearance many times but Kiran remained determinedly impervious to my hints. One day at breakfast I exploded. Kiran had come down ready to go to college in the briefest of minis. "What sort of fashion is this that makes you show everything but your panties? Go upstairs and change. You can't possibly go outside the house like that." Kiran stood her ground. "I shall wear what I am wearing." She charged upstairs to gather her books, and Gopal remonstrated with me. "Please don't get angry with my daughter. You may say what you like to me but not to her." But I was determined. At that time we also thought about returning home after a few months, and I knew we would have to keep our daughters under our control. But I failed in my attempt.

Meanwhile I continued submitting articles in Punjabi on marital problems, menses, menopause — the whole gamut of sexual anxieties afflicting Punjabi humanity. Thousands of British Punjabis subscribed to *Punjab Times* and *Des Pardes*, London-based weekly papers in which features by Kailash Puri now began to appear.

To the editor of *Preetlari* I sent an article entitled "Swargi Hular" (Heavenly Uplift). In a clean, readable language I wrote of the need for mutual love, care and interest if intercourse was to bring satisfaction to both husband and wife. If one partner was unhappy neither could climax in orgasm. Their relationship would be sexually unfulfilling because of imbalance in their love. From the editor of *Preetlari* I received a complimentary note, but, as ever, my contribution to his higher sales went financially unrecognised. Since no copyright legislation effectively protects the writer of Indian languages I was not surprised to see "Swargi Hular" appear subsequently in twelve more Punjabi publications, including Britain's *Des Pardes* and *Punjab Times* and papers printed in Canada and the United States. It was some reward to have people come up and assure me "Bahut vadhia si — it was a beautiful article." But their appreciation made no impression on our bills.

At first it had seemed unthinkable to accept factory work. Little did I realise how soon I would be desperate because none was offered to us. As weeks passed our financial worries outweighed other considerations. By now, as well as the rent and day to day living expenses, there were outgoings on the second hand car which we had bought. To survive the cold we had to buy woollen clothing and blankets. For me, as I searched for work, the car was not a luxury but a must, as my feet were often painful. Gopal's applications for university posts were fruitless. Crowded in our two rooms we felt suffocated and oppressed with anxiety. I had started applying to factories for work, any work, but no one would hire me. "What experience do you have? None?" But, I protested inwardly, neither had any of these unsophisticated Punjabi village women all around me, yet they were taken on. All over Slough Industrial Estate I trudged from factory to factory — Mars, Cadbury . . . At each the same question from the Personnel Officer. What was wrong with me? Why was I considered unfit for factory work? At night I lay awake, crying, hoping Gopal would not hear my sobs and asking "God, where have you thrown us?" I could not bear to imagine Gopal's state of mind. What was to be the future for our children? Should we stop Kiran's education and send her out to work?

One day I felt so hopeless that I put on Kiran's short dress and pencil-heeled shoes to try my luck with a new image. But I fared no better and despised myself. What the factories wanted, I told myself, was not a more Westernised Indian, but one who looked as if she would work passively, like a silent donkey.

We searched the newspapers every evening for positions vacant, and Gopal was by now sending applications for all the clerical posts advertised, but unsuccessfully.

Eventually Britannia Lard factory offered me a job, standing from 8 a.m. to 5 p.m. filling bottles with oil on a conveyor belt. At home, if I stood cooking for two hours, I had pains in my bunions and both heels. At Britannia Lard I had to stand all day. Indian and English girls were standing all around, uncomprehending of my distress. I worked without speaking, remembering the past, fearful for the future, crying with pain and grief. Surely, my fellow workers said, I should be happy. I was earning good money. It was £5 per week, but it felt like £50; my earnings were so precious to me in those days. One day, as I stood at the conveyor belt filling bottles, I fainted. An elderly Punjabi brought me a glass of orange juice and took me to the relaxation room for five minutes. As soon as I came round I insisted on going back. I couldn't afford to waste time.

When I went home I smiled and laughed as best I could, not wanting to distress Gopal or the girls. I was embarrassed that letters came to the house more often addressed to me than to my husband. I pledged with myself that as soon as Gopal started earning I would stop doing so. We had always previously managed on his earnings, and we would do so again. While standing on the factory floor and filling bottles I was constantly chanting shabdan (words from the Gurus' hymns) and praying to Guru Nanak to have mercy on us and grant a suitable job for my darling husband.

After some weeks at Britannia Lard I graduated to Chick's sweet factory. Here I was filling bags with sweets and small toys. The workforce were half white, half Asian. If you slowed down, your wages were cut. But I earned about £6.50p a week, and no longer had to stand. My supervisor was a friendly young woman who often came round for a chat. She was engaged and saving hard for a house deposit. I wondered then, "Why does she need to buy a house? Why can't she stay with her husband's parents after marriage?"

I had not realised that in the UK, unlike India, grown up men and women, especially married couples, live on their own.

In Slough shopping centre was Suiter's department store. One day I read in the local paper that they needed a sewing machine demonstrator. I had always enjoyed embroidery and dress-making for my daughters, and this sounded better than factory work. I was interviewed and, to my considerable amazement, was given the job. I hoped that this would be valuable experience for improved employment in the future. Meanwhile I earned £3.50 for two days work per week, Fridays and Saturdays.

Seeing me at work, one of the Directors of Sewmasters asked me if I would work for them. They offered me £4.50 to work the same hours. This I gladly accepted and I was sent to demonstrate Sewmasters in their Hayes branch. At Sewmasters I worked with Jacki. Late in life she had married the managing director. One day she said, "I'm sending Mum on a wonderful holiday for two weeks with all the pocket money she needs to buy herself what-ever takes her fancy. She never had a day's happiness with my father, always did just what he wanted. Now that he's dead I mean her to have a fling." She made a lovely embroidered sheet and pillow case and presented these to her mother together with cash as spending money. I had heard that sons and daughters in this country did not care for parents. And here was Jacki doing so much for her mother! She also amazed me by what she said about her father's attitude to his wife. All this was news to me.

Some of my colleagues' confidences resonated rather less with my own Indian experience of family life, as when, to my horror, a young woman informed me that her father had asked her to have an abortion; if he had a grandchild it would make him feel old. How funny! I did not understand how a father could give such advice to his daughter.

Custom was good and I received bonus payments. Then, shortly before Christmas, I returned home one evening unable to hold back my tears. I have been dismissed with no reason given. Gopal did his best to console me with his usual optimism. "You will get something better very soon. What's the use of worrying?" But I knew all too keenly how he felt about his own plight.

Then I remembered how a few weeks previously a friend in Hayes had told me of a crimplene factory on the local industrial estate. If I went from door to door with a polythene bag full of suit lengths I would earn commission. I followed her advice. We had no telephone and I would turn up unannounced on the doorsteps of our Indian acquaintances, often to be told, in typical Asian style, "Come back some other time." The recurrent embarrassment and the waste of my precious time galled me bitterly. Each week I was lucky to make £2.

By this time we had moved to a small house in Southall with monthly mortgage payments to honour. Here there was a growing population of Punjabis, many unable to communicate in even elementary English. Health workers, doctors, social workers and police were keen to learn the basics of spoken Punjabi. There was not even a court interpreter. I gave oral Punjabi lessons two evenings a week in Dormers Wells School in 1968 and once a week I taught Indian cookery. I have not been able to ascertain whether previously there had been courses in Indian cookery or Punjabi run by Adult Education Centres in London or elsewhere in Britain. I also worked part time as interpreter in a family planning centre. The gynaecologist, Dr Wiseman, and the Family Planning Director were the most understanding of English women. They understood my predicament and my anxiety. They sympathised and refrained from asking troublesome questions.

In the sixties some Punjabis were reluctant for their children to speak Punjabi. In any case children growing up in Britain tend to gravitate to English. By their attitude I feared that parents were creating enemies within their own houses, children who would refuse chapatis and dal, demanding steak and kidney pie or beef-burgers. On return visits to their villages such parents could show off their English children, boasting that they were sahibs who ate meat three times a day. I am convinced that children should be encouraged to feel pride in their parents' culture.

Along with the Britishers studying Punjabi in my class were two boys whose father was a staunch "comrade" active in the Indian Workers' Association, a pro-Marxist organisation which was more vigorous then than now. They showed little interest and lolled casually in their seats. When I asked one of them to say "ghagga", one of the first letters of the Punjabi alphabet, he made a noise as if something had stuck in his gullet. "What language do you speak to your mother?" I asked, pointing towards him with a ruler in my hand.

"She speaks Punjabi and I speak English."
"How long have you been over here?"
"Three years."
"And in those three years you have forgotten how to speak Punjabi?"
No answer.
"Say the word for horse."

This word, "ghora", begins with the letter "ghagga". He artic-ulated it effortlessly. I knew well that "gh" is a tongue twister, but it is our own language and we are used to pronouncing it correctly. The contemptuous attitude of such youngsters to their mother tongue boded ill for future family understanding. But I wasn't surprised at such an attitude because at that time parents who had arrived from villages in India rather relished seeing their children behave like a "gora sahib" (English person).

In Southall I was afflicted with arthritis. First fibrositis attacked my back, then, gradually, my shoulders and arms began to ache. If the dinner needed stirring I came to dread the excruciating pain in my elbow. Despite depression and this physical affliction I began editing a new magazine, with encouragement from local Punjabis. Little suspecting how my hard work would be exploited, and hardly knowing to whom I was addressing it, I started *Kirna Weekly* (Sunbeams Weekly). This literary venture was short lived. Life still seemed bleak and dark, but together we weathered the worst and thanked God for any rays of hope.

I desperately needed full time work and went to the Southall Employment Exchange. The DHSS official, a middle aged woman, instructed me, "Write your name clearly. You must write your application in good English, you know. If not you will not get a job." I left the office, humiliated by her patronising tone, her English assurance of racial superiority. Did she not understand that whatever the shade of one's complexion human feelings are the same? I was taken on by Westminster's, a tobacconist with branches all over the country. My job was in the Acton office, with fifty or more others, doing accounts. This was my first clerical appointment and I was terrified that I wouldn't learn quickly enough or would disappoint my employers in some way, an intolerable prospect, as I hated feeling incompetent. How would I cope? Soon I was used to working all day on the calculator and I worked overtime on Saturdays and Sundays. The realisation that I could still learn new skills and work reasonably efficiently gave me a deep sense of satisfaction.

One day in the gurdwara I met a girl who was in the Civil Service and she urged me to apply, despite my objections that the Civil Service would never employ such an uneducated person. "So what? You're working at Westminster's without qualifications, aren't you? There's nothing to lose. Just send in an application." She emphasised that I must send my application to her office which was in Harrow-on-the-Hill.

To my astonisment I was selected to work as Clerical Assistant for Harrow Land Registry. Within six weeks I was promoted to Clerical Officer, working on deeds and surveys. I concentrated diligently. In the lunch hour, while my colleagues relaxed, I took out a notebook and jotted down poetry in Punjabi. Rereading it the gloom and sorrow of that time again submerge me, but no English rendering can so sharply convey my mood:

> Sir, tan kadi akhiya nahi
> Hazur sada akhwaiya hai . . .
> I have never said "sir" to anyone,
> I have been addressed with respect . . .
> Now times have changed,
> I am behind the counter
> Saying "sir" to undeserving people.

And another one:

> Living every day,
> Dying every moment,
> Begging a ray of light from the sun,
> What sort of life is this?
> Between the stones of yesterday and today,
> Analysing.

I prayed hard that our rightful bread winner would soon get a position. One lunch time two colleagues asked, "Why do you keep mumbling something all the time?" They had noticed my lips moving as I recited words from the Gurus' hymns: Satnam Sri Wahiguru, Satnam Sri Wahiguru . . . Lord God, Whose Name is Truth. Their enquiry brought me back to Harrow Land Registry, with a jolt. I had been repeating the words unconsciously, resolved that my darling husband would find a suitable post and retire in great glory.

In this country your free time could be commandeered by nobody else. In the factories I had marvelled at the self-confidence of the most menial employee. Your superiors could not speak rudely or boss you about when you were off duty. How different from the conditions in Indian work places, where an officer would bark irritably at his subordinate, "Go away. Bring it later." And where employees were too scared of losing their meagre pay to utter the least complaint, no matter how unreasonably their superior behaved. It is an Indian characteristic to impress upon subordinates in the office and upon domestic servants that you are the boss. The employer is "Mai Bap" — like mother and father. The employee's life and livelihood depend upon his mercy. Indians love to be cruel. It is true that they are glad to give in charity to the victims of poverty or disease. But their motive is to secure a comfortable place in heaven. Their language is abusive to their peons and subordinates, and they lose their dignity and call them names.

This was the first time I had been one of a large work force, the first time I had alone faced a large community of English people. Everyone talked with me and I felt no discrimination. At Harrow Land Registry I had to deal with many enquiries on the telephone, but my ear was not attuned to local colloquial English. "Yes, what was that, could you please repeat what you said? Sorry, this line

110

doesn't seem very good." Would disgruntled members of the public complain to the Land Registry for employing someone whose hearing and comprehension were so defective? I was also scared of being even a few minutes late for work in the morning. Each day I got up at 6 a.m. and was out of the house by 8 a.m. I returned at 6 p.m. in the evening, never earlier, then cooked the evening meal before rushing off at 6.45 p.m. three evenings a week to Dormers Wells School to teach sixty or more students. Classes finished at 9 p.m. and by 9.30 I reached home again to collapse into bed, fearful of oversleeping.

Our furniture and other possessions had come from Liverpool; Risham and Kiran were doing well at their studies, and I had interesting, challenging work with no cause for shame. But I could not be happy until Gopal found employment, and employment as a scientist. Every month I hid my salary to avoid hurting his pride further. The knowledge of his feelings tore my heart. My only consolation came from struggling my hardest to help my dear ones in this time of need. My darling husband had always been so absurdly honest, loving and caring, totally dedicated to science and to his family. This was my only prayer, "God grant that my dear, dear husband reach his retirement still working as a scientist."

Both daughters worked hard at their studies and did well in their examinations. Kiran had passed her A levels and was to start at university. Baba was in Warsaw studying hydrogeology. Luckily our children were very understanding as well as being academically successful.

Our house was too chilly for comfort, so we were tempted by an advertisement for central heating. A few weeks later we were £300 poorer, and the house was equipped with heating which never functioned. Our attempts at contacting the firm concerned proved futile. We had discovered the hard way about "cowboys". In our respect for British integrity in business transactions we had not imagined such dishonest practices.

One evening as darkness fell Gopal and I were walking with our daughters along the road at the back of our house. A group of English lads were quickening their step behind us. As they caught up with us they swore obscenely, shouting at us "Go home!" This experience left me feeling sick and shaken. In West Africa we had been mixing as equals with British scientists and their families, all part of the same expatriate society of leisurely socialising. Now these louts were insulting and intimidating us for no reason, while I gave of my best to British society. On the buses the unoccupied places beside Indian passengers remained empty until all other seats had been filled. This petty discrimination was a new experience for me. I wondered at their phony standards and feelings of superiority.

Nearly eighteen months after our arrival in Britain Gopal was appointed to a lectureship in Liverpool Polytechnic. For the first time Liverpool meant more than docks and warehouses and became a place in its own right, a city in which to live, not only a point of arrival and departure. True to my private pledge I handed in my notice at Harrow Land Registry, to the puzzlement of colleagues who asked why I did not request a transfer to Liverpool. As Kiran was due to sit her A levels that summer we arranged for her to stay as a paying guest with a close school-friend who lived in Maidenhead. Gopal proceeded to Liverpool ahead of the rest of the family, leaving the car with me. There were a thousand and one arrangements to make and my classes were still running.

My colleagues could not understand my decision to resign from a job which commanded such a high salary and pension. But my mind was made up. I regarded my husband's salary as "barkat" (good luck), and knew that I would be able to manage. I would live like a lady and enjoy being a mother, wife and free-lance writer.

One day I was returning from Dormers Wells School, preoccupied with my own affairs. On the dual carriageway I noticed the drivers of oncoming cars staring at me. "What is wrong with me?" I wondered. Then a police van pulled up alongside. An officer jumped down. "What's happened? What are you doing? Don't you realise that this is a dual carriageway?" Sheepishly I said, "Yes, I do realise." I had been absentmindedly cruising along in the wrong direction on a perfectly familiar stretch of the dual carriageway. Luckily two of the police in the van had been studying Punjabi in my class, and they good-naturedly let me off with a heartfelt warning not to repeat the lapse.

Their good-humoured readiness to believe my plea of carelessness was inexplicable. I shall always feel gratitude to them.

9

Liverpool

Now that Gopal had secured a post in Liverpool we needed a house. So, with the help of an English friend through the Rotary Club, Norman Williams, who knew the different areas, he began looking. Armed with a list of promising addresses from the estate agent, he set out on foot in the rain. He rang the bell of the first house only to be told, "Sorry, this house has been sold." Gopal protested that he had only just been given the details by the estate agent. "Someone telephoned, and so it is no longer on the market. Goodbye." He fared no better with two or three more properties, and readily accepted Norman's offer to take him to prospective houses in his own car.

In May we moved to Bucklands. The house needed redecorating and I had no idea what materials were needed for ceilings, walls and windows. Again an English friend, Brian from London, came and stayed with us and he helped, guiding us through the mysteries of wallpaper, emulsion and gloss. The garden was overgrown with weeds, so on our return from the shops we embarked on the new experience of gardening. A man in his early sixties stopped outside the gate and said, "So you are the new owners of this house then?" We nodded. "Oh, I think you will be accepted here." We recoiled, stunned at the implications of his condescension. What sort of people were these who had to approve us?

After a few days our next-door neighbours called. Genial and welcoming they invited us round for sherry and light refreshments. We appreciated their gesture but our new-found friendship was to last only one week. During maintenance work on our central heating system some smoke drifted over the garden wall. My cooking was interrupted by an emphatic knock at the front door. "Am I speaking to Dr Puri?" a uniformed policeman demanded of my husband. "It has been reported to me that you are responsible for causing a public nuisance. The neighbours have registered a complaint concerning smoke from these premises." Was I supposed to gather up the smoke and store it in my own house, I wondered. We sent them a Christmas card but there were no more visits.

Blundell Sands is a gracious residential area of spacious Victorian houses, quiet, leafy, conservative. We were the first Indians to move into the neighbourhood, and our arrival did not pass unnoticed. In September the *Crosby Herald* gave us a favourable write-up. People might not speak to us, but they had read of our existence in the *Echo* evening newspaper. The *Southport Gazette* too wrote a feature on us. We were the talk of the town.

Both Gopal and I had served on the executive of the International Friendship Society in Ealing which turned into the Community Relations Council. In Blundell Sands I was preoccupied with maintaining a sizeable house and garden single-handed, with no idea what was happening in the great, unexplored world of Liverpool. However, someone gave my name at a general meeting of Liverpool council. We received an invitation to a meeting. By the time we returned the car to the garage I had been elected a founder member of Liverpool's Community Relations Council. A local social worker, who had, I later discovered, read about me, must have already paved the way.

Before long I was out three evenings a week, often till ten o'clock at Community Relations Council (CRC) meetings. As years passed more and more Asians and West Indians joined the CRC. Some Asian members came as representatives of fictitious organisations. Quarrels became endemic and, sadly recognising that I could no longer achieve anything useful through serving on the CRC, I resigned.

Kiran was studying Sociology at Liverpool Polytechnic. Risham was admitted to Crosby Manor High School. Gopal enjoyed considerable independence in his teaching and research at the Polytechnic. I was coping with the multifarious demands of family, home and journalism. Most bewildering and hurtful to me were the unfamiliar Western values unconsciously directed at me by our own children. I had, each time, to take stock, to analyse why I felt hurt, insulted or incensed, how far I

114

should take my children to task, how much I should accept without remonstrance. Usually underlying this tension was the West's individualism, the East's belief in the priority of family relationship.

When my second cousin came to Britain, Risham's confusion surfaced. "What have I got to do with them?" I feared such signs. Were they symptoms of family disintegration? I did my best to explain and reason. Or the telephone rang. "It's your phone call, Mummy." In Asian families there had never been any question of "yours" and "mine". Everything is "ours". But here were my children, with no thought of offence, saying matter-of-factly, "It's your friend speaking", instead of "It's Auntyji or Uncleji" as I would have liked. Or I had to ask myself, "Why am I hurt? Why do I mind so much?" when Risham or Kiran said, "Baba has invited us round." Wasn't Shammy their own brother? Why then this talk of "invitation"? In India we never said, "A relative has invited us", but only "We are going to his place." To be invited is like being thanked in the verbal English way. It means you are separate, formal, with no deep unquestioned claims as flesh and blood. Or I listened, shocked and baffled, as Britishers insisted on repaying each other a few pence. Such insistence over trifles would be insulting to an Indian, implying that he was deemed mean enough to expect even a penny to be repaid. Even with close friends and relatives the British appeared to keep exact balance sheets always in mind. Would we Indians follow suit?

In some ways, however, we were as British as any pet-loving Briton. With us at Bucklands we now had Stasha, a young collie. He was Kiran's pet in particular. Among the anonymous letters asking, "Why don't you go home and work for your own people?" was a note demanding, "Please stop your dog barking." I wondered how to stop our dog barking.

To fill a gap in the Punjabi literature readily available in this country, and to supplement our income, I started a new monthly magazine, *Roopvati*, which bore a strong resemblance to the successful *Subhagvati*. It catered for the whole family and included a few features in English. There were articles on religion, literature, immigration and legal rights. Gopal provided a language-teaching page, a chart showing the same words and phrases in Roman script, Punjabi, Hindi and Urdu. The Indian High Commissioner, Apa Pant, contributed articles on yoga, and the distinguished Sikh journalist and writer, Khushwant Singh, and others less well known, also wrote for us. I signed the editorial "Kailash Puri", and wrote other features under my other names, "Viranwali" on the children's page and "Vino" (always Gopal's name for me) among other pseudonyms. We carried advertisements for income tax consultants and yoga teachers, for import-export firms, health clinics, hakims, sari boutiques, private coach companies, travel agents and shops selling Indian musical instruments — the whole gamut of Punjabi enterprise in Britain. But Gopal and I differed over the running of *Roopvati* and would from time to time shout at each other and stop talking so that running the magazine smoothly became problematic.

Gopal was working full time at the Polytechnic, and I had a hundred and one claims on my time, but we produced *Roopvati* alone. We had no typewriter with keys for the Gurmukhi script in which Punjabi is written, so I wrote out every issue by hand and sent it for printing in Delhi. The magazines were airlifted to Liverpool, 5000 of them, for us to collect and distribute. Being in Liverpool with so small a Punjabi population we had no-one with whom to share any stage of the production. Had we been living in London or Birmingham we might have found proficient help. I dealt single-handed with the piles of readers' letters begging for advice or, heart warmingly, expressing thanks. "Dear Kailash Puri, when I read your editorial I feel that we are sitting together and you are talking to me . . . " I dealt with countless other letters seeking advice on different aspects of life, or complaining at the writers' unbearable circumstances. Domestic violence, alcoholism and children's problems were increasing rapidly.

Yoga began to take up more of my time. Yoga and meditation had long interested Gopal. For him a sound ecological balance was inseparable from harmony within the human psyche and between individuals and groups. At first he was invited — to Grimsby and Glasgow among other places — to speak on yoga and relaxation and I accompanied him to speak on health foods and waterless vegetable cookery. We visited many yoga centres all over the country to speak, demonstrate yoga asanas and cook.

In 1971 the Indian High Commissioner, Dr Apa Pant, attended a Day of Yoga and Relaxation which Gopal and I had organised as part of the Crosby Arts Festival. "This is the best and subtlest way of Indianising the British," he commented. That evening at home he shared generously of his vast learning, taught us pranayama, hatha yoga and surya namaskar (breathing exercises, postures for physical health and postures of greeting to the rising sun). As I absorbed Apa Pant's teaching I knew "This is it. I must find out and practise as much as I can." I borrowed all the books I could find by renowned yogis and practised pranayama and hatha yoga religiously. Gopal too helped me to learn and understand this art and science, which Patanjali, the first guru of yoga, and other yogis, gave to Indians thousands of years ago.

Sikhs will object that there is no place in our religion for yoga. Didn't Guru Nanak refute the yogis of his day? Fanatics denounce any Sikh who dabbles in yoga, or, worse still, teaches it, as Yogi Bhajan (alias Harbhajan Singh Yogi, also a Puri) did so conspicuously in America as the founder of Sikh Dharma of the Western Hemisphere. To these critical coreligionists I say, "Whatever brings true peace of mind is good. I am a devout believer in Guru Nanak and the Guru Granth Sahib from which I read daily. Through my faith will come my salvation, but my faith is not restricted to a narrow path." Gopal and I both practised this and learned a great deal both from Guru Granth Sahib and from yoga, the science of relaxation.

To those other critics who asked, "Surely yoga means strict self discipline, the capacity to live without food or drink, on air alone, or even without air" I replied, "If I decided to become a hermit, of course I should be able to do these things, to come out alive after two hours buried in concrete. I have children, bills and appearances to keep up. The yoga I teach can bring mental peace to others emotionally worn by the usual demands on time and energy." We carried on teaching yoga and meditation three times a week for twenty years, which blessed us with remarkable friends.

In the 1960s thousands of women turned to yoga to find inner harmony. They renounced and denounced meat and bought physical health expensively in health food stores. Family harmony suffered when hungry husbands and children were denied their fish and chips, ham or hamburgers. With no spirit of compromise to rescue them, marriages foundered on soya chunks and raw carrots. This was a mockery of yoga. The unmarried sadhu, with no mortgage, job or family pressures, may well live on air and prayer. But most yoga students in Britain are enmeshed in responsibilities to spouse, building society and employer.

One day a patient called, asking to see Dr Puri. "I am afraid Dr

Puri is away," I told him, "Can I help you?" The young man was clearly desperate, so I invited him in for a consultation, contrary to my rule of accepting no new patients in Gopal's absence. Gregory was a local civil servant. "I have been off work for six weeks. I can't drink, eat or sleep." He told me he had led a normal life until he had bought a book on yoga, convinced that he could enrich his life. Soon he was devoting three hours to yoga each morning before setting off to the office. On his return of an evening he put in three more hours. He switched his diet to a strictly vegetarian regime. Within three months he could digest nothing but pineapple, lettuce leaves and cottage cheese. Following a book without the help of a teacher can be misleading and harmful to health.

In India our fasts are a gentle discipline. Many Hindus observe one day a week with only fluid until sundown when the fast may be broken. In the West a keen yoga convert might fast for seven days without even water. Recuperation might take as many months. In India, at holy places like Allahabad's confluence, one sees yogis upside down, their heads buried in sand without breathing for many hours. But those engaged in this world's business show more common sense than their Western counterparts. No Indian would fast for a whole week while working eight hours a day. But I met an English woman at a Sunderland Day of Yoga who had decided to do just that. Her digestive system failed, she was miserable and had no strength. We took her under our umbrella, taught her regularly, but without harshness. She recovered and became a yoga teacher.

Yoga practitioners are conspicuously lithe and fit. But arthritic pains racked me at the time when I began my exercising. From my arms the arthritis had spread to my hands: my knuckles were swollen. The prospect of fixing a hairgrip in my bun daunted me. Pulling up my trousers meant excruciating pains in my thumbs and forefingers. My thumbs no longer bent: grating ginger or carrots was agony. The fear that I would be unable to clean the house, to dust, to rub fingerprints off the doors weighed on my spirits. The skin between my thumb and first finger resembled tissue paper and my knees were swelling painfully. The doctor I consulted told me, "Your muscles have begun to waste away. We know neither the cause nor the cure for this condition."

This verdict so disturbed me that I asked Gopal for treatment I had hitherto refused. He administered a traditional Indian remedy for osteo-arthritis. India's ancient medical science is called Ayurvedic medicine. Plant, animal and mineral material are ground down in the preparation of a range of tablets. In its insistence on a right balance between the humours of the body Ayurveda is closer to the approach of Hippocrates or to the doctors of Shakespearean England than to allopathic Western medicine. Gopal consulted his Indian "materia medica", now that he knew the GP's diagnosis, and prescribed a course of minuscule pills to be swallowed with butter morning and evening. I continued to take these conscientiously for two-month periods with intervals of several months between courses. Thanks to Ayurvedic therapy and daily yoga my health improved, the pain receded, my muscles never wasted away and I maintained a brisk pace, serving concurrently as executive member of fifteen organisations and teaching yoga with Gopal three times every week.

During December 1971 we were staying with friends in Neasden, North London. One night Gopal shook me awake to stop me crying so loudly in my sleep. As I woke from my dream it was still clear. I had been weeping because I could not stop someone dear to me from being swept skyward from me in a great black urankhatola, the heavenly airborne vehicle in which the gods of Hindu myth used to traverse the world. In my dream I had not seen the face of the dear one caught up in the urankhatola.

For the first time since settling in Britain, Shammy, Kiran and Risham would all be with us for Christmas. Excited by family reunion and the festive season they had invited their friends to a fancy dress party at our house. For the first and only time Shammy had donned an all black turban. In wild apparel, supposedly evoking the Dirty Thirties, guests spilled into the garden. The children suggested that we should go for a meal to escape their halla gulla (hullabaloo). When we returned from Southport at 11 p.m. the festivities were still in full swing. At midnight they all went to the middle of the road, holding each other's hands, singing and dancing. It was sheer joy for Gopal and me to see our children's merrymaking.

Next morning, preoccupied with celebrations past and yet to come, we did not immediately attend to the mail. Risham and I returned from shopping to be told by Gopal, "Darling, I have some sad news for you." My father had died in Delhi. I recalled the faceless dear one swept heavenward from me in my dream. I recalled my last parting from my father. Shammy tore off his black turban saying, "I've worn black only this once, and we receive news like this." I was distraught at losing my father when we were so far away. We could phone only through an operator, and the fact that I could not speak to my mother and brothers made the situation still worse.

I realised the full tragedy only when I met my sisters. Life had dealt our father many blows and his resentment built up as his eyesight failed. He disliked my mother participating in marriages and other family celebrations. He spoke roughly to her as if venting on her the disappointments of a lifetime. Unable to see, he spent his last days in hospital. With him were my brothers and sisters, who had come up from Bombay, and my mother, loyal but unloved. I was sorry for my mother who had cared for her husband for so many years, and this was what she got in the end. She was now at the mercy of my brothers and their wives. After India's partition my father had tried to establish businesses, but each had closed down after a big financial loss. My mother received nothing in cash or kind.

Although sorrowing in my bereavement, I still could not abandon *Roopvati*. We knew that the largest number of potential Punjabi readers gather in the gurdwaras for Sunday congregational worship. So we devoted our weekends to distribution through the Sikh temples of Yorkshire, London and the Midlands. We would leave Liverpool at eight in the morning and arrive in some gurdwara in Coventry, Leeds or Birmingham to find it still almost empty at ten o'clock.

Our visits to the gurdwara helped us to understand what we had assumed to be our own community. We had misunderstood them in more ways than one. Trying to be helpful one woman asked me why I was still selling the same book as I had been a year before. Why didn't I sell it at 10p instead of 20? Didn't I realise that there was plenty of work in factories? I was saddened to think that money was more important than the written word, whether in books or magazines. They did not want to read. Money was their only interest.

In the 1970s most of the men serving on gurdwara committees, including the presidents, were clean-shaven. To gain employment on their arrival in Britain they had dispensed with uncut beards, long hair and turbans. The ladies sitting in the gurdwaras were decked our in Punjabi salvar kamiz suits of glittering, synthetic fabrics. Their arms were well-covered by the sleeves of their kamizes and cardigans. I was dressed, as I had been for nearly thirty years, in a chiffon or silk sari, with the end drawn up over my head in the presence of the Guru Granth Sahib. I wore a brief, sleeveless sari blouse. As we drove from one Midland gurdwara Gopal told me that my dress had inadvertently caused offence. "People will stare at her bare arms," a gurdwara official had said. I wept in humiliation: were these people so narrow-minded or so hypocritical? They did not want to read, were interested only in making money and had got the barber to remove the visible symbols of their faith, and now they were criticising my dress. As a small concession to their sensitivities I decided that from now on I would don my salvar kamiz when we promoted *Roopvati* in the gurdwaras. I had no intention of corrupting their wives and daughters. But Gopal was emphatic: "You remain true to your own style: don't change because of these ignorant people. You are what you are and I would not like you to change for these hypocritical people who do not know what they are or what they want."

These "sardarnis" (Sikh women) were strangers to me in dress, dialect and outlook, but we were sisters in deeper ways. In the gurdwaras they opened their hearts to me. "Do you think we will have to leave this country?" "Do you think life here will become unbearable?" "We don't want to lose our children in this society." "I don't want my son to marry a gori" (white girl). "My daughter wants to choose a boy for herself, not the spouse we have selected from the village." They ignored the fact that they were now living in the Western world where values were less rigid and children chose their own partners.

After several years *Roopvati* was paying for itself financially and looked set to yield a profit. It had always paid for itself in the wealth of insights it gave us into our own British Punjabi community. It had also won a place in its readers' hearts. A gurdwara leader in Nottingham told me, "When *Roopvati* comes out all the family fight for it, but I always make sure I get hold of it first." The Comrades were less appreciative. These self-styled communists, members of the Indian Workers' Association, whose politics and factions controlled many gurdwara committees, dissuaded potential subscribers. "Don't read what Kailash Puri writes: she's a Tory, a member of the bourgeoisie." Nonetheless our readership continued to increase.

One Sunday morning we set out in chill fog for the gurdwara in Nottingham, leaving Risham alone in the house. We needed only ten minutes to promote *Roopvati*. Having been invited to join the congregation we had requested an opportunity to speak before the dhadd-players and ragis commenced their hymn singing programme. Their performance might last hours, and we had no wish to set out unnecessarily late on our return journey through the fog. However the management committee was unmoved by our preferences. We sat among the congregation as the dhaddis' fingers frenziedly struck their little hand-drums, the shape of egg timers: their voices filled the building. Soulfully their rough, peasant voices proclaimed the familiar words of the Gurus while the harmonium waxed and waned and small children ran about among the congregation. After saying our piece and selling a few copies of *Roopvati* we made a hurried getaway. In such poor visibility the drive was no easier than we had feared. As we pulled into our drive, relieved at being safely home, we wondered why the outside light was on. Risham came to the door, tears streaming down her cheeks. Shakily she told us she had been chatting to a friend on the phone when Stasha had slipped out of the open gate. There had been no sound, but Stasha never returned. Two minutes later he was lying unconscious by the roadside. We took Risham with us to see Stasha at the veterinary surgery where a friend had taken him. Stasha was very poorly and the vet explained that he would not last the night.

10
Writing and Public Speaking

From West Africa we had been able to visit our relatives annually. This was no longer feasible. We had known that our stay there was only temporary, but now we had a settled home of our own. Gopal, as the eldest son, felt acutely his responsibility for his mother. Indian parents look forward to the security of care in their sons' homes in their declining years. Gopal, Harbans and Surinder had all moved overseas to follow successful careers and Beyji, their mother, was becoming older and more frail. Contrary to Indian custom she was staying with her daughter. It used to be unheard of for parents to take any financial help from their daughters — indeed they would pay for any service rendered in their daughter's house. Anything else would reflect on their sons' shameful neglect. At least Beyji was not financially dependent upon Gian, as Gopal made sure his mother received money each month. A friend in Allahabad owed us money and, at our request, sent it in monthly instalments to Beyji in Calcutta where she was living with Gian, Nanak Singh and their five children.

Now that we were all established in Liverpool for the foreseeable future, Beyji must, we agreed, join us without delay. We wrote to Gian's daughter, Gudi, a doctor who worked for a clinic in New Delhi, asking her to get Beyji's passport ready, and assuring her that we would call Beyji as soon as we had obtained her visa. We sent a formal application to the Home Office and received an official letter asking why we wanted Gopal's mother to live with us in Britain when she had lived for so many years without us. The Home Office needed to know how many years we had been away from India. The Home Office needed evidence that she was Gopal's mother and that she was dependent upon us. The Home Office required us to forward our whole history, documented with a receipt for every payment made to Beyji. We had no such receipts. Gopal became increasingly upset as months slipped by and the interrogation continued. He appealed to our Member of Parliament, and another six months elapsed before the news arrived that permission had finally been granted.

The Saturday after receiving this glad news Gopal and I again visited Birmingham to promote *Roopvati* in the gurdwara. Before setting off homeward we telephoned Risham to say that our departure had been delayed. Her voice trembled as she told us that four strangers had arrived from Southall. We had not been expecting guests and Risham had no idea what to do with them. Over the phone we calmed Risham. "Just take some food from the fridge and freezer, show them where we store the flour for chapatis, and let them take charge of the kitchen. We'll be back as soon as we can."

Wondering who our guests might be, we set out on our homeward drive. We found Risham less anxious and the visitors happily looking after themselves. We were delighted to discover their identity: Giani Joginder Singh Sarl, his wife, son and a friend had been giving programmes of devotional music, kirtan as we call it, in gurdwaras in the Midlands, and had decided to visit us — a heart warming surprise. (At that time, Sikhs further south wrote Liverpool off as a dreary, vandalised city with few business prospects, a benighted mix of dock strikes, black ghettos, vice rackets and weather even gloomier than the British norm.)

To our joy we would have Sunday kirtan in our own home. I telephoned more than a dozen Sikh families, inviting them to join us for kirtan followed by langar, the traditional vegetarian hospitality. Late that Saturday night we busied ourselves in preparing vegetables, lentils, puris and khir, our favourite creamy rice pudding. Before we retired wearily to bed Gianiji sang a melodious shabad, verses from Guru Granth Sahib, and at Gopal's suggestion he sang kirtan for us at six in the morning in our family prayer room where the Guru Granth Sahib was always enthroned. For the sangat (congregation) later that morning we would carry the scriptures downstairs to our largest room.

After our dawn kirtan upstairs I was serving our guests their breakfast when the doorbell rang. Gopal came into the dining room, looking drawn, clutching a telegram. He said simply,

"Beyji died in her sleep" and handed me the telegram. That very week, the week that permission had been granted for her to join us, Beyji had passed away, weak and depressed by the long wait. She had not received our news. None of her sons had been with her. We had not been informed of her illness and our only solace was knowing that she had died in her sleep, peacefully, and without suffering.

If only she had lived long enough for proof to reach her of our continuing concern. Our hopes, so high after obtaining her visa, were shattered. In our grief Gianiji and his family comforted us. He sang shabads for the departed soul and shabads of consolation for us, the bereaved.

Meanwhile friends were arriving for the morning kirtan. Our devotional music reached its joyful conclusion in the hymn of gladness, the Anand, for which all stand, and the solemn words of the Sikh prayer, the Ardas. After the formal recitation Gianiji spoke of our recent bereavement. Everyone was stunned, eyes shone with tears, and our guests asked why we had made no reference to Beyji's death when inviting them to the kirtan.

We explained that we had then had no inkling of what was taking place in New Delhi. But of this we were sure, that some divine power had prompted Giani Joginder Singh Sarl to travel to Liverpool, where his services would be needed. What more appropriate homage to our dearest Beyji, whose days had been devoted in large part to reciting the words of scripture? To her we owed everything, for her unremitting struggle to educate her sons. Now with her blessing her grandchildren were prospering. As Beyji was dying in her sleep, could she sense that prayers were being uttered in her beloved son's house so far away? Our early morning hymns and the kirtan on hearing the devastating news sustained us in our sorrow as nothing else could. But Gopal did not forgive himself for failing to provide even a few months' comfort for his aged mother, who had sacrificed so much for his education. Words can aggravate a hurt, and silently I shared Gopal's guilt. If only I could have served, however briefly, the lady who gave birth to the loving person who became my husband. But it was too late.

Ever since it began I wrote regular features for the Punjabi monthly *Kaumi Ekta* (Communal Unity). I sent my articles by registered mail and later saw them in print. The editor never acknowledged my contributions or paid a single paisa.

However he came to Liverpool and asked me to write on "sej ulajhana" (sexual problems), the title of one of my books, which proved to be the first of a series of ten which I compiled on sexual matters. Readers of *Kaumi Ekta*, devout Sikhs no doubt, wrote demanding how he could publish such pornographic stuff. He published my articles for three months, then under pressure from the "holier than thou" he conducted a referendum. Overwhelmingly readers replied that they did not find my contributions vulgar, let alone pornographic. "From these essays we gain gyan — true knowledge." "Previously," one wrote, "shivshakti (creative force) has been despised as something dirty." Not one of the many letters I received was in bad taste. More than fifty per cent of the letters to *Kaumi Ekta*'s editor expressed appreciation for my column. Many letters blessed me, urging me to carry on producing such illuminating articles. "Kailash Puri has brought this subject into the drawing room, where we all share this great information."

Punjab Times, *Des Pardes* and *Sandesh Weekly*, three major Punjabi newspapers published in Britain, to which I also contributed frequently, subsequently conducted similar surveys. Such feedback helped me to write pertinently. Again not a single unpleasant letter reached me.

Meanwhile, speaking engagements brought more personal satisfaction than I would have obtained from factories, shops, hotels or offices. However inadequate our income might be, I could not exchange my precarious earnings for the secure monotony on offer. Many a time I wondered why I continued to accept invitations to speak.

Audiences asked the same questions with only minor variations. How fruitful could my attempts at answering be when some questions betrayed such ignorance and lack of imagination?

> "Do you have to walk five steps behind your husband? No?
>   I'm glad to hear your husband respects you." (How
>   condescending!)
> "Does your husband wear a turban in bed?"
> "Do you have curry for breakfast?"
> "What sort of food do you give to your grandchildren?"
> "What language do you speak to your grandchildren?" (None
>   of your business!)

And, in one form or another, "Why don't you go home?" It may be phrased more delicately, "You must miss your family. Surely you would like to retire among you own people?" or "Don't you find the British weather horribly cold and wet? Wouldn't you prefer to live in India?" With all these questions I tried to deal patiently and honestly. But why did I have continually to justify living in a country to which I had given thirty of the most productive years of my life? Not only that, but my husband and children made their own substantial contributions to the professions here. It seems that too many of the people who came to hear me speak had a fixed stereotype of Indian women. Whatever I said, and despite my appearance, they heard it coming from the lips of their mental image, a woman, impoverished and abused in a hot, dirty, dangerous land of inferior people. My audiences addressed to me the questions that they wanted this imaginary person to answer. Few comprehended that in a land where many millions toiled on the land, lived in simple village homes and were unable to read, millions also studied at universities, worked in city offices and inhabited teeming twentieth-century cities. Indians were scientists, professors, architects, philosophers, cutting edge researchers, they were doctors, accountants, dentists and in the highest echelons of the Civil Service.

One day I was to address an Inner Wheel meeting in a hotel. I apologised for arriving a few minutes late. Mrs Smith, a spindly, sharp-nosed, elderly lady asked if I had come on foot. "No, I don't walk. It isn't one of my hobbies" was my response.

"Oh, how did you get to the hotel then?"
"My car is just outside the hotel."
"Do you drive?"

I looked away, remarking, "I have been driving for the last twenty-five years."
There was a vase of flowers on the table. "What lovely flowers," I said appreciatively.

"Do you have a garden?" Mrs Smith enquired again.
"Yes, we do."
"You must be growing vegetables?"
"No, we have flower beds."
"Oh, so you like flowers then?"

I did not tell her that my husband was a scientist, that he was teaching English people, or that in India we had employed two full-time gardeners. Mrs Smith was still bubbling over with pent-up questions that she had to ask me.

As overseas chairman of Abbeyfield I had been inviting the elderly residents turn by turn to spend an afternoon in our house and garden. I decided to ask Mrs Smith if she could join us. I knew she would love to see inside an Indian's home. The day was windy and a big red rose had fallen in the middle of our doorstep. I saw Mrs Smith coming down the path, her grey hair plaited and coiled round in earphone style. Through her round-rimmed glasses she was peering at the rose. I opened the door to welcome her inside. "Oh, is that one of your customs? A red flower on the doorstep? How lovely! Do you want me to step over it or walk round it?" "Just come inside," I told her. I must not show amusement or irritation. She was a widow, she had informed me, with a daughter who would, she hoped and prayed, never get married and leave her on her own. She probably met few people, and she was good at knitting squares for charity. I subsequently heard that her daughter had left her to live alone.

One evening I had been invited to address police cadets who were passing out: the theme was Multicultural Britain. With only minutes to spare I took a wrong turning. Stopping my car I lowered the window to ask an elderly lady for directions to the policy academy. Her reply was not helpful: "I don't want to talk to you. What business have you to be here? I never talk to immigrants." Her views saddened me. My family and I were serving the country well and were proud to be doing so. I managed to keep my calm and performed well at the passing out ceremony.

With *Roopvati* and speaking engagements taking every available minute I could not make enough time for the books I felt clamouring inside me to be written. Well-meaning friends assumed that I was keen to earn more money. I was. "Why don't you become our partner in running a big hotel and restaurant?" they asked. "Wouldn't you like to run a smart Indian boutique in Southport?" All I had to do was stand there and I would take home £500 a week. There were plenty of people ready to capitalise on my proven capacity for hard work, and I would no doubt earn a lot more than at present. But I had no intention of selling my soul. £5 for an occasional lecture meant more to me that £50 at the cost of my self-respect. Behind though we were with our mortgage repayments I could not make myself work for money alone, and it was with mixed feelings that I wound up publication of *Roopvati*.

In 1971, East Pakistan had become the separate country of Bangladesh. The plight of thousands of Bengali refugees challenged many in Britain to send aid. I was secretary of the local Inner Wheel Club, the female counterpart of Rotary International. We obtained sewing machines, three hundred cotton reels and fifteen hundred yards of material and made up white baby bags, each containing half a dozen shirts for a small child. We sent these and blankets to Bangladesh free of charge, thanks to the generosity of the captain of the ship.

Sometimes a speaker would come to arouse the good ladies of the Inner Wheel Club to further feats of charity. One such speaker had visited India many times and went around schools and organisations promoting the work of a charity in South India which particularly assisted homeless boys, giving them the skills to earn a decent living. While setting up his projector and screen the speaker caught sight of my sari. "Are you Indian?" he asked. "I am sure you will understand. My wife and I have visited India eight times and always enjoy it very much. Of course I've visited wealthy homes as the guest of the Rotary Club members, but tonight I am talking about the poorest of the poor." He showed his slides, commenting all the while. When he showed us the picture of a snake, bulging with a rat which it had just swallowed and remarked how grateful the local people would be for this extra protein I gazed in disbelief. Did he believe that South Indians, to whom even eggs are often taboo, would even dream of eating a snake? Or was he cracking a distasteful joke?

"I have visited a hundred schools," he informed us. "I tell the boys and girls, 'You have beds, mattresses, central heating, but all that these boys have is a little jute mat. They are fortunate to wake up alive as there are cobras and scorpions all around where they sleep. You have lovely clothes, but these children, the same age as you, are all in tatters. They are lucky to have a loincloth. When you get up in the morning you have a bowl of your favourite cereal and some bread and butter to eat, but these people have to collect fuel first. By midday they may have collected enough twigs to cook themselves a handful of rice.'" He was happily developing his favourite subject while I was boiling inside.

At question time I spoke up.

I am from India, and a pucka Indian. Of course it is not news to us that thousands of people there live in poverty, but I feel I must make a few points to clear up any misconceptions. We had servants. They were not well off but they always slept on beds. I have yet to hear of people who sleep among cobras and scorpions. No-one would survive under such circumstances. I am surprised at your talk and the material you have used. I am glad that the poor are receiving assistance to lead lives of dignity, but if speakers use this style when addressing schools they will do untold damage. Their young audiences will grow up looking down on Indians. We need Asian children to feel self-respect and all to learn respect for others. In a country as racist as Britain such patronising talks will not enhance mutual understanding. Poverty can be seen in any city of the world.

I wrote a letter to the Archbishop of Canterbury complaining about one such preacher. Dr Ramsay answered me politely in a letter dated 13th February 1979:

Thank you for your letter. As one who has travelled in India and who has a doctor daughter in Pakistan, I can appreciate better than some the richness of the ancient civilization of India.

I know also the immensely valuable work that many of our missionaries have done and are doing in India and elsewhere, but I realise that some have been and are insensitive to the feelings of the people of that great country. We must do all that we can to warn them of any such insensitivity.

It was during my 1972 visit to New Delhi that I again met Mrs Indira Gandhi, this time by official arrangement. We conversed for twenty minutes and I presented her with copies of my books. She spoke of the responsibility of expatriate Indians to commit themselves to being good citizens of their adopted country, while enriching its corporate life by sharing their cultural wealth. As she talked her eyes darted about. Her thoughts seemed to be in several places at once. Though she was slight in build and of only medium height some uncommon power emanated from her.

Kiran graduated in Sociology from Liverpool Polytechnic and returned to Slough as Assistant Community Relations Officer. To our delight in August 1973 she married one of her brother's friends. After working briefly as Research Officer for the Runnymede Trust she settled in her childhood home, Ghana. Here they worked at the university and lived in Achimota. Ghana had changed tragically since our departure. Corn, yam and other staples were scarce; Ghanaians starved, and for weeks electricity was cut off. The shortage of water was another big problem. Many foods were scarce or not available. We sent food parcels through our friends who were visiting Ghana at the time.

Upstairs at Bucklands I continued writing on sexual matters. As my interest grew I read more and more, borrowing books from the library. I cannot read Sanskrit, but I read Vatsyayana's Kama Sutra in Richard Burton's translation. To the sage Vatsyayana my debt is immeasurably great and a pioneer, closer to me by two millennia, also inspired my efforts to help alleviate the sexual ills troubling so many of my readers. I read and reread the writings of Dr Marie Stopes. No other Cambridge fossil botanist can have so shaken contemporary society. Fifty years on, my post bag was remarkably similar to Marie Stopes's, and as I read about her campaign to educate women in ways of limiting their pregnancies, and of the hostile response from some respectable quarters, I recalled my own efforts via *Subhagvati*. What Marie Stopes was doing in the 1920s I was doing in the 1960s and 1970s, and I was persecuted much as she was. But she won in the end. Another similarity with Marie Stopes was the fact that her husband, like mine, was a palaeobotanist.

Once Risham's school friends were discussing pornography: "Your mother would never read anything like that, would she?" they asked, doubtless imagining me as a prudish, retiring Asian lady. Risham enlightened them. "There's hardly a book on sex that my mother does not have in her library. My mum researches all the world's books on sex and love-making."

As I wrote, I forged a clean Punjabi vocabulary of sexual terms, drawing on Sanskrit roots, the words of Vatsyayana. I avoided the bawdy words of Punjab's oaths and jests, bringing my subject, as one reader had remarked, "into the drawing room". To quote: "We have never had such an experience to read, learn and adopt such a healthy sexual relationship as it has always been termed as a dirty side of life. For heaven's sake continue Kailash Puri's enlightenment for the young and old equally."

One day I was writing in my bedroom with *Playboy*, *Forum* and other explicit publications scattered on the floor around me. Through the window I saw Shammy driving through the front gates. I scooped up my periodicals, piled them by the fireplace and covered them with a newspaper. Shammy came upstairs to see me, and I left the room to make him some coffee. I returned to catch him poring over my unsuccessfully hidden reading matter. My daughters too would slip in to borrow books surreptitiously, then furtively slip them back to their places on the shelf. We never discussed my subject matter, but they knew it well. But with Gopalji I would discuss it and he gave me sound advice. He was my teacher and guru throughout our married life.

Ever since our arrival in England in early 1967, Gopal and I had been struggling. Often the mortgage repayments were in arrears. I needed money, but I also needed to be challenged by my work, to feel that I was making a contribution worthy of my talents. When our overdraft was too heavy, however, depression extinguished all incentive to look for creative stimulus. It was during this period that the telephone rang: a gentleman from Marks and Spencer had read Kailash Puri's *Highlights of Indian Cookery* and wished to speak to her. He explained that his company had decided to offer a range of Indian dishes and had been advertising unsuccessfully in catering journals for an Indian cookery consultant. Would I be free to meet him for further discussion? Perhaps, he suggested, I could recommend an Indian restaurant where we might meet. "But I never go to Indian restaurants," I answered without thinking. The gentleman from Marks and Spencer sounded ever so slightly taken aback.

We arranged to meet at the Adelphi Hotel and I was taken on as consultant from 1973 to 1975. We visited London's best Indian restaurants, tandoori specialists in Mayfair and Euston, and investigated what the Taj Mahals, Rajdoots and Koh-i-noors of the metropolis had on offer for their predominantly non-Indian clientele. In fact few Indian restaurants are truly Indian, being run in most instances by Sylheti Muslims from North Eastern Bangladesh, who have both moulded and catered to a British notion of India's cuisine. St Michael favoured introducing ready-cooked and frozen chicken korma, lamb rogan josh, mixed vegetable curry and, the hottest of the series, pork vindaloo. Four of us were involved in creating this new line and we frequently laughed over my low opinion of Merseyside's Indian restaurants.

Spices are imported whole to factories in London for grinding and mixing. We went to half a dozen spice warehouses. Some did not meet Marks and Spencer's hygiene requirements. Some did not have spices of a sufficiently high quality. Finally agreement was reached with a spice dealer in the East End. His unmixed coriander, turmeric, cumin and chilli were satisfactory, but I insisted that the garam masala should be mixed to my own specification from ground clove, cardamom, cumin, black pepper and cinnamon, and that it should not be the mix of turmeric powder, cloves and ground coriander that was available to Indians in grocers' shops.

My years of culinary experience and accumulated knowledge were being recognised — and by a distinguished company, noted for its excellence. My flagging spirits responded to the challenge of producing a set of dishes to their satisfaction. I am a workaholic and was happy to be associated with a team of workers all doing their best. My good fortune buoyed me up.

Each of the prospective dishes was prepared for an expert review panel. Its appearance, flavour, texture, nutritional value were minutely analysed. After many months of diligent effort our Indian range was introduced to stores suggested by advance market research. Indian housewives will no doubt continue to prepare their own infinitely varied provincial dishes with their own individual blend of spices. But Marks and Spencer may have succeeded in adding variety to a few Western dinner-tables. Perhaps Indian bachelors appreciated St Michael's gesture to the Orient. Nowadays ready Indian meals are available in almost every supermarket. But Marks and Spencer was the pioneer!

One day another telephone call came as a result of my cookery publications. Angrily, my caller demanded whether the food prepared in an Indian restaurant was supposed to make the customer ill. He intended reporting me to the weights and measures department. Marks and Spencer were better satisfied and in December 1974 *St Michael News* featured the Indian Frozen Food Range under the headline, "The Mystery of the East".

In the spring of 1975 I realised a wish I had nursed throughout my travels, for the thirty years since Gopal had first described the fairyland beauties of Kashmir and given me the plot of "Situ di Nilam". Thanks to the generosity of the Dhingras, who paid our fares, Risham and I had the holiday of a lifetime overlooking Srinagar's Dal Lake. I marvelled at the clear blue skies, the snow on which we could go sledging, without even needing cardigans.

133

I visualised Gopal there as a young man, hunting for fossils, romance in his soul, and I wrote a poem wishing he was with me now. Our hotel was high about the lake. It was mid-April and the birds were singing.

Whenever we visited India from Britain I was profoundly moved by the wretched condition of the poor, huddled asleep under dirty coverings along the station platforms. I was outraged by the arrogant rudeness of officials to their subordinates in the offices we had to visit. It annoyed me to see householders delaying rightful payments. The gardener might have to return repeatedly to beg for his meagre monthly wage. A workman is fobbed off with "I have no change. Come back later." For Indians life in the West opens their eyes to the injustices of Indian society, the compound suffering of the powerless. I admire the caring concern of welfare workers from Britain and elsewhere. The Welfare State looks after every individual "from the cradle to the grave".

In Britain I noticed that the indigenous British may not be in the habit of inviting Indian neighbours round for tea, but they love to give in charity. In 1974 the Liverpool Community Relations Commission housed sixty Ugandan Asian refugee families who had been temporarily billeted in wartime army quarters. A Gujarati couple, thin and sickly in appearance, were housed with their nine children in Blundell Sands, before they shifted south to join their community in Leicester. On Christmas day local Liverpool people anonymously left presents for them on their doorstep. Some were curious to see inside an Asian home. Eugene, one of our neighbours, loved visiting them but his wife stopped him, demanding, "Why do you go to the Asians' house? We don't eat curry. We have nothing in common with them." Eugene was saddened by his wife's remarks. He just wanted to help an Indian family who had been uprooted from their home. He wanted to help them do their shopping and get their children to school. Regardless of his wife, Eugene carried on helping the family.

Whatever the attitude of Britain's householders, during the 1970s her politicians increasingly realised the importance of wooing Asian voters. In 1975 I was one of fifty people invited to the House of Commons for drinks. At a cocktail party a few weeks later I asked Mrs Thatcher's secretary if I could be allowed to interview her as the recently elected leader of the opposition and so Britain's next Prime Minister if the Conservatives won the next election. A few days later a cordial letter arrived to inform me that Mrs Thatcher had consented to be interviewed.

My conversation with the Conservative leader appeared in *The Spokeswoman Weekly*, a Sikh English language paper published from Chandigarh, and in the *Liverpool Weekly*. In Punjabi translation it was printed in *Panj Pani* and *Des Pardes*. Mrs Thatcher answered my questions on women's family responsibilities, on racial discrimination, single-sex schools and on a Community Relations Commission report suggesting that Asian voters sympathised with Labour. I questioned her on the entry to Britain of UK passport holders currently in Africa and asked her what career she would have followed had she not been a politician. As she dealt with each question I sensed the same quiet authority that had impressed me in my brief encounters with Indira Gandhi. The two leaders had much in common, and neither did much for the women of their respective countries. Intolerably, Mrs Gandhi turned her back on "bride burning".

Later that year I sent Mrs Thatcher a copy of my *Mysteries of Indian Cuisine Explained*. In acknowledgement her private secretary wrote that she hoped "that during the Christmas Recess when she might get one or two days away from all the pressures she will have the chance to try out a recipe." I like to imagine the kitchen of No 10 was occasionally scented with garam masala and turmeric powder.

Marks and Spencer passed my name on to Leiths School of Food and Wine where I was invited to give demonstrations of Indian cookery from 1977 to 1980. Again I rose to the challenge, this time the challenge of sixty student caterers watching my every move. I was delighted to be demonstrating Indian cookery to young people with their lives ahead of them.

In 1977 I devoted several weeks to yoga in ashrams in Delhi and Hardwar. I was fortunate enough to go back the following year. Daubed prominently in public places I read:

> Agla bacha aje nahin,
> Tin de bad kade nahin.
> Your next child — not today;
> After three — never.
> Pahila jaldi nahin;
> Duja hali nahin;

Tija kade nahin.
Don't have the first one quickly;
Don't have the second one now;
Don't have the third one ever.

In 1982 I demonstrated Indian cookery in a West Midlands hospital. I hope that my efforts resulted in menus a little more tempting for the many Hindu, Sikh and Muslim patients. The particular challenge was improvising with the ingredients and utensils available in a hospital kitchen. At about the same time I was appointed nutritional adviser for *Spectrum*, the journal of the British Wheel of Yoga. 1981 *Cosmopolitan* included a feature entitled "Cool down with Curry". Alongside my recipes for mushroom bhaji, seekh kebab, tandoori chicken, rogan josh, pilau rice and carrot halwa is a photograph of Risham surrounded by enticing dishes. To my considerable surprise, I had numerous telephone calls from many quarters asking about her.

1981 was UNESCO's International Year for the Disabled. For the North West Women's Association I ran classes in relaxation for victims of multiple sclerosis. The students, of all ages, appreciated the opportunity to practise yogic breathing technique and postures. In class they felt relaxed and in less pain.

1981 was also the year our first grandchild was born; Kiran came back to London for the delivery of Shivan in May, then flew out to Ghana again. Shivan was God's gift to us and we were over the moon, but I worried about shortages, infection, and all possible mishaps. Sending regular food parcels hardly alleviated my fears as a grandmother.

11

"A shoulder to cry on"

"Modhe da asra, a shoulder to cry on." That's what is said about my work as an agony aunt, supporting many, many people who felt that they had no-one else to turn to. Often it was hard for them to make a phone call undetected, and they would slip out to a telephone booth to tell me their life's tragedy. Halfway through a heartrending story we would be cut off. A letter with more of the story might arrive weeks later.

To me the saddest thing about Western society is the nuclear family. You cut yourselves off from your parents and grandparents. You have no-one to share your troubles, no-one's shoulder to cry on. For teenagers too this is very sad. There can be a strong link of understanding between grandparents and grandchildren, but they allow themselves no opportunities to discover this.

Reading my name in the Punjabi press people would contact me from India, Canada, California and from Germany and other European countries. Sometimes their parents had sought advice from me nearly forty years before in India. Human problems bear a striking similarity across the continents and the decades and certain patterns emerge: domestic violence, alcoholism, adultery and gambling and husbands neglecting their wives and children to spend money on themselves.

I cannot forget one phone call from an Indian bride in California. An Indian girl still knows that she will marry her husband's family, not only her husband, and may well spend the first years of her married life in the joint household. In this case her husband's elder brother was head of the house and expected more than sisterly love from her. Frustrated by her rejection of his advances he claimed that her recently conceived child was his, and that he would disclose his secret to his brother if she did not agree to please him. She was distraught, too terrified to confide in her husband. If she did so his elder brother threatened to throw her out. He would ensure her rejection by her own family by spreading shameful lies about her. She knew my name and telephoned, weeping hysterically. What could she do but end her life? Day after day she called me and I encouraged her in her loyalty to her husband and in her silent determination to resist her brother-in-law's advances. This was no easy case, but I advised her almost every day and eventually she and her husband moved out to set up their own business.

Often women are women's worst enemies. A young wife rang and told me that her Asian workmates made her life hell with their taunts and prying. "What is wrong with you? Why haven't you got a child? Is something the matter with your husband?" In our folk songs, especially those sung in the bride's home during the run up to the wedding day, the stereotyped mother-in-law is the bane of the young wife's new life:

> The hen that crows is worth having
> But I don't want to go to my mother-in-law's house
> Because she goes on grumbling.

> The hen that lays eggs is worth having
> But I don't want to go to my mother-in-law's house
> Because she keeps taunting me

Here is one real-life daughter-in-law's plight: "My mother-in-law purposely does not buy the washing machine, although we can afford it, but she likes me to do all the household chores, even though she stays at home and I work in a shop. Twice a week I now wash the family clothes, which requires a lot of energy and hard work. It makes me very angry because my husband, who is educated, doesn't support me and thinks his mother knows best. I can't have any more of it and go on breaking my back. I don't mind cooking and washing but cannot do the family washing twice a week. You think I should go on like this to keep peace in the family?"

I dealt with many similar cases, but (despite what I have said about nuclear families) the greatest problem in such cases is the joint family system which means that young women cannot access help and no-one can write to them.

However much their husbands drink and beat them up, Asian

women here, especially those brought up in the East, continue to suffer behind closed doors, rather than to leave and claim their legal rights. One day Mrs X telephoned me. She was the mother of a small child, and lived with her husband, his elder brother and sister-in-law and his parents above the shop which they ran jointly. She was grief-stricken because her husband had told her to leave; he wanted nothing more to do with her. She had come to Britain in order to marry, and had only one relative, an uncle, over here. She refused to leave and her husband disappeared. He had in fact told his mother and elder sister-in-law his where-abouts, but they accused her of driving him away, they didn't know where. Mrs X phoned me again, begging me to intervene, but I pointed out that the family would then behave more cruelly, accusing her of spreading their bad name. After some days the husband returned, but would have no more to do with her, and she was debarred from serving in the shop. When she last rang me I advised her to call her uncle, and ask him to meet all the family together, so that he could ask her husband what fault he now found in her. If the worst came to the worst she should leave the house, but only after getting her legal share. Two years later she called me with the news that she had remarried and was enjoying life with her second husband.

Well-qualified girls wrote to me, frustrated because their parents expected silent acquiescence to their marriage plans. They had let them study and follow careers — to enhance their marriageability. The girls' awareness had been developed, but when the time came for them to marry they must keep quiet. Parents might insist on choosing their job as well.

"They wish to achieve the highest honour by learning, but try to convince me that my fate must remain in their hands. I do not have the right to choose a job or husband of my liking. I don't think I would be able to honour their feelings but at the same time I do not wish to hurt their feelings." So wrote one intelligent, well-educated girl who did not want to yield to her parents' choice of husband. She left home and married an English husband of her own choosing.

The dowry system, and all the problems so intricately bound up with it, create considerable distress. Dowry cropped up repeatedly in the letters I received, like this one from a young Asian wife living in Wembley: "I did not have the courage to write to you before but now I have to ask your advice. My parents gave a lot of dowry in my marriage to please my parents in law and my husband but as soon as I came to England with them they began ill treating me. No-one talks to me, including my husband, and I sit alone in my room after coming back from work. My mother-in-law takes my entire weekly wage and gives me only travelling expenses and nothing for tea or lunch. My husband is not at all bothered about me. If I try to speak to him he walks out of the room. The family all sit together, laugh, joke and enjoy themselves but they never ask me to join them. If I try to help my mother-in-law in the kitchen she shouts at me and tells me to go to my room. I am not allowed to go out on my own or meet my friends. I would like to go back to my parents but don't know how to manage it. Please help, otherwise one of these days I'll kill myself. I have nothing to live for."

Such a letter takes courage. Having taken the first step I felt she was in a better position to take some action to improve her life. I advised her to get in touch with the social worker in her area or a welfare officer and explain the situation. If, after that, she decided to leave the family but stay in Britain, she should contact the police to prevent harrassment from her husband and in-laws. She was luckier than some. She had a job and friends. She could support herself without cutting herself off from other people. It is a grave step to break away from one's husband's family and one which can never be taken without much thought. To manage on your own in a strange country is not at all easy. In such cases a woman has to be strong, educated and confident of her ability to live one her own.

In Gujarati Hindu communities in Britain marriage without a dowry was the exception rather than the rule. In terms of hard cash, even by 1980, £500, £1000 even £5000 was not an unusual amount to change hands. One of the reasons a girl was allowed to go out to work was often so that she could contribute to her dowry. In poorer families her earnings might make up the greater part of the dowry. And again the Patels (as well as Punjabis) can be considered responsible for the inflationary dowry trends in Britain. Among their community dowries are exorbitant; each father trying to outdo the other in a public display of wealth. Such showing off cannot be dismissed as simply materialism. There was much insecurity among Asians in Britain, particularly among those who came as refugees from East Africa. Since dowry is a reflection of status, they turned to money to soothe bruised egos.

Amongst younger Asians in Britain, men and women, there was already an increase in feeling against the dowry system. "Why should parents consider it a disadvantage to have borne a daughter?" one young man asked me. "I will not ask for a dowry and my parents are totally opposed to the system as well." Parents, still clinging to their Indian traditions, were not always so supportive. One young Asian girl told me that she would refuse a boy who asked for a dowry but felt her parents would give the gifts. "My parents have already collected jewellery and money for when I get married." But what about those parents who cannot afford expensive clothing, jewellery and furniture plus cash? I think that education is the first requirement. Girls must think about themselves and their marriages.

The new-found wealth of families who had emigrated to Britain, America or in the past, East Africa, brought about a strange phenomenon, that of buying sons-in-law. Parents of daughters would return to India to find a suitable husband, and hope to attract families in higher society by means of their riches. They could be seen at airports, literally shaking the bags of money as if to draw good husbands by the jingling of their gold and by entertaining lavishly in expensive hotels.

I can generalise from a distance and say that certain problems fall into certain categories. But when I was helping a particular family I never generalised. Each situation is unique. Some parents would never countenance their child marrying an English person. Some will encourage their daughter to find an English partner, knowing that no dowry will be expected, and thinking that English men are more easy-going. In human behaviour every rule has its exceptions. I was not surprised when an alcoholic's wife admitted that she told her daughter to "marry a good gora (Englishman)" as he would not beat her and stay in bed after drinking.

I would point out to parents, distressed by their son's intention to marry an English girl, that they too can make affectionate daughters-in-law. My advice to the boy who left home to be with his English girlfriend was, "Speak to your parents. Tell your girl-friend that being part of a joint family isn't as bad as outsiders imagine." Some girls become proud of the family. Others grab the jewellery and expensive clothing but keep away from their Indian in-laws.

This Indian parent spoke for a growing number:

My son has decided to live with an English girl without getting married which is a great embarrassment for us. As you know it is not our custom even to go around together before marriage. First of all we do not want him to marry someone other than an Indian, because the British are not as much family minded and those girls are far too permissive. It feels as though we are going to lose our son. Since he disclosed this I haven't been sleeping well and do not wish to go out or meet anyone. Is there a way to convince my son about the wrong thing he is doing to himself and the family? If he married her, this will be the end of our culture, traditions and celebration of Divali, Gurpurab, Raksha Bandhan and Vaisakhi. Those people do not like us for what we are. We love our family and they like to keep away from the family.

An English mother wrote:

Do you believe in cross breeding? My son is married to one of your kind and that is how I got your address to let you know that your people must stop marrying British men and women. If your people wish to live here, better leave us alone and carry on your arranged marriages.

I must let you know that I am not looking forward to holding a mix-blood child.

I wrote back:

I do not know what you mean by cross breeding. Would you use the same expression for a Britisher married to an American, German or New Zealander? . . . If you have ever been in love yourself you should know what it is like . . . Does love see the colour or creed? As regards arranged marriages — if left to Asian parents they will definitely prefer this.

If I risk any generalisation from my experience as agony aunt in the 1960s, '70s and '80s, it is that an English wife tended to clash with her Indian husband whereas an Indian wife was more likely to compromise, less likely to explode. Marriages between Indian girls and English boys were less turbulent as a rule that those between English girls and Indian boys. Rabindranath Tagore said: "Woman is not a competitor of man but she is his complement." When an English girl marries an Indian they often clash. As we say in Punjabi, "Do bhande tarkrande ne" (two pans are bound to clash together.) English girls do not like the extended family system. In fact they run away from the family and just keep to their husband.

Another general observation is this. Feminism has harmed marriage more than any other single pressure. For woman life without a man is abnormal and every wife should show her husband how uniquely important he is to her. This does not mean that the wife is without freedom. Nor does she lack the complex challenge of creating a harmonious home for her husband and children, and of bringing up children who will in their turn know how to behave with their spouse and in-laws.

To Westerners India's arranged marriages are sometimes synonymous with marriages of convenience or the forced marriage of two strangers against their wills. In our experience love grows after marriage. Surely this is no worse than marriage in which love evaporates after romantic courtship? Our philosopher president Radhakrishnan said: "We do not marry the woman we love but we love the woman we marry" and elsewhere, "If love without marriage is illegal, marriage without love is immoral." As Hindus and Sikhs constantly recall, husband and wife should be "ek jot doi murti — one flame in two bodies". That is the Gurus' teaching to bear in mind after marriage, no matter how many differences you have.

The Rig Veda, a religious composition, so ancient that no-one can know to which century of the first millennium before Christ to attribute it, says that the bride's father selected for her a husband whom she mentally admired. This was too seldom the case during my years as agony aunt.

Indian fiancés would arrive in British cities from rural villages to marry girls with different values. The girl's religion, caste and area of origin accorded with his, but she had grown up part of British society. At school she had been encouraged to voice her point of view in discussions. She had been taught to question the need for arranged marriage and for marriage itself. Her white contemporaries would go out freely with the boys of their choice. She spoke in the local English idiom and she knew the ropes. She was going out to work and running the home. Her husband was uncertain, insecure, confused by the rapid patter of native English, and he had not found work. He would worry because she was more competent and assured. To compensate he might become aggressive and start beating her up. It would be an unforgiveable insult to his pride if she complained to the police. Between 1978 and 1979 I received numerous, often lengthy letters from male fiancés, and an equal number from brides who had been victims of domestic violence. In India it is widely assumed that in Britain girls sleep around. When village men come over to marry an Indian girl who has been brought up in Britain they all too easily suspect her of loose living. In moments of disagreement the husband taunts his wife with her permissive past, despite having no evidence to support his accusations.

Here from my postbag is one such case:

Respected Auntyji
I have been married two years and we have a year old daughter. My husband is an MA. I started working in a factory when I was fifteen. He came from our village for marriage. On the very first night after our wedding he asked me if I have had boy friends like English girls. Foolishly and honestly I told him that I used to be very fond of an Indian bloke who worked in the same factory but am happy to be married to him. Since then he has been very suspicious of me and accuses me for no apparent reason. So much so he has started calling me a prostitute and says that he is going to say in the presence of his elder sister and her husband that I go out with English men, Jamaicans and Pakis just like a prostitute. I can tell you honestly Auntyji I have never in my life gone out with any man. Why is this man torturing me so much? He is threatening to take away my baby to India because he says, "I don't want my daughter to become a prostitute under your filthy influence."

Too many Asian men feel they can have a good time with white girlfriends, then ditch them to marry an Asian wife. On a television phone-in during the 1980s an English woman called me. She was two months pregnant and her Indian boyfriend's father had arranged a marriage for him in Bombay. Her boyfriend had told his parents about her and offered her £1000 for an abortion. He threatened to tell her father that the baby was not his. After all she had been seen with other boyfriends. He didn't want a confrontation with his own father and was prepared to go through with the marriage in Bombay.

After marriage husbands, Sikh, Hindu and Muslim, increasingly spent time with white mistresses, or even Asian girlfriends. For wives there was less latitude even if they were so inclined. Women used to contact me in acute distress, no less so when their husband had told them of the affair himself. In some cases the husband had no intention of giving up his girlfriend when he accepted an arranged marriage. For a bride fresh from the Indian sub-continent, ignorant of her legal rights, ignorant perhaps of English as well, with few if any relatives in Britain, the discovery was devastating. One came to Britain to get married but her husband spent all his time with his white girlfriend. Her only relative in Britain, an aunt, was pressurising her to file for a divorce and to marry another man whom my client disliked. It turned out that the aunt had promised a friend that she would fix up a marriage for her son.

Some Asian husbands would go out drinking night after night. Whether their wives wanted sex or not they demanded to be satisfied every night. So many desperate wives phoned me to ask how they could put an end to this vicious cycle of drinking and sex. Very often the best advice I could give was, "Communicate with your husband. Don't speak angrily to him, but stop being passive. Make sure he knows how you feel. Tell him that if he does not change you will consider leaving him."

When husbands complained to me of their wives' frigidity I would say, "Treat your wife with patience and gentleness. A kind and understanding man will not ask his wife to do anything distateful. If they explore their own bodies lovingly their enjoyment will grow. You must realise that your love life can never improve if only one party is enjoying it."

Along with the cries for help came tokens of gratitude, a gift on the birth of a son or a letter of appreciation:

I have never been interested in sex but I do love my husband. Somehow I have never liked his touch on my body and the penetration has always been so very painful. After discussing this problem with you on the phone and having read your book on your recommendation my sexual life has changed tremendously. If I was told by anyone about such a terrific change I would never have believed. My husband has always been loving but the attention, love and affection I get now are fantastic. I want to thank you, thank you a million times for enriching my life.

145

One woman wrote that she had not seen me but kept my photograph in her bedroom and bowed before it each morning, because "you have helped me throughout my marriage crisis and I faced all the problems with confidence. Now I have everything. We are very happy. Thanks ever so much. I owe you a lot of gratitude."

But another wrote:

> You have been God to many people, but if you don't solve my problem I'll say you're useless. Though I suspected it long ago my husband has become a great philanderer. I'm heartbroken. He tells me the stories now. I cry all night.

I wrote back: "I am not God, no-one is God. My humble service is to help. Tell me more detail and I'll give advice." For a year no reply came, then the phone rang. A voice asked if I remembered her. I never let people feel forgotten. "Yes, yes I do, but refresh my memory." She shared her grief with me; she had no-one else in whom to confide. Her husband's girlfriends had begun coming to the house. All I could give her was the emotional relief of having found a sympathetic listener.

One day a woman rang me from Leicester: "Do you do abortions?"

"No."
"Do you deliver babies?"
"No. I don't do such jobs."

She had called a niece over to Britain for marriage only to discover on her arrival that the girl was in an advanced state of pregnancy. Her aunt wished to keep this secret in order to avoid prejudicing her chances of matrimony. I advised her to ensure that the baby was delivered in hospital and immediately put up for adoption. I could think of no other option.

A girl rang me and asked, "Respected sister, do you perform jadu?" Jadu means magic.

"No, I don't. What is your problem?"
"A man keeps following me; he's a distant cousin. People say he's casting the evil eye on me."

146

I questioned her further, fairly sure that at some time she had encouraged his advances.

I never accept what I am told purely at face value. Family crises involved more than one person, each with his or her feelings, weaknesses and a point of view. But I rarely heard from more than one party. While questioning I would piece together the others' points of view and the essential details initially withheld by my caller. By reading between the lines I could make out more or less who was at fault. For example a girl rang me weeping from Oxford police station: "My husband has driven me out of the house, Aunty. What shall I do?" Gradually I elicited the cause. He had found her sleeping with another man.

A young wife, married only the previous year, was upset because she had not conceived. She was contacting me on the recommendation of a friend who had conceived a son after consulting me. From her over-anxiety I guessed the reason: "May I ask you one question? Tell me, did you have an abortion before marriage?"

"Yes, are you a jyotisht (astrologer)?"

I asssured her that I relied not on the stars but on my own common sense.

Sometimes my patient probing met with only denials, but my suspicions remained. A Pakistani husband complained that his wife and child would have nothing to do with him; they would not even prepare his meals. "She is enjoying her life by neglecting me entirely." I suggested, "You must have done something to prejudice her so much." He never called back and I remain unconvinced that he was a blameless victim.

Time is not always on my side to permit my proffering constructive advice. One caller telephoned from a public call box two hours before his lavan (Sikh marriage rite) to say, "Can you help me?"

"Help? What sort of help do you want?" I asked.
"I am getting married."
"When?"
"I am on my way to the gurdwara for the marriage now."
"What sort of help are you looking for?" I persisted.
"I'm impotent, what shall I do?"

"God, how foolish you are. If that is the case, and you knew my
telephone number, why did you not seek help months ago?"

His mother came on the line: "Please do something."

Anxiety about a couple's sexual performance is not a purely
private matter. A mother rang to ask, "Shall I get them single
beds? Should they make love every night? How many times a
week? Will it make him weak?" As an Indian I understand her
concern. Traditionally men and women have slept separately
except when the husband desired intercourse. Double beds were
regarded as a sign of the West's soft over-indulgence in sex.
According to ancient Indian wisdom a man is weakened by the
emission of sperm and strengthened by drawing it upwards
towards his brain.

Most of the letters appealing for my help were in Punjabi, but
I received many in Hindi and English and a smaller proportion
in Urdu. One came from an English lady of twenty-one who had
read my *Mysteries of Indian Cuisine*. She wrote:

> I am very fond of Indian food. . . . As I have a taste for Indian
> food and admire your traditions, I think I must have been an
> Indian in my last incarnation. I am most impressed by Indian
> men, their looks, manners, everything and want to marry an
> Indian. Can you find me a nice Indian guy? Really, an arranged
> marriage. I would love to have an Indian husband.

A five-page letter arrived from an Army Officer. He gave
details of his parents and interests and asked me to find a suitable
Indian wife for him. "I feel they make better and stable homes and
remain faithful to their husbands." He had not been reading
Mysteries of Indian Cuisine, but an interview with me published in
the *Telegraph*. I had been questioned about arranged marriages
and the tragic death of Indian girls at the hands of their parents.

During the early seventies several such tragedies occurred.
Parents were struggling to establish small businesses. They
worked round the clock with all too little time for their children
who were impressed by the freedom of their white peer group.
When English friends wanted to go out at night their parents did
not interfere. Asian youngsters resented the restrictions imposed
by their parents. They could not even participate in after-school
activities, leave alone keep dates. If a daughter came home late

from school or showed dissatisfaction with family constraints her parents panicked. Without consulting her they arranged a marriage. Her protests were construed as proof that she had a boyfriend. They dreaded the unbearable social embarrassment of community gossip. A girl might be kept indoors, prevented from slipping out to the Social Services Office or the police. In a few cases parental fury at the daughter's adamant refusal to cooperate resulted in murder by her father or brother. The family's "izzat" (honour) must be guaranteed even by the most drastic means. There was a stir in the British community, outraged at this violence. Few comprehended the Asian parents'dread of losing their children, their horror of disgrace in their own community.

All Asian families in Brtain have experienced the tension between Eastern morals and Western mores. Here is another letter which speaks for many more:

Respected Kailash Sister
My daughters of sixteen and seventeen have adopted English ways. They don't want to listen to me. If I stop them from going out they threaten to leave home and live on their own. I lie awake worrying till they return. Please can you tell me how to convince my daughters that they are not English and must live within the Indian family system? We do not encourage going out with strangers in the evening. More so with the boys. I am very upset and worried about my daughters. Please guide me.

I replied:

I have all sympathy for your frustration, but as parents we have to understand our children's position. They are educated and brought up in a multicultural and multiracial society and spend most part of the day in schools. Girls and boys discuss all sorts of topics and arrange their meetings also.

You have to give them some liberty. Win them over with patience and love. Understand the outside social presures on them. Let them talk to you. You will find they are normal kids who need love and understanding. If you have an open mind they will discuss all their problems with you. I am sure you will agree with me.

Sometimes it is the daughter who writes:

I am very much in love with my boyfriend and we both want to live together before we decide to marry. At the moment we are trying to know each other because I am Indian and he is English. We have a lot in common and get along very well. But I can't break this news to my parents, they will never allow me to marry any one other than a man from our own community. I am terrified of my father who will hit the roof and probably pack me off to India to marry someone of his choice and this is the last thing I want to happen. Please advise.

I advised her to do nothing hasty and to speak tactfully to her mother who might then win her father round, as wives often do.

Many love affairs develop between Hindus or Sikhs and Muslims. Culturally, especially when compared with surrounding white society, they share so much. Neither party can bear to hurt their parents, yet they know that, religion apart, their chosen partner would be acceptable in every other way to their family. Had they fallen in love with such a member of their own religious community they know that their parents would have sanctioned the marriage. But for most families marriage across this particular religious frontier is still inconceivable.

Parents can pressurise their daughters in many ways. An unmarried, twenty-five year old Pakistani woman wrote:

When I was seventeen my parents wanted me to marry a chap from our village in India who was illiterate and I did not want to marry him. There was a lot of shouting, crying and cursing but I did not give in and kept on working in a factory. Then they wanted me to work at home in case I fell in love as some girls did and left their parents.

I have been working at this wretched machine it seems all my life sewing for nearly twelve hours a day. I am a money-making machine for my parents. Now they do not talk about my marriage because they do not want to lose the weekly money I make for them. I want to get married but they don't let me go out. How can I get rid of this miserable life?

The problem is that parents get used to the income which their daughter is generating. Parents do not realise their daughter's boredom and they ignore her sexual urges and need to get married.

Many parents have consulted me as if I were a marriage bureau rather than an agony aunt. From Ilford a Sikh father telephoned, a Ramgarhia by caste. Ramgarhias are from families traditionally engaged in carpentry, ironwork and building. Most of the Ramgarhia families in Britain came here from East African countries and in the larger British cities they have set up Ramgarhia gurdwaras. My caller informed me that he had two unmarried daughters, both working as hospital doctors. "I want only Ramgarhia Sikh boys for them, Ramgarhia Sikhs sporting uncut hair and beard." Two weeks later the Ramgarhia father again phoned, saying he would like to break his journey in Liverpool to meet me. With him came his two daughters, good-looking women in their early thirties. I had a long talk with them in their father's presence. When he left the room I asked each daughter if she would agree to marry her father's choice of husband. Both assured me, "We'll marry whoever he chooses. We know he has our best interests at heart."

From a Midlands hospital a doctor wrote, giving pages of his family history, details of his uncles' property and so forth. Could I, he requested, find him a suitable Sikh wife. "I don't mind whether she knows English or not, but she must be extremely religious, reciting the Sikh prayers morning, afternoon and evening. I won't accept any dowry and I want a simple marriage ceremony. I don't wish my wife to go out to work." I was surprised at his specifications for his bride and I felt that he must be a strange young man.

Many Sikhs and Hindus venerate living, spiritual masters. Some have a reputation for miraculous cures. All draw huge congregations on their increasingly frequent visits to Britain. By devotees such men are lovingly referred to as Babaji. Their impact upon followers extends far beyond the spiritual to influence such practical matters as matrimonial alliances. One day a young girl contacted me. "I was called over to the UK by Babaji for marriage. I saw the boy and like him. But now Babaji says that if I marry him I will bring him bad luck. What can I do?"

Other requests for help ranged from personal hygiene, appearance, diet and the menopause to difficulties and suspected racial discrimination in the search for paid employment, immigration and citizenship problems and frustration with temple committees and Asian community organisations. Here is what a Sikh man wrote, fearful of deportation:

I came here as a male fiance and got married two years ago. We are divorced now. But I have received a letter from the Home Office for deportation. I cannot understand this because my ex-wife is a UK citizen and I had been granted permanent residence. How can they deport me? Can you kindly advise me?

Not every letter was written in distress. Mr Kumar wrote from Southall:

I am not really an educated person, but I do understand every-thing happening around. I feel very sad when Asians whose life is fairly comfortable in this country compared with what they were back home, but they never seem to acknowledge the facil-ities they have in this country. I cannot understand this mentality. I am most grateful and shall remain so because my children are having the best education, best medical aid and we live very comfortably. I like to be fair and honest and like to show my gratitude because I was untouchable in my own country and am equal to everyone in my adopted country. There have been a lot of problems before I found this happiness but it has all been very worthwhile.

BBC television gave me a weekly slot as an agony aunt and this ran successfully for more than six months. I also visited Central Television, Granada, Thames and Channel 4 regularly. On Breakfast TV and Pebble Mill at One I appeared with English agony aunts, Anna Raeburn, Virginia Ironside and Claire Rayner.

12

Pakistan

While Gopal worked full-time as a lecturer we could not realise one longstanding ambition, to visit Pakistan, our birthplace. Over the years the hope persisted that one day we would return, this time perhaps on a lecture tour. In 1982 we were thrilled when Gopal received an invitation to lecture in Lahore and Rawalpindi. Although Kiran was in Ghana we were excited at the prospect of taking Risham and Shaminder to our ancestral home. We longed to show them where their grandparents had lived and, above all, to take them to our village, Kallar. Sadly the Indian government saw fit to issue a warning that it was unsafe for Indians to cross to Pakistan. Once again we were deprived of the pleasure of taking our children to the land of their ancestors.

At least I could see my mother, now failing in health, and constantly repeating, "I must see Mukhpal's son married before I die. I must see Bikhu married before I die." Unlike her sons and daughters-in-law, my mother read and commented on my novels, poems and articles.

In 1982 we also took the opportunity to revisit Dehra Dun and catch up on news of friends of thirty years ago. A very different highlight was the honour of receiving the Woman of the Year Award from the Bhai Mohan Singh Vaid Sahitya Kendra, a Punjabi Literature Centre, in appreciation of my writing on love, sex and marriage. This was followed in 1988 by the Shiromani Sahitkar Award ("supreme writer of the year") from the Bhasha Vibhag (Department of Language) in Patiala. Next, the Institute of Sikh Studies awarded me the "Sahitkar [writer] of the Year" award in Delhi in 1989.

Our 1982 trip temporarily diverted my thoughts from increasing anxiety about Risham. She wanted to marry, and to marry a Sikh, but no-one seemed suitable. Since taking her A

153

levels she had studied for a year at Southport Polytechnic, then qualified in Arts and Textile Design at the North East London Polytechnic. She had worked briefly for the British Council before being appointed Administrative Officer at Thumb Art Gallery. She met innumerable people, but her problem was no nearer solution.

Third parties informed us of a succession of professional Sikh bachelors — doctors, solicitors, accountants, businessmen. In turn Gopal and I met them all, and the parents of eligible young engineers employed in Canada. Once we were out of the room Gopal would wink at me and repeat happily, "It's okay this time." Each time I answered, "No." As we drove away he would voice his irritation at my fussiness. "You don't like anybody. You and the children gang up and reject everyone." I was adamant. If, as Risham's mother, I had misgivings about a prospective son-in-law, I refused to introduce him to her. Night after night I lay awake worrying and arguing with my husband about our daughter's prospective grooms.

In 1983 Gopal was invited to lecture on Ecology in Delhi and Punjab. We arrived in Delhi in December 1983 to participate in preparations for my nephew Teetoo's marriage. With us was Risham, thanks to her brother who had bought her the ticket. Marriages are always exciting, the more so when one is reunited with relatives usually several thousand miles away. All the anticipation and anxieties reach their natural climax as bridegroom and bride walk solemnly around the Guru Granth Sahib. The married recall their own wedding days, the unwed wonder about their own as yet unknown life partners. After Teetoo's lavan we were glad to relax in the garden, appreciating Delhi's bright winter sunshine, warm as an English June. Beside me sat Gurdip Kaur Dhingra, the friendship between our two families undiminished by the passage of thirty-five years. In front of us were several men, one of whom immediately caught my attention. "Who is that young man?" I asked Gurdip. His name was Asjit, and Gurdip added, "They're very pucka Sikhs." I nudged Risham, "Have a good look at that boy." Gurdip had found Asjit's mother. We sat and chatted. Everything we gleaned concerning his family background, education, prospects and attitudes reassured us that here was an ideal son-in-law. Once the subject had been broached with Asjit he confessed that he had been unable to take his eyes off Risham during Teetoo's lavan. As Teetoo's bride followed him, linked by the pink scarf that symbolised their union, Asjit's thoughts had been elsewhere.

Risham's leave had nearly expired. Before her return to Liverpool Asjit visited us several times for a couple of hours with her. Both agreed to a betrothal ceremony before Risham's departure. Our anxiety had given way to glad anticipation.

In late January Gopal and I reached the Punjabi city of Ludhiana where I had been requested to speak about the problems and pleasures of Asians in Britain. My audiences seemed surprised and delighted that I spoke Punjabi rather than English. Immediately there was a bond between us and, as a Punjabi writer, I welcomed every opportunity of speaking in my mother tongue.

The students were interested to discover that life in Britain was not problem-free for Indians. I explained about discrimination, housing, unemployment and told them that many Indian pupils failed their O or A levels, and joined their parents on the growing list of jobless. I told them of the increasing incidence of divorce among Asians and the disintegration of families. In some Women's Colleges my audiences were all female. Uppermost in everyone's minds were the appalling instances of bride burning and dowry deaths publicised by the Indian media. A young wife's nylon sari would catch fire as she cooked over the kerosene stove in her cramped Delhi kitchen. It was not always clear whether she had committed suicide or been murdered by her in-laws. The reason was invariably the mounting pressure on her to win more gifts from her parents for her parents-in-law — money, a fridge, a television or a scooter. Sometimes the girl could no longer bear the financial strain and taunts loaded upon her struggling family. Sometimes a callous mother-in-law had decided to dispose of her and extract the second dowry from her next daughter-in-law's parents.

These shocking cases were relatively rare, but all these students were worried about excessive dowry demands before or after their marriages. I suggested that young unmarried men and women should form organisations and pledge themselves not to enter into any marriage that entailed dowry. They should not involve their parents as this would mean a stigma on the family. Outsiders would spread word that these parents did not wish their daughter to marry.

After one of my lectures an undergraduate stood up and

unburdened herself. "Auntie, I am facing such a dilemma. My elder sister is married. Her in-laws have been asking my parents for more gifts. My father and mother are arranging my marriage to my sister's younger brother-in-law. I feel very upset and do not know what to do." I advised her to speak openly to her parents, to point out that they had already suffered one set of degrading demands for dowry. "You must tell them that you are unwilling to marry someone who was almost certainly more interested in money than in their daughter as a person."

The college principal, Mrs Kahlon, was keen to capitalise on the enthusiasm generated by my visit. "We will call a meeting while you are here and start an organisation along the lines you suggest. Otherwise their zeal will fade. Everyone is so afraid of family pressures." The meeting was announced and press and television reporters turned up to photograph the girls taking their anti-dowry pledge. I hope these students stood firm in their resolve and influenced their peers in the same direction.

From Ludhiana Gopal and I proceeded to Amritsar. The narrow streets around the Golden Temple were choked with India's distinctive traffic. Every bicycle bell, every scooter rickshaw hooter made its own mad din. Away from the congestion and sanctity of central Amritsar is the pleasantly quiet campus of Guru Nanak Dev University where Gopal was to lecture.

"What are you plans for the weekend?" Professor Thind, Head of the Department of Punjabi, asked us on Friday. We had no plans. "Why don't you go to Pakistan? We can always alter Professor Puri's lecture schedule to give you a few days there." "But," we responded, "How can we go? We haven't written to anyone." "No problem. I will send word to two writer friends there, and they will look after you impeccably." The Wagah border is only fifteen miles from Amritsar and a university car was soon at our disposal. The hope of seeing our birthplace again after fifty years filled us with delight.

We left Guru Nanak Dev University that chill January morning to find that thousands were surging forward for visas, pushing, pulling and periodically beaten back by the soldiers' lathis (sticks) which they wielded indiscriminately. There was to be a cricket match that weekend, a powerful attraction in its own right. It was also a God-given opportunity for intending smugglers. We had heard of the daily illicit traffic over the border where police could grow fat on the bribes. In return for enough cardamoms, tea and fine woollen shawls Indians could come home laden with the televisions, videos and consumer durables which were imported unrestricted into Pakistan, a country poor in industry but rich with money hard earned by expatriate labour in the Gulf States. There was a frosty nip in the air. Muslim villagers from Uttar Pradesh, the women in heavy silver chokers, squatted motionless, huddled together under their blankets and shawls, sustained by the hope of reunion with loved ones. Day after day they had watched the more literate, moneyed and well-connected pass ahead of them in the queue.

We were given priority and drove straight to the office for our visa. "Sit down please." Round numerous tables hungry-eyed customs officers drank tea and eyed me up and down. While we were answering questions some Muslim villagers were summoned. They had been waiting for two weeks. "I must see my brother before I die," the woman told me. "I haven't seen him for thirty years. I have sold every piece of jewellery in order to see him again. Every day these officers have demanded dollay (dollars) from us on some pretext or the other. We have no money for food. How can we afford to come back again?" It was painful to see these poor old men and women handled so cruelly. I longed to shout at the soldiers that they should show these innocent people some mercy.

From Amritsar we travelled to Lahore, to stay with Dr Jamal in his house in Shamnagar, Charbuji. My sole aim here was to revisit the house in Dharampura built by my father over fifty years before. He had built our family house in the shopping centre of Lahore. Until then we had lived on the edge of the cantonment. During our absences in Kallar and Rawalpindi the house had often lain empty, but the shops on the ground floor, four on each side, had all been rented out. One shopkeeper used to live on the ground floor below our rooms and we had lived upstairs. Memories of girlish curiosity, forbidden viewing of the bazaar, unmentionable nightly eavesdropping, all flooded back.

Our hosts gladly acquiesced with our eagerness to revisit my former home and so we set off after tea. Vividly in my mind's eye I saw the house fronting the Mayo Road, emblazoned with the double-bladed sword of Sikhism over the words "Puri Nivas" and a verse of Sukhmani Sahib, the hymn of peace composed by our fifth Guru, the martyr Arjan Dev. The words ran through my head:

. Jeh prasad basih sukh mandir . . .
In your head continually meditate
On the One by whose grace
You dwell happily in your home.
Throughout the eight watches
Let your tongue repeat the name of the One
By whose grace you live in happiness with your kin.

As we drove along crowded, unrecognisable streets I visualised the baithak with its glass doors from floor to ceiling and its magnificent curtains.

The car stopped: we had arrived and my memories shattered at the reality of Puri Nivas 1983. The whole facade from the first floor down was covered with jute matting, the doors and windows were smothered. The house was unoccupied and derelict with wooden struts to prevent it from collapsing into the street. There was no light, no way of entering. The verses of Sukhmani Sahib had been scraped off the wall. Instead of the purposeful bustle of successful businesses the area felt run down and desolate. My spirits plummeted. How could such a beautiful residence have been so neglected? Why did no one live there? I would never know. Why had I been so eager to return? A small crowd was gathering around us and a shopkeeper was enquiring, "Did you live here once? Was this your house?" I was too upset to answer and grateful for the tea he brought. "Times are such, don't worry," he said to comfort me. I recalled Kazan Singh's fruit and vegetable shop and the cafe with its nightly banter and oaths, and I remembered Gopal visiting his teenage bride.

Gopal and Dr Jamal were sad, and I wept inconsolably because such a beautiful building had been reduced to debris.

Dr Jamal told us, "There are no husbands in this part of Lahore. All the men are earning money in the Gulf States and the women look after their children. That is the Sunni life."

In Lahore a Parsi lady heard me speaking on the radio. Knowing that we were staying with Shakila Jamal, she telephoned to arrange a meeting. From our conversation I learned the sad story of her life. Like most Indian Zoroastrians she had grown up in Bombay. Here she had met a Muslim barrister, kind, intelligent and handsome. They fell in love. Her parents reasoned with her to no avail, and eventually ostracised her. In Lahore she married her lover and began a new life with his two older wives and their children. In their husband's presence the two women treated her well, pouring her tea and praising her effusively. While he was in court they quarrelled with her and maligned her.

After a few years her husband died, leaving her childless and friendless. Disowned by the Pakistanis around her she nonetheless felt it would be wrong to return to her parents and revive sad memories. Here in Lahore she lived alone in a pleasant bungalow with servants in attendance. She busied herself in reading, social work and attending conferences.

Satnam's story was different. Her Sikh parents had finally consented to her marrying a Muslim. She had an impudent, obstinate zest for life. Satnam (Nama for short) was the daughter of the famous poet, Charan Singh Shaheed, the editor of the weekly *Mauji* ("Full of Mirth").

When her father-in-law reproached her, "Nama, don't ride on a bicycle, it brings shame to our family" she was unrepentant. "Then buy me a car, Abbaji, and I won't cycle" was her reply. If he told her that so much spiced betel nut would ruin her teeth she retorted, "First you stop smoking then." Satnam too was now a widow in Lahore.

Our host, Dr Jamal, was a poet and sang melodiously, but he was suffering unnecessary physical discomfort. Doctors had diagnosed a hernia which required specialist treatment in India or Britain. Several times his wife had been to India to make arrangements, but the Pakistan government refused him a visa on account of his supposed political sympathies.

One evening two Sufis came on bicycles. They were poor and unpretentious, their souls alive with the divine music which they shared with us throughout the night — Sultan Bahu, Bulleh Shah, Gulam Farid, mystic poets of centuries long past, as well as Iqbal and Faiz. We bathed in their love for God, swept along by the singing of these two untrammelled, wandering saints.

Dr Jamal's daughter, Nina, slipped away at midnight as she was preparing for examinations in medicine. Dr Jamal was a sick man, but he listened and recited his own compositions, then sank back on his cushions and slept. At half-past five the sky began to lighten from the East. A new day had dawned, and Yasmin, Nina's sister brought fish and freshly baked nan (unleavened bread) from the bazaar for our breakfast.

From Dr Jamal's house Gopal telephoned the local Forestry Department to which he had been invited to speak the previous year. Would anyone from his generation be in the office? Would he find former students, now middle-aged? We had little time to speculate as we were immediately invited over. Divisional Forest Officers and researchers gathered to meet Gopal, all asking questions, begging him to stay longer so that others might meet him.

Gopal explained that we hoped to proceed to Rawalpindi, and the Forestry Department officers promised to make all necessary arrangements. In the meantime we were feasted on cakes and pastries, samosas and pakoras.

Sardar Liaqat Khan, the local Forest Officer, arranged for us to visit Panja Sahib. Gopal and I sat in the front of his jeep beside the driver, while Sardar and his assistant took the back seat — very self-effacing behaviour for a Divisional Forest Office I thought. In case we felt uneasy eating out in an unfamiliar Pakistani restaurant he had, without our knowledge, packed up home cooked tandoori chicken, home-made halwa and the finest of sweet pastries in a big basket. There were also, he told us in our own Pothohari dialect, red blood oranges from Kallar, our own village. Moved by his kindness we looked forward to our first glimpse of the gurdwara where my mother had prayed so earnestly for a son more than half a century earlier. I recalled too the local specialities of Panja Sahib, ambras and kattalama, made by deep frying a rich dough layered with clarified butter.

The sacred pool, renowned for its striped fish, was nearly empty, and the precincts, once thronging with countless brightly clad pilgrims, were deserted. I remembered the devotees joyously bathing in the holy water and the clatter of the langar where a free meal of chapati, dal and spiced vegetables was served to all who sat in line cross-legged on the ground. But the white marble pavement around the pool was still cool underfoot, and there before us was the rock bearing the impress of Guru Nanak's right hand. According to legend the rock had been hurled at him in fury by Pir Wali. Pir Wali had refused Guru Nanak's disciple Mardana's request for water from his spring and was incensed when fresh water sprang up to quench their thirst. Pictures show Guru Nanak staying the rock in mid-air with one upraised hand. We proceeded over the bridge to the central shrine, white picked out in yellow. There were no carpets on the floor, but our hearts were gladdened by the signs of continuing daily devotion. An Afghan Sikh was caring for the shrine. Everything was clean and well-maintained. Most important of all, we found the Guru Granth Sahib fittingly enthroned. It had been ceremonially opened that morning and we shared, thankfully, in the freshly prepared karah prashad. The shrine of the holy hand print had escaped the sadder fate of so many Sikh and Hindu temples in Pakistan that now stand neglected and derelict. Great must be the joy of the thousands of Sikh pilgrims allowed to cross the border to celebrate Baisakhi here each April and to commemorate Guru Nanak's birth each November.

Despite the disappointment of Puri Nivas, Lahore, my heart was set on seeing our Rawalpindi home once again. As we drove along I looked excitedly for remembered landmarks — the Arya Samaj College, the Modern Cambridge School, the Chadha family's gurdwara and the hospital. I looked out for the three steps leading to the front door and the little grey letterbox ("Sardar Sohan Singh Puri") and for the distinctive baithak protruding on one side of the house.

We had identified the house at last. It was well maintained, hardly altered from how I had imagined it. We knocked at the door and were cordially welcomed inside, strangers in what had been our own home. The women and girls hid at the sight of a strange man and woman entering. We were offered refreshments and left bearing tiny gifts. After so many years my memories were fresh and I was deeply moved.

My father had built his house near to Gordon College, which Gopal was curious to revisit. At reception we asked if we might see the Principal. When Gopal gave his name and the years in which he had been an M.Sc. student there the Principal sent his PA for files and back copies of *The Gordonian*. The Principal welcomed us enthusiastically, and the entire staff joined us. Greetings were exchanged and each of the lecturers looked at us with awe and happiness, as though they were meeting dignitaries. At once the Principal ordered cakes, samosas and pakoras.

The PA returned bearing *The Gordonian*, Vol XIX, 1939, No. III. My heart leapt with pride at the sight of the full page photograph of Gopal as I had first seen him, above the caption:

Mr. Gopal Singh Puri, Demonstrator Gordon College, got a first class, first M.Sc. for work on the Pleistocene Flora of Kashmir under the guidance of Dr. R. R. Stewart.

We were taken to see the palaeobotanical samples. From

locked, glass-paned cupboards one of the staff brought out the fossil collection. On nearly every exhibit was the label, "Collected by Dr. G. S. Puri". Scientists and researchers flocked around us, asking for Gopal's autograph. As he signed the visitors' book my heart swelled with the glad knowledge that here, as in many other institutions, my husband had experienced loving recognition for his life-long services to science.

Above all Gopal and I longed to see Kallar, home of both our families and of the great Bedi dynasty. Early in the morning Sardar came with his assistant to prepare refreshments for our journey to the village. As we drove along in the jeep powerful emotions mingled, distancing the immediate present and trans-porting me to my childhood with my grandmother, among neighbours early at the riverside, at the holy marble shrine of Damdama Sahib. Girlhood and marriage flooded back. How could I be that ignorant little girl, cross-legged on the dusty jute mat at Nidhan Kaur's school? Now I had travelled the world, but I could not rest until I again saw Kallar.

The car drew into the bazaar. Gopal was looking around for a familiar face or landmark. I recognised nothing. We saw a school where Khalsa College had once been. As we left the jeep we saw a haggard, frail gentleman in silver-rimmed spectacles. He was leaning on a stick. Sardar and Gopal approached him and gave the names of Master Hara Singh Puri and Sardar Sohan Singh Puri, his father and mine.

"Yes, yes, I knew them, but who are these people?" Soon over twenty people had gathered around us. We set out to revisit our family homes. As we walked the procession following us kept increasing. We saw the well, Shankre da khuh, near the orchards where I had swung as a girl. "There used to be another well too," I said. "Yes, there is, but no one uses it." So its evil reputation had survived Partition.

Another forty yards on the uneven rocky galli and we had reached Gopal's house. We knocked at the door. Two women opened it and quickly ran to shelter inside. A man appeared at the door. On learning our reason for coming he invited us inside. Instead of the bamboo step-ladder to go upstairs there was a brick-built staircase, and the floors were no longer hardened earth. The low-ceilinged rooms were unchanged except for an extended veranda. Three brothers lived there, who were all by coincidence, like Gopal's parents, teachers. All was spick and span, and set with indoor plants. There was an indoor water-tank and, wonder of wonders as I visualised the old days, a washing-machine. We asked if we might take a photograph of our house. "We'd like the ladies to join us too."

"No, we are in purdah," they told me.
"Don't worry. My husband and his family used to live here. He is your brother. This will be the picture of a lifetime for us to take away."

I embraced them and, tentatively, the ladies joined us on the charpoy. They insisted on serving us with tea or sherbet and mithai. Not wanting to hurt their feelings we accepted gladly.

We proceeded next to my family's house. From a distance I could see the topmost room, with its three carved doors. As children we had loved to hide and bounce on the bedding that was stored here. Many a time I had fled here to sulk or hide my pocket money.

As I saw the tredera again, after forty years, a strange sensation invaded me, as if I had returned from another world. Before my eyes my life seemed condensed in a moment. I was once more the girl-bride waiting upstairs for the bridegroom who would not come, with the barber's wife fussing in and out of the room, and all the guests wondering what was going to happen to "this girl", me.

But I could not show my emotions with this friendly, welcoming, inquisitive crowd milling around us. We climbed the two concrete steps to the massive carved doors. Were they still secured of a night with a wooden bar fixed across inside? We were invited inside and in my mind's eye I saw Beyji on her palang and Lalaji's framed photograph dominating the room from the mantelpiece.

"We still have your fan, sister," the house-owner was saying. I remembered the pankha, the wooden frame draped with thick khaki cloth, hung across the room and worked by the pankhawala's invisible efforts outside. What a lovely, soft breeze it had created. A doctor and his wife and their six children now lived in our house.

The procession was still increasing as news of our return spread, but, apart from a few elderly women, only men were visible. "Brother, come to our house just for a short time," someone was begging. Gopal said we must now have our lunch. Chairs and tables appeared outside and we had our food before again starting.

Along the way we met a woman who said, "My father played the baja (harmonium) at your marriage." He was Punnu, the flute player, and he had known my grandfather as well as my father-in-law. The woman insisted that we must visit her, but we pleaded lack of time. A young man continually reiterated his invitation. "My father can't come out. Please come." We allowed ourselves to be persuaded. The old gentleman, tall and thin, was lying in bed waiting for us. As soon as he saw us he burst into tears, lamenting the politics which had divided the country. Gopal touched his feet as a sign of respect, and the old man could hardly speak for emotion.

A reporter also would not take "no" for an answer. In Pothohari dialect he said, "We will never have such a day in our lives again." In his house sweetmeats, fruit and a fine tea set were set out on a coffee table. On the mantelpiece were photographs and plastic flowers. Again the women would not venture out of purdah and a man made tea for us. As we drank it we heard what had happened since we had left.

The standard of living had risen strikingly over these four decades. Not every house had its own water supply, but all had electricity. Houses were well-maintained and full of luxury items. The earnings of Pakistanis in the Gulf States have brought previously unimaginable material comfort. We noticed cars parked in the gallis.

Our pilgrimage could not be complete without again seeing Damdama Sahib and the palace and I wondered what had become of the shop where we bought yoghurt and milk, revrian, malok and roasted chickpeas, all for a few paise. There was no sign now of the shop where Sital Singh had glowered at us from below his turban of rolled white cloth. I remembered his rage when he caught us plundering his behr tree.

Now, in 1983, Damdama Sahib was in ruins. The gurdwara had been destroyed. All that remained was a dusty shell. Yet the marble platform where we had venerated Palang Sahib and Nishan Sahib had survived. A crack testified to the efforts of the Muslim iconoclasts. We were told, "A man took a pickaxe, but the axe struck him and he died there and then. In turn two others attempted to smash the platform, but with the same result. Then people realised that some holy person must lie there." On one side I spotted two blackened divas. Someone must still have faith and come secretly after dark to leave their oil lights, like the jotan that I and so many other devotees used to light so many years before.

Sir Raja Gurbaksh Singh's palace had fallen into disrepair. The palace, we learned, now housed a primary school. We were shown the ground floor. The colours of the religious murals on pillars and ceilings were as vivid as my memories. Upstairs we again saw the rooms that had been Tika Sahib's and Mataji's, but they were now unrecognizable.

We wished to show our gratitude for the kindness we had been shown, and so decided to give money to buy sweets for the children in school next day. As we had no small change Gopal asked a man standing near us where we could change a note. A middle-aged man thrust his hand inside his shirt pocket and brought out two or three thousand rupees. Our hundred rupee note looked meagre indeed in today's affluent Kallar.

Back in Delhi my mother listened attentively to my accounts of places she had never thought to leave and could never hope to revisit. She became sad when I described the wretched state of our house in Lahore, commenting, "During your father's life a letter came asking him what rent he had charged. Why, we never discovered. In any case property rates would have changed since 1947."

We called on Risham's future in-laws, who received us most hospitably. "Please arrange the marriage soon," they implored laughingly. "Otherwise we shall be bankrupted by the telephone bill. Asjit and Risham are talking to each other for hours every day."

Back in Blundell Sands we eagerly awaited the return of our six reels of film from the processors. When we heard that not a single photograph had come out we could not believe it. In years of globetrotting our camera had never let us down and never had photographs meant so much to us. There was no explanation. We had our memories, but these are harder to share with our children who have not seen Pakistan. At least our tape-recorder had not failed us. We could relive the night with the singing faqirs at Dr Jamal's and Shakila's house in Lahore. Not long after our return a letter from Dr Jamal informed us that one of the two Sufis had passed from this earth. "Make sure you keep the tape," he wrote.

Our most pressing concern on our return from India and Pakistan was preparation for a double wedding. Risham's marriage to Asjit Singh had been finalised and Shaminder and Sheila, a PE teacher whom he had met in Indonesia, decided to marry at the same time. Double marriages are unusual in our families, yet first my two sisters had shared their wedding rites and now my eldest and youngest child would share theirs. Almost forty years separated the two wedding days, but in the frenzy of hectic planning my thoughts returned to Gurcharan and Amrit's marriage at Kallar. How strange it would have seemed then for a girl to be married from her parents-in-law's home, a girl who had known her future husband (Shammy) over a number of years.

Happy though we were at Risham's marriage to Asjit, and often as our family had been separated, I wept at her departure to her in-laws' residence in New Delhi. How, I wondered, would she feel at the sacrifice of independence, career, a London life? I advised her to behave circumspectly, especially during the first six months as a daughter-in-law. "You've been going to work like an English girl, owning your own flat. All eyes will be on you to see how you behave. If you go out don't have anything alcoholic to drink. If your husband has one glass too many, never say anything. Everyone there is bound to have various preconceived ideas about you, coming from this permissive society. So it is extra important not to give offence in any way. Make sure you do not neglect your mother-in-law. From now on you have two mothers. Consider her the more important as you have to spend your life with her. One mother gives you birth. With the other you have to spend most of your days. The bond between you and me can never disappear. Your mother-in-law must be convinced that you love her, respect her and will look after her in her old age. These first six months will be the real test. Then if your husband feels that you genuinely love his mother he will be happy. He will not be torn by divided loyalties." Sending Risham to another country (even though it was our own country) was very hard.

Risham sent us cheerful letters from New Delhi and sounded vivacious as ever on the telephone, yet my worries would still surface in case she regretted her lost freedom, in case she could no longer go swimming, could no longer enjoy life as she had. "Are you really happy, darling?" I asked her on the telephone.

When she replied brightly in the affirmative I feared she was reassuring me to comfort me, and during one of our conversations I burst into tears. "Why are you crying Mummy?" Risham asked. She put Tayaji, her father-in-law's elder brother on the line and, unable to speak coherently, I passed the receiver to Gopal. Tayaji assured him, "Risham is queen of the family, we all love her and she does whatever she wishes to do."

In February 1984, I flew to Delhi to be with Risham to be with her for the birth of her first child. Ten days after my arrival Seerut was born. Joy at the safe delivery of our second grandchild combined with the glad realisation that Risham had made the necessary adjustments in lifestyle, and was happy in the evident affection of her husband's family. My fears had been baseless.

Shammy and Sheila were also far away from England. His current assignment was in Lima, Peru. Kiran and her husband had settled rather nearer home, but too far away for us to meet as often as we would wish.

In 1984, when Shivan was four years old, Gopal and I were leaving Kiran's house to return to Liverpool when our grandson snatched my chunni and hid it. He did not want his granny to leave. I needed my chunni to cover my head when we paid our respects in the Nishkam Sevak Jatha gurdwara in Birmingham on the way home. "Granny has to go to the gurdwara, she needs her chunni," I cajoled him, "See, here is another lovely chunni for you if you give me that one."

"I need your chunni," retorted my grandson, "I'm going to the gurdwara too." (Little as he was, Shivan covered his head with one of Kiran's chunnis when he mumbled the words of Sikh prayers in front of the picture of Guru Nanak, in imitation of his mother.) There wasn't time to change my clothes, so I had to leave my green chunni in the rose bushes and take another from my suitcase, whether or not the colour agreed with my salvar kamiz suit. In the car Gopal reflected on the quirky coincidences of life. Forty years earlier, before I had joined him in London, he had come as a young ecologist to Boxhill station to collect soil samples from the neighbouring countryside. With him he had always brought my green chunni.

So life's motifs recur in ever changing patterns, some beyond our imagining, some of our own deliberate choice. So, when my grandchildren were older I would teach them arati, just as Kallarwali Beyji had taught me. They would sit in Babaji's room, the little room above the front door, where the Guru Granth Sahib lay, covered with a silken cloth. We would sing in Punjabi:

> Gagan mein thal rav chand dipak bane tarika mandal chand
>   moti . . .
> The sun is your silver tray,
> The sun and moon your oil wick lights,
> The galaxy of stars are the pearls that stud it.
> The sandalwood is your incense . . .

and I would remember Beyji's specially soft chapatis and wonder if my grandchildren would one day think of me in Liverpool as I think of her in Kallar.

When my grandchildren came I would light the Divali lamps and prepare the festival delicacies. Without the family around me there seemed so much less point. Why maintain traditions in isolation, why cook goodies for myself and Gopal to put on unnecessary weight? We were surrounded by people who knew nothing of our festivals, people leading very private lives. Sometimes I thought, "If we die will anybody notice or come to look for us?" This was a frightening thought, this thought shared with all our private neighbours. Without our work, our articles and books, and with no talks to give, our life would indeed have been lonely. That is why I still say, "Let Asians live among Asians." Then at least they may be glad together at festival time, neighbours may knock at their door and their death will not pass unremarked.

Changes there must be and I have no right to dictate to my children and grandchildren. So my heart rejoiced all the more when I saw the traditions that survive in their homes. When at Divali I noted that Kiran had placed coins in a steel thali in front of Guru Nanak's picture I felt happy. Such delicate strands will unite my grandparents with my grandchildren.

My speaking commitments continued, and the same questions were asked. One day one of the audience said, "Madam Chairman, may I ask the speaker if she would go back to India if she had the option?"

"No," I replied, "Liverpool is my home, where my husband and I have lived for so many years. We are busy here and our work is our life. I need privacy to work and am no longer in a mental state to stand having servants and other people around all the time. I have become more British in attitude and want to concentrate on my work without distractions. At my age I can't afford to waste time. In India people have also changed from how they were twenty or thirty years ago. I don't fit in there any longer. In any case I doubt if we could afford a decent flat in Delhi. They have become so expensive. My roots are certainly in India but my home is Liverpool."

Even after Gopal's retirement life still left us little leisure. Sometimes I wished I more often found time to accompany him to the seafront, a two-minute drive along empty, well kept roads from our house, with residences standing in immaculately culti-vated gardens, their trees and hedges sculpted by the driving sea winds. Couples walked hand in hand, dogs were let off the leash, joggers in blue tracksuits ignored the elements. We would park and watch the silhouetted shipping soundlessly moving towards Liverpool, a collage of silent rectangles to our left. We would remember the first glimpse of Liverpool from the sea so many years ago, and the many subsequent arrivals and departures from those docks.

As I looked at the dry blown grass and the clean driven sky and the sand folded by wind and wave I was back at Kallar, a child once more beside the Kanshi river, the future before me.

Afterword

Kailash's story is part of the Punjabi, and more broadly the South Asian, history of Britain. More specifically, she identifies strongly throughout as a Sikh and, while open and receptive to insights from beyond this specific heritage, it is Sikh devotion that recurrently upholds her in crises. With this in mind, the Afterword focuses on the years 1983 to 2013 primarily in the UK's Sikh community.

Kailash's 60-year memoir breaks off just before two turning points in the story of Sikhs in the UK: a statement in the House of Lords and a military operation in Punjab. In 1983 a landmark ruling in the House of Lords defined Sikhs as "almost a race, and almost a nation". The Law Lords' verdict overthrew the decision of a lower court in the Mandla v. Dowell Lee case, which had resulted from Birmingham lawyer Seva Singh Mandla's complaint to the Commission for Racial Equality after an independent school refused to admit his son unless he removed his turban. As a result of the Law Lords' ruling, Sikhs (like Jews, but still at that time unlike Hindus and Muslims) gained the protection of the UK's Race Relations legislation.

The following year, in early June 1984, simmering unrest in India's Punjab state climaxed in Amritsar with the storming of the sacred precincts of Harmandir Sahib (the Golden Temple) by the Indian army, and the deaths of hundreds of pilgrims as well as the militant spiritual leader, Jarnail Singh Bhindranwale. He had amassed weapons and taken refuge in the Akal Takht (the highest seat of Sikhs' temporal authority) in the Golden Temple compound. Almost five months later, on 31st October, India's Prime Minister, Indira Gandhi, was shot dead by two Sikh bodyguards and in the next four days thousands of Sikhs in Delhi died in orchestrated violence.

In Britain and North America these events in India galvanised Sikhs' sense of collective identity as victims of persecution. Men who had cut their hair and shaved their beards now increasingly asserted a visually Sikh identity. Gurdwara committees no longer included short-haired members. Gurdwara elections were dominated by the growing campaign for a Sikh homeland, Khalistan, free from the "tyranny" of a "'Hindu government". Pro-Khalistan organisations, such as the Babbar Khalsa and the International Sikh Youth Federation attracted followers. The curriculum materials representing Sikhism for students of religious education in British schools began to include paragraphs on the Sikhs' rights to Khalistan. Relations between Hindus and Sikhs were more strained than before. At the same time lines of fission also ran through the Sikh community: for example, most of the gurdwara congregations that demonstrated support for Khalistan were predominantly Jat by caste. (Sikhs from other castes sensed that any future Khalistan would be Jat-dominated.)

By the mid 1990s violence in Punjab had diminished, but the destruction of the twin towers in New York on 11 September 2001 impacted on the lives of Sikhs in the UK as well as in North America. Among the first victims in the USA of the subsequent crescendo of Islamophobia was a turban-wearing Sikh, gunned down at his petrol station. Incidence of verbal and sometimes physical abuse intensified because of a widespread assumption that the turban and beard signified Islamic sympathy with al-Qaeda. Subsequent terrorism (such as the bombings of 7 July 2005 on London transport) deepened public anxiety.

Quite apart from tendencies for negative stereotypes of turbaned Sikhs to harden after acts of terrorism with which Sikhs were totally unconnected, male Sikhs in the UK have faced successive challenges when employers in different sectors required Sikh employees to dispense with their turbans. (This seemed particularly unreasonable to those Sikhs whose knowledge of history included the fact that during the period of British rule soldiers enlisted in the Sikh Regiment of the British Indian army had been required to maintain the outward markers of Sikh identity, including uncut hair covered by a turban.) By the early 1980s Sikh campaigners had already won the right for Sikh members of bus crews to wear turbans and for turbans to be accepted in lieu of motor-cycle crash helmets. In 1989 Construction (Head Protection) Regulations allowed Sikhs to wear their turbans instead of the hard hat that was now statutory on building sites in the European Union. However, in 1992 the Personal Protective Equipment at Work Regulations (giving legal force to the Council of European Communities 1989 directive) allowed for no exemptions for Sikhs in other types of employment.

When Kailash visited countries of mainland Europe the number of resident Sikhs was negligible, but during the past thirty years communities have formed in many other western European countries, gurdwaras have been established, and periodically problems arise for turban-wearing Sikhs. Thus the turban fell foul of France's ban in 2004 on religious clothing in its public schools and Sikhs in France are also required to remove their turbans for official identity photographs. In 2010 Dr Shaminder Puri, Kailash's son, a University of Warsaw graduate, challenged in court the intransigence of the Polish Border Guard which insisted that Sikh travellers remove their turbans at the airport security. As a result of the highly publicised Court case and Sikhs' efforts, in February 2012 the practice was halted. Revised EU-wide procedures have eliminated the need for a practice so insulting to Sikhs.

Sikh protests have been directed not only at public institutions but also, in the new millennium, at other Sikhs. Notably, in December 2004, an angry protest led to the cancellation of performances of the Sikh writer Gurpreet Kaur Bhatti's play *Behzti* (Dishonour) in Birmingham Repertory Theatre, because of its scene of an imaginary rape in a gurdwara (Singh and Tatla 2006; Thandi 2012). Similarly, alleged disrespect for the Guru Granth Sahib has triggered the disruption of marriages on the grounds that the Guru Granth Sahib has been installed in hotel premises where meat and alcohol are served.

Distress at perceived disrespect for the Guru Granth Sahib also lies at the heart of protests against marriages of a Sikh to a non-Sikh. Such protests were unheard of when Kailash and Gopal's children got married. In 2013, in line with a 2007 pronouncement in Amritsar, the Sikh Council (an umbrella body) ordered gurdwaras in the UK not to allow mixed marriages, unless the non-Sikh partner assumed the name "Singh" or "Kaur", attended a two-day course on Sikhism and affirmed belief in one God. Only a minority of Sikhs marry out, but 'mixed-faith' families are steadily increasing (see Nesbitt 2009).

By 2011 Sikhs in England and Wales officially numbered 423,000 (UK Census). Gurdwaras have increased not only in number but also in scale, visibility and the levels of expenditure on new buildings. There are more than 250 gurdwaras in the UK and one very large gurdwara, the Sri Guru Singh Sabha Gurdwara in Southall, cost £17 million to build (Singh and Tatla 2006: 70).

In 1998, in compliance with an edict from Amritsar, chairs and tables were removed from gurdwaras that had adopted their use in the langar hall. Once again all present would sit on the floor, in line with the Gurus' emphasis on equality and with practice at that time. However, in many British gurdwaras, provision has subsequently been reinstated in the langar area for those who cannot easily sit on the floor. Another obvious change, this time in the worship hall, is the use of prominent powerpoint screens on which words from the Guru Granth Sahib appear in roman script, and in English translation, while the verses concerned are being read or sung in the congregation.

The facility that has, since 2000, made this possible is the website sikhtothemax. However, well before 2000 the availability of the scripture online had enabled Sikhs to access the Gurmukhi text as well as its rendering in English and contemporary Punjabi, and to hear each day's scriptural bidding from Harmandir Sahib. Previously, only a minority of Sikhs had been able, like Kailash and Gopal Puri, to house the Guru Granth Sahib (the 1430-page Gurmukhi text) with appropriate respect in their own homes, as this entails setting aside a separate room where the scriptures can be installed and read. Otherwise Sikhs would simply keep a small book of the passages used in daily prayer and, more rarely, an English translation of the scripture.

The internet's impact on the Sikh community extends far beyond its facilitation of instant access to the Guru Granth Sahib. By providing information, discussion forums and other online communication the worldwide web has engaged a generation who otherwise risked feeling more distanced from Sikhism, and it has linked Sikhs in transnational networks united by particular devotional or political styles and stances.

Kailash's narrative includes her acknowledgement of the spiritual impact of certain individuals. Many devout Sikhs report the catalytic effect of an encounter with a person of widely recognised spirituality. In the development of the UK's Sikh community several such personalities, referred to as "Babaji", have played a distinctive role. Gurdwaras have been established by their followers, while other Sikhs condemn reverence for a Sant or Babaji as bordering on regarding the individual concerned as a Guru.

The years 1983 to 2013 witnessed the popularity of increasingly influential religious groupings: the Damdami Taksal (associated with Sant Jarnail Singh Bhindranwale), the Akhand Kirtani Jatha (inspired by Bhai Randhir Singh) and the Nihangs (who trace their style of Sikhism back far before the reformist movement that began in the late nineteenth century). All three groups appeal to young Sikhs who are searching for "authentic" tradition and finding their own identity. Both male and female adherents of all three groups wear tall turbans known as "dumala".

Not surprisingly, the same three decades have seen not only an upsurge in some Sikhs' zeal for aspects of their heritage and spirituality but also concurrently, in the case of many families, a decline in religious commitment. Moreover, as Kailash perhaps anticipated, a younger generation is largely unaware of ancestral cultural traditions. However, young people still self-identify strongly as Punjabi and as Sikh, regardless of their levels of religious observance or of familiarity with the Punjabi language. Meanwhile, and with the disapproval of the more religiously zealous, many young Sikhs and other South Asian youth have been attracted by bhangra, music and dance that combines the characteristic drum beat of Punjab's harvest dance and contemporary Punjabi lyrics with elements of western styles of popular music (see Singh and Tatla 2006: 198–204).

Popular culture and sport have been positive for British Sikhs' sense of self, while also crossing and blurring boundaries. These three decades saw the rise of the cricketer Monty Panesar (Mudhsuden Singh Panesar, b. 1982) and international fame came, in his nineties, to the record-breaking Marathon runner, Fauja Singh (b. 1911). Two Sikh women — the director, Gurinder Chadha, and actor Parminder Nagra — created the best-known image of a Sikh in football, as millions watched Jesminder ("Jess") Bhamra realise her dream in the film *Bend It Like Beckham* (2002). Ten years later two other fictional Sikh women, the schoolgirl Sukhvinder Jawanda and her mother, the local councillor and General Practitioner, Dr Parminder Jawanda, entered the consciousness of the millions who read *The Casual Vacancy*, thanks to the imagination of non-Sikh author, J. K. Rowling (2012).

Kailash's delight in her children's professional success has been widely paralleled in families of South Asian background as young men and women have entered the professions, especially law and medicine. The standard of living in many families has risen, and Sikhs are strongly represented in the "significant South-Asian middle class exercising greater leverage in the economic, cultural and political arenas" (Thandi 2007: 183). Since the early 1980s family businesses have grown up while factory jobs have dwindled. The ongoing expansion of South Asian enterprise in fashion, cuisine, and South Asian weddings (including catering, photography and make-up) was unimaginable when Kailash wrote her Indian cookery columns, taught her classes and advised Marks and Spencer on its rogan josh and vindaloo.

British Punjabis increasingly visit India to do their wedding shopping for gold jewellery, dazzling outfits for the couple and close family members, and other requirements. The expectation of dowry, on which Kailash comments in chapters eleven and twelve, remains widespread, and families compete in the opulence of marriages, which are celebrated more and more lavishly (see Menski 1999).

A small minority of Sikh families live jointly, with elderly parents, their sons, daughters-in-law and grandchildren in a single household. However, grandparents increasingly spend the last years of their lives living independently, staving off a loneliness for which their earlier experience has seldom prepared them. Many retired Punjabis spend winter months in Punjab; relatively low air fares allow frequent travel between the UK and India as well as to the many other countries in which relatives have settled.

Family life has accommodated adjustments and compromise. Nonetheless, Kailash has gone on being consulted by distressed callers; spouses' suspicions, South Asian families' preoccupation with izzat (family honour), and associated intransigence regarding the marriages of their sons and daughters, continue to cause suffering. Driven by their own bitter experiences some women have not only published their stories (Shan 1985; Sanghera 2007) but also campaigned and set up projects to help other South Asian women. Among such projects is Karma Nirvana, established in 1993 by Jasvinder Sanghera to support victims and survivors of forced marriages and honour-based violence. At the same time, it must be stressed that such cases are the exception. Moreover, Kailash emphasises the fact that in many UK-based families parents have lost, or at least loosened, their authority and control in a shift that was already well underway by the 1980s.

One of Kailash's major concerns is her observation, as an agony aunt with "over 50 years of correspondence recounting tales of love and loneliness, misery and mistreatment, joy and sorrow" (Puri and Whittington 2012: 154), that the UK's communities are as divided as ever, indeed possibly even more so because of religious hatred. Telling each other our stories and sharing the lessons of each other's lives is one way of helping to weaken these divides. Certainly *Pool of Life* is being published in this hope.

Suggested Further Reading

The Introduction includes pointers to autobiographical writing by Sikhs and other Punjabis. Readers looking for scholarship on the experience of Sikh women in India and the diaspora are recommended to read the studies edited by Doris Jakobsh (2010), including the opening discussion on Sikhism and women, which we co-authored. Satwant Rait's reflections on Sikh women in the UK (2005) will also be of interest.

Accessibly written scholarship on Sikhs and their religious tradition includes introductions by Owen Cole (2004), Doris Jakobsh (2011), Gurinder Singh Mann (2004), myself (Nesbitt 2005) and Nikky-Guninder Kaur Singh (2012). For a mapping of the dynamics of Punjabis' religiosity I commend Roger Ballard's work (1999). Nesbitt (2012) is a detailed exploration of the complex relationship between strands that are often separated out as "Sikh", on the one hand, and "Punjabi Hindu" on the other. Harjot Oberoi (1994) provides a historical perspective by demonstrating the relatively undemarcated religious activity of Punjabis until the rise of a reformist movement, the Tat (i.e. "pure") Khalsa at the end of the century.

Tat Khalsa discourse emerged in the 1880s within the Singh Sabha, one of whose founding members was Khem Singh Bedi, whose family inspired widespread devotion, as recalled by Kailash in chapter two. Devotion to the descendants of Gurus, however, came to be strongly disapproved of by the Tat Khalsa activists. For more on this subject and on the standing of Khem Singh Bedi see Oberoi (1994: 248ff.). Images of the palace in Kallar where Kailash glimpsed his son, Baba Gurbaksh Singh Bedi and family are available online at:

www.chohakhalsa.com/folder_2/khem_singh_bedi.htm
(accessed 19 March 2013).

Throughout her life Kailash has drawn inspiration from the words of the Sikh Gurus embodied in the sacred volume, Guru Granth Sahib. This scripture is accessible in an English rendering online, for example at www.srigranth.org. Many readers will find it helpful to read anthologies of key passages interpreted by contemporary scholars. Two such collections are Nikky-Guninder Kaur Singh's (1996) and the work of Christopher Shackle and Arvind-Pal Mandair (2005).

177

Suggested Further Reading

Kailash has spent the major part of her life in the UK, much of it serving the South Asian community as an agony aunt. For sharply observed glimpses of South Asian experience see Sanjay Suri's *Brideless in Wembley* (2006). For an amply illustrated account of South Asian settlement in one Midlands city see Virdee (2006). Scholarship more specifically on Sikhs in the UK includes Singh and Tatla (2006) and Nesbitt (2011). Shinder Thandi sets the UK experience in the wider context of the European Sikh diaspora (2012). As context for Kailash's memories (in chapter five) of the UK's first gurdwara, the Bhupindra Dharamsala or Shepherds Bush gurdwara see Bance, Singh and Anand (2008).

Most of Kailash's impressive output in Punjabi has not been translated into English. However, Rana Nayar's (2002) collection of short stories by nine British Punjabi writers commences with "Behind the Open Doors" in which Kailash Puri "casts an angular, suspicious glance at the contradictions and unresolved paradoxes of an unorthodox open society" (xvi–xvii). In Puri and Whittington (2012) Kailash herself shares in English her thoughts on community relations. Sanjay Suri (2006: 237–280) shares more of Kailash's correspondence on relationship and sexual problems.

References

Bains, T. S. and Johnston, H. 1995: *The Four Quarters of the Night: The Life-Journey of an Emigrant Sikh*. Montreal & Kingston: McGill–Queen's University Press.

Ballard, R. 1999: Panth, Kismet, Dharm te Qaum: Continuity and Change in Four Dimensions of Punjabi Religion. In P. Singh and S. S. Thandi (eds.). *Punjabi Identity in Global Context*, New Delhi: Oxford University Press, 7–37.

Bance, B. (Peter) S., Paul, S. S. and Anand, G. S. 2008: *Khalsa Jatha*. London: The Central Gurdwara.

Barton, R. 1987 *The Scarlet Thread: An Indian Woman Speaks*. London: Virago.

Butalia, U. 2000: *The Other Side of Silence: Voices from the Partition of India*. Durham, NC: Duke University Press.

Cole, W. O. 2004: *Understanding Sikhism*. Edinburgh: Dunedin Academic Press.

Jakobsh, D. 2010: (ed.) *Sikhism and Women: History, Texts and Experience*. New Delhi: Oxford University Press.

Jakobsh, D. 2011: *Sikhism*. Honolulu: University of Hawaii Press.

Johnston, H. J. M. 2011: *Jewels of the Qila: The Remarkable Story of an Indo-Canadian Family*. Vancouver and Toronto: UBC Press.

Mann, G. S. 2004: *Sikhism*. Upper Saddle River, NJ: Prentice Hall.

Menon, R. and Bhasin, K. 1998: *Borders and Boundaries: Women in India's Partition*. New Jersey: Rutger University Press.

Menski, W. (ed.) 1999: *South Asians and the Dowry Problem*. Stoke-on-Trent: Trentham.

Nayar, R. 2002: *From Across the Shores: Punjabi Short Stories by Asians in Britain*. London: Soma Books.

Nesbitt, E. 2005: *Sikhism A Very Short Introduction*. Oxford: Oxford University Press.

Nesbitt, E. 2009: Research Report: Studying the Religious Socialization of Sikh and "Mixed-Faith" Youth in Britain: Contexts and Issues. *Journal of Religion in Europe* 2 (1), 37–57.

Nesbitt, E. 2011: Sikh Diversity in the UK: Contexts and Evolution. In K. A. Jacobsen and K. Myrvold (eds), *Sikhs in Europe: Migration, Identities and Representations*, Aldershot: Ashgate, 225–252.

179

References

Nesbitt, E. 2012: Hinduism and Sikhism. In K. A. Jacobsen (ed.), *The Brill Encyclopaedia of Hinduism*, vol. 4, Leiden: Brill, 573–587.

Oberoi, H. 1994: *The Construction of Religious Boundaries: Culture, Identity and Diversity in the Sikh Tradition*. Delhi: Oxford University Press.

Purewal, N. 2010: *Son Preference: Sex Selection, Gender and Culture*. Oxford: Berg.

Puri, K. with B. Whittington 2012: *The Myth of UK Integration*. Caithness: Whittles.

Rait, S. K. 2005: *Sikh Women in England: Religious, Social and Cultural Beliefs*. Stoke-on-Trent: Trentham.

Rowling, J. K. 2012: *The Casual Vacancy*. London: Little, Brown Book Group.

Sanghera, J. 2007: *Shame*. London: Hodder.

Sanghera, S. 2009: *The Boy with the Topknot: A Memoir of Love, Secrets and Lies in Wolverhampton*. London: Penguin.

Sato, K. 2011: *Mrs Jasvir Kaur Chohan: Life Story of a Sikh Woman and her Identity*. Tokyo: RCHRCD, Meiji University.

Sato, K. 2012: *Mr Sarup Singh, MBE and Mrs Gurmit Kaur: Life Stories of a Sikh Artist and his Wife*. Tokyo: RCHRCD, Meiji University.

Shackle, C. and Mandair, A-P. 2005: *Teachings of the Sikh Gurus: Selections from the Sikh Scriptures*. London: Routledge.

Shan, S-J. 1985: *In My Own Name: An Autobiography*. London: The Women's Press.

Singh, G. and Tatla, D. S. 2006: *Sikhs in Britain: The Making of a Community*. London: Zed.

Singh, N-G. K. 1995: *The Name of My Beloved: Verses of the Sikh Gurus*. SanFrancisco: HarperCollins.

Singh, N-G. K. 2012: *Sikhism: An Introduction*. London: IB Tauris.

Suri, S. 2006: *Brideless in Wembley*. New Delhi: Penguin.

Syal, M. 1997: *Anita and Me*. London: Flamingo.

Tandon, P. 1969: *Punjabi Century 1857–1947*. Berkeley: University of California Press.

Tatla, D. S. 2004: Preface. In A. Chandan, Gopal Singh Chandan: A Short Biography and Memoirs, Jalandhar: Punjab Centre for Migration Studies. Available at: www.sikh-heritage.co.uk/heritage/sikhhert% 20EAfrica/GSChandan-BioFinal%20with%illustrations-%20May%2006.pdf Accessed 20 March 2013.

Thandi, S. S. 2007: The 1980s and After: From Adversity to Celebration. In M. H. Fisher, S. Lahiri and S. Thandi (eds) *A South-Asian History of Britain: Four Centuries of Peoples from the Indian Sub-Continent*, Oxford/Westport, Connecticut: Greenwood World Publishing, 183–214.

Thandi, S. S. 2012: Migration and Comparative Experiences of Sikhs in Europe: Reflections on Issues of Cultural Transmission and Identity

30 Years On. In K. A. Jacobsen and K. Myrvold (eds), *Sikhs across Borders: Transnational Practices of European Sikhs*, London: Bloomsbury, 11–35.

Virdee, P. 2006: *Coming to Coventry: Stories from the South Asian Pioneers.* Coventry: Coventry Teaching PCT & The Herbert.

Virdee, P. 2009: Negotiating the Past: Journey through Muslim Women's Experience of Partition and Resettlement. *Cultural and Social History*, 6 (4), 67–84.

Publications by Kailash Puri

(Most were originally published by Arsee Publishers, New Delhi.)

Novels (Punjabi)

Main, ik aurat
Katehre wich khari aurat
Umi udhal gahi
Viki viah kiun kare?

Novel (Hindi)

Suzi

Collected stories (Punjabi)

Ik sawal (A question)
Do tazweezan (Two suggestions)
Kalankani (The accursed one)
Ledi Margaret (Lady Margaret)

Poetry (Punjabi)

Bibini
Lahoo da safar
Na sima na sammati
Paigame muhabat

Sexology (Punjabi), all reprinted 2002 by Gyan Books, New Delhi

Sej ulajhana
Sej anand
Sej hular
Sej sansar
Sej sanjh
Sejan di sej
Sej sumel
Sej shastar

References

Sexology (Hindi)

Saiks ki ulajhane

Sexology (Urdu)

Saiks and saiks

Essays (Punjabi)

Subhagvati
Kala manaka
Gharon par ghar
Sunanda sah nahin sakdi
Bratanian vich Panjabi sabhiachar
Parivaran dian samasiavan

Autobiography (Punjabi)

Meri sahitak savai-jivani
Bari jau lakh beria

Anthologies

Flame
One word
Light years
British South Asian Poetry

Cookery

Rasoi kala
Highlights of Indian Cookery
Mysteries of Indian Cuisine: An Englishman's Guide to Indian Cookery

Index

agony aunt, 3, 4, 137–52, 178
Agra, 48
Akhand Kirtani Jatha, 174
Allahabad, 85, 92–3, 123
Amar Das, Guru, 56
Ambala, 74
America, 69, 86, 99, 101, 104, 137, 141, 170–1
Amritsar, 64, 74, 76, 156–7, 170, 172
Amsterdam, 100
Anand, viii, 56, 125
Appiah, Joe, 95
Appiah, Peggy, 95
arati, viii, 10, 21, 22
Ardas, ix, 56, 99, 125
Arjan Dev, Guru, x, xvi, 20, 29, 167–8
astrologer, 86, 96, 147
award, 1, 153
ayurvedic medicine *see* traditional remedies

babaji, ix, 84, 151, 173–4
Babbar Khalsa, 171
Baisakhi (Vaisakhi), ix, 29, 41, 142, 161
Balewa, Sir Abubakah Tafawa, 94
Basant Panchami, ix, 35
beard, 23, 50, 151, 171
Bedi (family), 4, 21, 44, 99, 162
Bedi, Gurbaksh Singh, 8, 9, 21, 44, 165, 177
Bedi, Khem Singh, 8, 21, 22, 177
Bedi, Sahib Singh, 8
Behzti, 172
Bend It Like Beckham, 174
betrothal, 43, 44, 45, 155
Bhago *see* Mai Bhago,
Bhatra, ix, 1, 69

Bhatti, Abdullah *see* Dulla
Bhatti, Gurpreet Kaur, 172
Bhindranwale, Jarnail Singh, 170, 174
Birmingham, 120, 124, 167
birth, 3, 6–7, 12, 27, 68, 80, 84, 136, 145, 146, 167
birth control *see* family planning
Bombay (Mumbai), 18, 65, 71, 72, 82, 144, 158
Botanical Survey of India, 82
Brahmin, ix, 26, 30, 31, 59, 83, 86
bride burning, 135, 155
bride-price, 90–1
British, *passim*, 15, 37, 42, 60, 79, 89, 134
British Raj, 17

Calcutta (Kolkota), 18, 73, 93, 123
Canada, 2, 104, 137, 154
caste, ix, xii, xv, 4, 15, 26, 44, 143
    see also Brahmin; Jat; Khatri; Ramgarhia
Central Botanical laboratory, 85–6
Christian, 1, 2, 9, 14, 96
Christmas, 107, 119
clothes, 91, 100
    men's clothes, 9, 11, 53
    women's clothes, 10, 13, 18–19, 31, 35, 37, 53, 57, 58, 67, 90, 91, 95, 103–4, 105, 120–1, 167
community relations, 4, 114, 130
cookery, 4, 19–20, 76, 82, 95, 107, 116, 132–3, 135, 136
cosmetics, xii, xvi, 27, 39–40
Crosby Herald, 114

Damdama Sahib, 4, 21–2, 81, 99, 100, 164–5

Index

Damdami Taksal, 174
Dassehra, 36
dastarbandi, x, 22, 82
death, 9, 18, 119–20, 125
Dehra Dun, 73–82, 86, 153
Delhi, 75, 116, 123, 130, 135–6, 154–5, 165, 166–7
Des Pardes, 104, 126
Devika Rani, 79
diva = jot, x, xii, 21, 22, 36–37, 39–40, 168
Divali, x, 30, 36–7, 39–40, 168
domestic architecture, ix, xiv, xv, xvi, 7, 11–12, 32, 40
dowry, 28, 37, 43, 139–41, 151, 155–6, 175
  see also bride-price
dream, 81–2, 119
dress *see* clothes
drum, x, 9, 49, 70, 122
Duggal, Sardar Bhagat Singh, 15
Duggal, Sardar Gurdit Singh, 15
Dulla, 35

Ealing, 1
East Africa, 2, 4, 140–1
engagement, 27, 44, 46–7
  see also betrothal
English, 109, 111, 143
  see also British
English (language), 48, 58, 107, 143, 151
Europe (mainland), 70, 98, 100, 137, 171, 172
  see also Amsterdam; Poland
evil eye, 26, 27, 40, 79–80, 146

family planning, 83, 98, 107, 135–6
fasting, 30–1, 118
female infanticide, 3, 27
Femina, 82
festival, 28–30, 34–7, 76, 85
  see also Baisakhi; Christmas; Divali; Holi; Hola Maholla; Lohri; Tiyan
food, xvi, 10–11, 12, 16, 25, 26, 29, 30–1, 32, 33, 34–5, 56, 57, 70, 90, 108, 126, 129, 131, 134, 148, 161

  see also cookery; fruit; langar; sweets; yoghurt
Forest Research Institute, Dehra Dun, 75ff
forestry, 79, 160
fruit, 7–8, 23, 96, 158, 160
funeral, 9–10, 79, 92

games, 38
Gandhi, Mrs Indira, 81, 130, 135
Gandhi, Mohandas Karamchand, 97
Ghana, 92, 93–101, 131, 136, 153
Ghanaian Times, 95, 97
Gobind Singh, Guru, 8, 17, 29
Golden Temple, 64, 170
Gordon College, 32, 38, 161–2
Gujarati, 103, 134, 140
Gurdwara, xi, 11, 36, 42, 109, 120–1, 147, 171, 172–3
  Birmingham, 124, 167
  Chadha's (Kallar), 42–3, 54–6
  Nottingham, 122
  Southall, 178
  see also Damdama Sahib; Golden Temple; Panja Sahib; Shepherd's Bush
gurdwara
Guru Granth Sahib, xi, 6, 7, 8, 21–2, 29, 30, 40, 44, 54–6, 69, 76, 84, 86, 88, 98–9, 124, 154, 161, 168, 172, 173, 177

hair, 22, 26, 39, 40, 61, 120, 151, 171
Harrow, 109–110, 112
Hindu, ix, xiii, xvi, 1, 2, 3, 4, 9, 29–31, 34, 36–7, 44, 71, 85, 118, 119, 140, 143, 145, 150, 170–1, 177
Hola Maholla, xi, 36
Holi, xii, 35–6
honour *see* izzat
hymn, Christian, 14
  see also Guru Granth Sahib; Sukhmani Sahib

Ibadan, 88–93
illness, 13–14, 15–16, 17, 21, 26, 41, 108, 118–19, 136, 159

Index

Indian Workers Association, 121
International Sikh Youth Federation, 171
izzat, xii, 50, 149, 175

Jain, 25
Jalandhar, 102
Jat, xii, 4, 69–70, 103, 171
jewellery, 46–7, 49–50, 53, 59, 65, 141
jot *see* diva
Jullundur *see* Jalandhar

Kallar, 4, 7–11, 17–20, 21–31, 34, 36, 37, 43, 44, 50, 52ff, 71, 74, 153, 162–5, 167–8, 177
Karachi, 45, 47, 66, 70
Karwa Chauth, xii, 31, 76
Kashmir, 11, 59, 83, 133–4
Kaumi Ekta, 125–6
Khalistan, 171
Khatri, xii–xiii, 4
Kirna Weekly, 109
Kulu, 76, 79–80
Kumasi, 93–8

Lahore, 7, 11, 13, 18, 40–5, 59, 71, 74, 153, 157–9
Lakshmi, xiii, 37, 45
langar, xiii, 70, 124, 173
Leiths School of Food and Wine, 135
Liverpool, 1, 65, 72, 88, 101, 111, 112, 113ff, 165, 167, 168–9
    Polytechnic, 112, 114, 116, 130
Lohri, xiii, 34–5
London, 48, 63, 65–71, 102–12, 119, 120, 136, 171
    see also Harrow; Southall
Lucknow, 48, 58ff
Ludhiana, 155–6

Mai Bhago, 17
Mandla v. Dowell Lee case, 170
Mankiala, 8, 50, 52
Marks and Spencer, 132–3, 135
marital relationships, 11, 28, 31, 61–2, 64, 67, 82, 84, 95, 104, 120, 137–9, 142–8

marriage, xii, xiii, xiv, xvi, 7, 25, 27–8, 42ff, 48–50, 52–7, 91, 143, 147, 154–5, 164, 166, 172, 175
medicine, 16
    see also traditional remedies
milk, x, xi, xiii, 16, 19, 23, 31, 37, 39, 57, 67, 90
    see also yoghurt; sweets
mother-in-law, 16, 28, 44, 46–7, 56, 57, 65, 84, 87, 123–5, 138, 140, 155, 166
musical instruments, ix, x, xv, 53, 54, 70, 116, 164
    see also drum
Muslim, 1, 3, 18, 36, 58, 66, 71–2, 83, 85, 90, 96, 145, 150, 157, 158, 164, 170

Nagra, Parminder, 174
Nanak, Guru, 4, 6, 8, 9, 10, 21, 37, 69, 70, 106, 167, 168
Naushaira, 21, 37
Nehru, Pandit Jawaharlal, 75, 81, 85, 95, 97
New Delhi *see* Delhi
Nigeria, 86, 88–92, 94
Nihang, 174
Nishkam Sevak Jatha, 167
Nkrumah, Dr Khwame, 96–8
Nkrumah, Madam Fathia, 96–8
Nottingham, 1, 5, 121, 122

Pakistan, *passim*, 1, 4, 7, 153, 156–66
Panesar, Monty (Madhusuden Singh Panesar), 174
Panj Darya, 82
Panja Sahib, 6, 160–1
Pant, Dr Apa, 115, 116–17
Partition, 1, 3, 5, 7, 71–2, 73–5, 120
Patiala, 69, 75, 81, 86
Peshawar, 21, 43, 60
Poland, 100, 111, 172
police, 99, 112, 128, 147
Poona (Pune), 82–5
Pothohar, 21
Pothohari (language), 102–3, 164

prayer, ix, 6, 37, 41, 64, 56, 66, 73, 99, 110, 125, 151
  see also Anand; arati; Ardas
Preetlari, 82, 104
Punjab, *passim,* 1, 4, 8, 71, 81, 102, 154
Punjab Times, 104, 126
Punjabi (language), viii, xi, 103, 107–8, 112, 115, 131, 155, 156
Puri, Professor Gopal Singh, *passim,* 1, 2, 43, 161
Puri, Master Hara Singh, 9, 43, 162
Puri, Kharak Singh, 8
Puri, Sohan Singh, 7, 32, 162

racism, 69, 111–12, 113–14, 115, 127, 128, 130, 142, 155, 170
rakhi, xv, 30
Raksha Bandhan, xv, 30, 142
Ram (Rama), xv, 9, 36
Ram Das, Guru, xiii, 55
Ramgarhia, xv, 2, 4, 151
Rawalpindi, 6, 7, 15–19, 32–40, 44, 153, 161–2
religious experience, 41
  see also dream; prayer
river
  Beas, 102
  Ganges, 59, 85
  Gomati, 58–9
  Jamuna, 85
  Kanshi, 7, 24, 25, 29, 169
  Saraswati, 85
  Satluj, 102
Roerich, Nicholas, 79
Roopvati, 115–16, 120–2, 128–9

Sahni, Professor Birbal, 58, 60
Sahni, Professor Ruchi Ram, 58, 60
Sandesh Weekly, 126
Sathya Sai Baba, 86
school, 14, 129, 143, 149, 171
  Crosby, 114
  Dehra Dun, 81
  Ibadan, 89
  Kallar, 9, 18–19, 43, 71, 162, 165
  Poona, 82
  Rawalpindi, 32–3, 161
  Slough, 102

Solan, 14–15
Southall, 112
  see also Gordon College
seeds, xi, xv, 26, 27, 39
servants, 74, 168
  Gheba, 15–16
  Bidiya, 87, 92–3
Shepherds Bush gurdwara, 69–70, 178
shop, xi, 23, 66–7, 71, 89–90, 103, 128, 158, 164
shraddh, xvi, 30
Sikh, *passim*, 1, 3, 4, 8, 21, 37, 44, 71, 84–5, 96, 124, 126, 143, 145, 150, 153–4, 157, 170–5, 177–8
Singh, Maharaja Bhupindra, 69, 81
Singh, Sardar Gurbaksh, 82
Singh, Indarjit (Lord Singh of Wimbledon), 69
Singh, Khushwant, 115–16
Singh, Professor Mohan, (poet), 32, 82
Singh, Bhai Randhir, 174
Singh, Maharaja Ranjit, 8
Singh, Sital, 23, 71, 164
Singh, Sundar, 45, 50, 53, 57, 64, 74
Singh, Maharaja Yadavindra, 81, 86–7
Singh Sabha, 8–9, 177
Slough, 102–7, 130
Solan, 14, 17
son preference, 3, 6–7, 12, 35
song
  Lohri, 35
  marriage, 48–9, 53–4, 56–7, 138
  see also hymn
Southall, 107–12, 124, 152, 173
Southport Gazette, 114
Spokesman Weekly, The, 135
Stopes, Dr Marie, 60, 131
Subhagvati, 82–3, 115
Sufi, 159, 165
Sukhmani Sahib, xvi, 21, 157–8, 158
superstition, 13, 14, 24, 162
  see also evil eye
sweets, viii, ix, x, xi, xii, xiii, xiv, xv, 19–20, 22, 23, 36, 37, 40, 49, 163
Tagore, Rabindranath, 79, 142
Tat Khalsa, 177

television, 92, 95, 144, 152
Thatcher, Margaret, 134–5
Tiyan, xvi, 30
traditional remedies, ix, 26, 79, 119
turban, x, 17, 22, 23, 35, 66, 82, 88, 91,
 120, 126, 171, 172, 174

university, 43, 63, 111,
 Agra, 48
 Guru Nanak Dev, Amritsar, 156
 Ibadan, 86, 88–90, 93
 Kumasi, 93–4, 100
 London, 63
 Lucknow, 48, 58–60
 Warsaw, 100, 111
 see also Botanical Survey of India;

Central Botanical Laboratory;
 Forest Research Institute; Gordon
 College; Liverpool Polytechnic;
 Ludhiana
Urdu, 60, 115, 148

Vaisakhi *see* Baisakhi
Vatsyayana, 131

wedding *see* marriage
writing, 59, 82–3, 95, 104, 115, 125–6,
 128, 131

yoga, 4, 116–18, 119, 135, 136
yoghurt, x, xiii, 23, 39, 67, 85
Yoruba, xiv, 90–1

0131 2402065

Jill Cowan

Dégrad

0131 2002360

DAVid Ritchie
0131 07761753488